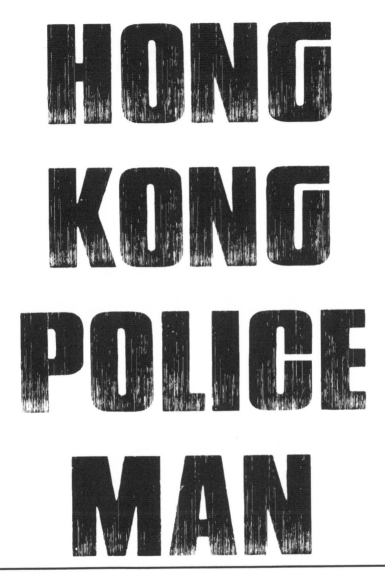

HONG KONG POLICE MAN

Law, life and death on the streets of Hong Kong.
An English police inspector tell it as it was

Chris Emmett

EARNSHAW
BOOKS

Hong Kong Policman

By Chris Emmett

ISBN-13: 978-988-1609-03-8

© 2014 Earnshaw Books

BIOGRAPHY & AUTOBIOGRAPHY / Historical

First printing July 2014
Second printing November 2014
Third printing February 2015

EB051

Published by Earnshaw Books Ltd. (Hong Kong)

For Philip Bruce

ACKNOWLEDGEMENTS

In researching this book I drew on two important works: *The Royal Hong Kong Police (1841-1945)* by Colin Crisswell and Mike Watson; and *Asia's Finest* by Kevin Sinclair. I also wish to thank those serving Hong Kong police officers who took the time to share with me their personal experiences of how it is to work in today's Hong Kong.

FOREWORD

Cliff Bale, journalist and Hong Kong resident since 1979

A POLICEMAN'S LOT is not easy, they say. It becomes that much more difficult when an officer from the Merseyside town of Warrington decides to up-stakes and join the police force in distant Hong Kong. This was the case with Chris Emmett in 1970, when he decided he needed a radical change of scenery. He served with the Hong Kong police until his retirement as a senior superintendent in 1998, seeing the city transform from a colony in a diminishing British empire to a special administrative region within the People's Republic of China.

This book is based largely on Chris' experiences between the time he arrived in Hong Kong until 1977, but there is a section on the historic 1997 handover and his experience attending a banquet hosted by the Chinese People's Liberation Army in the former main barracks of the British armed forces close to the Central business district.

With great humour, Chris takes us through his impressions upon arrival in Hong Kong, his first day at the police training school as a probationary inspector and his first encounter with the Wanchai bar scene and its pretty but predatory bar girls.

There are descriptions of his battle to learn Cantonese, his relations as an expatriate officer with his Chinese colleagues – who had intimate knowledge of the crime scene in the rough areas of Hong Kong such as its many public housing estates – and his brush with corruption, not brought under control until the Independent Commission Against Corruption was created in 1974.

Chris details his experiences in the various locations in which he served in the 1970s, including the then new town of Tsuenwan, where he gained his first experiences as an inspector. He was involved in a dramatic rescue at the height of deadly Typhoon Rose, which killed 130 people in 1971. There was also the discovery of a World War II bomb, something that – like typhoons – still happens today.

He also writes about his time in Frontier district, which brought him face to face with the Chinese military in the town of Shautaukok, where the border is an open road called China-England Street – an area still off-limits to most Hong Kong residents and tourists. He details feuds between rival villages in the New Territories that he observed and sometimes played a role in settling.

There are chapters on Chris' time with the anti-riot police and on Hong Kong Island, where he was involved in operations involving gambling and drugs and in detective work. He also gets to meet a young Li Kwan-ha, who in 1989 would become Hong Kong's first Chinese commissioner of police. This was an important development as the British colonial government sought to localise the various arms of government, including the police, in the run-up to the 1997 handover. Indeed, in 1994 the government stopped recruiting expatriate police officers, which meant there would be no more Chris Emmetts coming to Hong Kong. In time, as existing overseas officers retire, the force will become entirely Chinese, except for a few locally-born non-Chinese officers.

Today, the lot of the policeman in Hong Kong is becoming more difficult, as the special administrative region becomes more politicised. The police force is accused of siding with the government against protesters, something it denies. But that is another story. This one is about the police force in a colonial Hong Kong, when British and Chinese worked together to keep the peace on the streets of this extraordinary city.

CHAPTER 1
SOME FOREIGN FIELD

IT IS TWO HOURS *after dawn and my morning shift has started. The sun is still low but already the cab of the police Landrover is a sweatbox. I open the vents below the windscreen but there is no release from the heat. The back of my bush shirt is damp and my cap feels a size too small. A Colt .38 Police Positive revolver drags at my hip; the stiff leather of my Sam Browne belt bites into my waist. On the Landrover's rear bench, my sergeant is updating the mobile patrol log. The driver turns off the highway and the sergeant curses as we jolt over a pothole.*

We roll into the Kwaishek public housing project. Towers of drab concrete surround us, soaring twenty storeys and more. Once, their walls had gleamed white, but now mildew and grime streaks them grey and black. Laundry, drying on poles that poke from the windows, provides a sprinkle of colour. At ground level, practical shops offer hardware, dry goods, stationery, and plywood furniture. Rowdy teahouses serve up dim-sum and pots of treacle-dark, boh-lei tea that bites the tongue. On the street, unlicensed hawkers have set up handcarts laid out with fresh vegetables, stringy meat, fake designer T-shirts, cigarettes, and plastic toys. At the sight of the police Landrover, they shoo away their customers and scatter.

The housing project has a noise unlike anything I have ever known. It is the roar of thousands of people in tight concentration getting ready to face the day. Now, it is time for work; crowds throng the sidewalks. Around the bus station, newspaper vendors and cooked food sellers enjoy frantic trade. Oil bubbles and smokes in flame-blackened woks balanced dangerously on hissing gas burners. The smells interweave: stewed beef, custard and egg waffles, creamy bean curd. Each arriving bus prompts a jostling, elbowing, cursing scramble to be first to board. Unruly minibuses dart in to poach the bus company's custom and one blocks the road ahead of us. My driver bips the siren and the minibus moves on.

'Dai sap-yat joh (Block Eleven),' I tell my driver in Cantonese. He nods and we bully our way through crowds that spill onto the road. He stops beside a refuse point, its rank stench filling the Landrover's cabin.

The sergeant calls in a radio check. The radio crackles back at him. 'Nothing,' he snorts. We are in a radio blind spot.

The sergeant and I step out of the Landrover just as the rising sun slices between Blocks Eleven and Twelve. Sweat stings my eyes. I take off my cap and use it to shade my eyes as I scan the upper floors. The sergeant nods to the driver who crunches the Landrover into gear and moves further down the road. We cross a stretch of uneven paving and step into Block Eleven's lobby. In the airless gloom, the heat is even more oppressive. A mishmash of noise hits us: shouted conversation, blasting Canto-pop music, televisions running at full volume. The lobby floor is bare concrete. Chipped tiles cover the walls; once they were red but now they are just an anonymous dark hue. There are four lifts, three of them out of order. Corridors stretch left and right. Iron grilles mark the apartments, giving the corridors the look of a third world cellblock. In single rooms measuring twenty feet by twenty feet, families of two, three and four generations live, eat, love, quarrel, and sometimes work. We turn left. Our footsteps ring off the bare concrete. The corridor smells of mould and stale urine. Humidity dampens the walls; water drips from the ceiling and puddles the floor. A child watches us from behind a door grille, her eyes wide, her mouth open and questioning.

At the end of the corridor, a broad staircase leads to the upper floors and we begin to climb.

On the first floor landing, a neon light flickers and strobes. In a corner, a man squats, head down in the gloom. A line of smoke drifts across the landing. He looks up and his eyes widen. Then he is away, sprint-

ing up the stairs. The sergeant picks up a strip of tinfoil from the floor. There is a treacly residue on one side, the other side is flame- blackened.

'Jui lung,' the sergeant says. 'Chasing dragon. Fucking do yau.' Do yau -- drug addict. He crumples the tin foil and tosses it into a corner.

There is a scuff of feet on the stairs. I flatten myself against the wall and peer up to the next landing. There is movement; someone steps back from the staircase. I signal to the sergeant and he puts his back against the other wall. Together, we edge up the staircase. I strain to listen. Above us, someone is whispering. There are two of them but I can make out no words. A shape appears on the staircase. There is a hard CRACK. It rings off the concrete, numbing my ears. A rush of adrenaline courses through me. I drop to a crouch, my hand is on my revolver. Without thinking, I unclip the holster flap. There is a child's laughter and the sound of running feet. The sergeant picks up scraps of shredded paper from the staircase. It is the crimson remnants of a firecracker. I suck in a breath and take a moment for my heart to slow. We continue up to the next floor where, at the sound of our footsteps, a woman steps from a doorway. Her lips are a smear of scarlet; she wears hip hugging shorts; her breasts push against an undersized t-shirt. At the sight of our uniforms, her eyes widen and she darts back indoors. The iron grill rattles shut and the door slams closed.

On the tenth floor, two young men loiter by the lifts. They spot us and make to walk in opposite directions.

'Kei jue!'-- Stand still, the sergeant shouts. They stop and turn towards us, their eyes sullen, hands on their hips. One squares his shoulders and points a finger at me. He speaks in English. 'In here, police mean nothing. Better you go.'

I step up to him. 'Jue bin do?' -- Where do you live?

He smirks and looks me up and down. 'M' gwan lei si.'-- None of your business.

I grab his shoulders, spin him round and force his arms up against the wall.

'Jo m'yeh?' he snaps.-- What are you doing?

I kick at his ankles, forcing his legs apart. 'Jue bin do?'I ask again.

He jerks his chin towards the corridor. 'Ya' ng ho.'-- Number twenty-five.

I run my hands around his waist then along his arms and legs. No weapons. I turn his pockets inside out, I order him to take off his shoes then open his mouth wide. No drugs.

My sergeant has searched the other man. He looks at me and shrugs. 'Gon jeng, Ah Sir.'-- The other man is clean.

We walk on. Behind me, there is a shout. 'Fuck you! Fuck all police!'

The sergeant turns, his fist balled. The two young men hunch their shoulders and melt away.

'The noisy dog has no bite,' the sergeant says. He flashes me a smile. 'Is my English right?'

It's fine, I tell him.

We make our way back to the street. As we walk back to the Landrover, I wander from the shade of the awning. Too late, I see a glint of light and there is a 'swhack' on the ground beside me. What looks like a scoop of crushed ice lays strewn across the sidewalk. That is what happens to a bottle when it falls a dozen floors or more. The sergeant raises an eyebrow towards me. We board the Landrover, the sergeant tries the radio and this time gets through. 'High-rise patrol Block Eleven complete,' he says. He grins at me and adds, 'Nothing unusual.'

The driver guns the engine. 'Where next, Ah Sir?' he asks.

Good question. Where next indeed?

But, I get ahead of myself. They say it's a funny old life, and so it is.

In the autumn of 1970, I did not have a care in the world. I was an English Bobby in a bustling little Merseyside town called Warrington. I was twenty-two years old, had my own little patrol car and so long as I kept one step ahead of the sergeant, life was sweet. It was not too exciting, but so what, who needs excitement? Then one weekend, I thumbed through the Sunday papers and there it was. I could not take my eyes off it. I read it several times, there was even a picture. It was a pen-and-ink drawing of a British officer leading a group of Hong Kong policemen up a dark staircase. He wore a smart bush shirt and a leather Sam Browne belt. A shoulder strap supported the weight of a pistol on his left hip. He looked like something out of Boys' Own comics. Above the picture, a headline declared: '2 a.m. in Kowloon is a fine time for self-discovery.'

I cut the advertisement from the newspaper and carried it around for days. I showed it to one of my section's older constables, a crusty veteran with twenty years service. He held it at arm's length and frowned. 'You're a bit young for an inspector,' he sniffed. 'And what's Hong Kong got that Warrington hasn't?' He thrust the advertisement back at me. 'Waste of time, if you ask me. You'll probably have to learn Japanese.'

I tucked the advertisement back in my pocket and checked my pigeon-hole for messages. The only one was from my sergeant, chasing me for a report on a broken street light. Outside, autumn had set in. There was a light drizzle and the days were getting shorter. I made my way to the station charge office and typed up the broken street light report. The charge office constable was sipping tea and reading a day-old copy of the Daily Mirror. He nodded to me. 'Nice and quiet,' he said. 'Let's hope it stays that way.'

I thought for a moment, then fed a sheet of paper into the typewriter. I checked that nobody was watching and began to type:

Dear Sir,
In response to your recent advertisement ...

On Friday, November 13, 1970, a harassed official from the Crown Agents met me at Heathrow Airport's departure lounge. He checked my paperwork and pointed to a group of young men standing at the bar. 'You're the last,' he said. 'Introduce yourself and make sure you don't miss the bloody plane.' He wished me luck, hunched his shoulders and scurried off.

There were thirteen of us, all young and eager in our charcoal Terylene suits and our drip-dry shirts. There were a few ex-UK policemen but the rest were a mixed lot: a wide-eyed bank clerk, a bright and friendly journalist, an ex-medical student, an impish Irishman and Curly Briggs. Curly was a sunny Tynesider, a stocky boulder of a man with an open face and a laugh like a donkey trapped in a strawberry patch. His neck was as thick as a tree stump and he had a pink shaved head. Curly was not one for suits, and instead he wore patched jeans, a leather jacket over a white T-shirt and the kind of industrial boots favoured by English street brawlers.

There were a few self-conscious handshakes and some guarded conversation. Nothing special, just the usual: where are you from, what was your job? Someone asked why we were all there.

'Looking for a change.'

'Weather seems nice.'

'A bit of excitement.'

'Dunno,' said Curly in his musical Tyneside accent. 'Ah was at a bit of a loose end after university, like.' He pronounced it, *Yoon-i-vahsity*.

That shut us up; back then, university graduates were rare creatures.

Curly grinned. He raised a foot and pointed to his boot. 'What do you reckon to these then? Ah've sorted oot a few troublemakers with these lads.'

The conversation died. As one, we checked the boarding time; still half an hour to go.

'Ah reckon we can get in two or three pints before they call us, like,' Curly said.

And who were we to argue?

Twenty-four hours later, our Boeing 707 crossed the west Kowloon shoreline and made its final turn towards Kai Tak airport. We were so low, I could see people walking along the narrow streets below. The buildings crept closer and the starboard wingtip skimmed the rooftops as we made our final turn. I said a silent prayer as I saw TV screens flickering in the top floor flats. There was a flash of blue water on both sides of the plane then a thump as the wheels touched down. I waited until we came to a stop before opening my eyes, unclenching my teeth and prising my fingers from the seat arms. Minutes later, the door opened and a wall of heat hit us as we stepped onto the airport tarmac. I shielded my eyes against the sun and felt my shirt dampen. Two airport ground staff looked us over. They were cool and relaxed in linen shirts and slacks. Reflective sunglasses hid their eyes. They swapped a few words, laughed and went back to work.

We stepped onto a shuttle bus that took us from the tarmac to the airport terminal. There, we made our way through the arrival gate and into the terminal building. I loosened my tie and unbuttoned the top button of my shirt, luxuriating in my first taste of air-conditioning. We followed signs pointing to immigration control where an impossibly young British police inspector came forward to meet us. He wore a khaki bush shirt, matching shorts and a gleaming Sam Browne belt. The peak of his cap was glossy and all but hid his eyes. I found myself staring at the cross-draw holster hanging at his left hip, the butt of a revolver just visible under the holster's button-down flap. His face was without expression. 'Hong Kong Police?' he asked.

We nodded.

He eyed our crumpled suits and sweaty faces. 'Figures,' he sighed. He held out his hand and snapped: 'Passports.'

We handed over our passports and followed him to a side office where a Chinese immigration official sat behind a metal desk. He called us forward one by one. He glanced at the photographs, stamped the visa pages, then handed us our passports and pointed to a door behind him.

We gathered in the baggage hall and after a short wait, our

luggage arrived. Baggage identified and collected, we followed the inspector like a troop of ducklings. He nodded to the customs officers who waved us through.

The heat hit us again as we stepped into an open-air car park. We stared awestruck as a Swissair jetliner skimmed nearby rooftops. Without thinking, I ducked as it roared overhead. It was so low, I felt I could reach up and touch it. The inspector rolled his eyes and pointed to a navy-blue bus with the word, 'POLICE' written on its side in stark white. 'Good luck,' he said then returned to the terminal building.

Good luck? Strange thing to say, I thought.

I turned to the bus where a Chinese constable stood grinning by the door. We clambered aboard and squeezed onto cramped seats upholstered by a blacksmith. The constable climbed into the driver's seat then grinned over his shoulder. 'Police Training School. Very good,' he chuckled and gave us a thumbs up.

The bus rolled out of the car park and past a row of faded tenements. Another jetliner screamed overhead. 'The airport's in the middle of town,' someone gasped. 'It's right in the bloody middle of sodding town.'

Minutes later, we were in a tree-lined boulevard of low-rise apartment blocks with art deco frontages and broad verandas adorned with potted plants. On the sidewalks, the men wore slacks and neat cotton shirts; the women looked serene in patterned frocks. We crossed a busy junction and the road narrowed. We rattled across a pothole and the traffic slowed. Now, the buildings were shabby, their renderings cracked. Paint peeled from their doors and window frames. Open back lorries jammed the road. Hard-faced men sat in the lorries' freight compartments, steadying unsecured cartons and sacks. They wore shorts and grubby singlets. Sinewy muscle covered their arms and shoulders. We stopped behind a lorry with yellow squares painted on the corners of its tailgate. Stuck to the back of the driver's cab was a tattered poster of China's ruler, Mao Tse-tung.

The lorry's crew glared at us.

'Bloody *jaw-jai*, bloody commies,' our driver growled. He held his nose and flushed an imaginary toilet chain.

The traffic started to move. We turned onto a broad transport basin then rumbled aboard a roll on – roll off ferry that would cross the harbour. As the ferry pulled away from the jetty, we took the chance to wander around the deck. The sun glittered off the water and a cooling breeze came over the forward ramp. The harbour smelled of saltwater and spilled diesel. The ferry blasted its horn as a small *sampan* cut across its bow. A woman, dressed in pyjama-like britches and tunic, stood at the *sampan's* prow. She used a single oar to scull the little craft in a jerky, fishtail action. Beside her, a dog barked at us.

Sprawled across the harbour, ships lay anchored to mooring buoys. The ships had names like *Asia Conveyor*, *Santo Maru* and *California Dawn*. Aboard, ropes squealed through pulleys as derricks lowered bulging cargo nets down to lighters clustered around their hulls. A US Navy destroyer, bristling with guns and missile launchers, sat at a mid harbour mooring. Beyond the ships, the upper slopes of Hong Kong Island were green and lush with a sprinkling of white villas. At the mid and lower levels were high-rise apartment blocks that became more tightly clustered the closer they were to the shoreline. Moored to the harbour wall lay a British frigate, a paler grey than its American counterpart. Behind it, Hong Kong Island's business district was a mix of modern high-rise and colonnaded Victorian and Edwardian grace.

The ferry bumped against the jetty and its ramp clanged against concrete. The bus rumbled off the ferry and headed east, past the business district and the Royal Navy dockyard. It slowed to walking pace in the narrow streets of Wanchai. We gawked at the crowded streets, the grubby tenements, the clutter of Chinese signboards, the open fronted shops, the rowdy hawker bazaars, the rattling trams and the unruly traffic. From the sidewalks, people gawked back at our doughy faces and our charcoal Terylene suits.

'*Jesus*, it's the bloody *Orient*,' I heard myself say. And it was; it was the mystic east, famed for inscrutable villains, steamy nights and dark-eyed women. It was the stuff of schoolboy fantasy.

We drove past the racecourse then up a winding road leading to a gap between two peaks. Beyond the gap, the road meandered through lush greenery and dropped down to the coast. The air was clear and there were views out to scrub-covered islands. We passed a beach with a lido style cafe and sailboats moored offshore. The driver turned into a narrow side road and within minutes, we came to a drop-arm barrier beside a businesslike guard post. A Chinese constable raised the barrier and waved us through. His face and arms were tanned, his khaki uniform crisp. His boots shone and around his waist was a webbing belt of pure white. The belt's brass fittings dazzled.

Built in the late 1940s, the police training school was a pleasant collection of broad lawns and boxy buildings that gleamed white in the sunshine. There was a drill square, outdoor shooting ranges and a dusty football pitch. The school nestled at the foot of the oddly named Brick Hill and in the coming months, we would learn to hate the winding path leading to the hill's summit.

Two Europeans wearing PT kit ran towards us, a log slung between their shoulders. Another European bellowed commands at them. The epaulettes of his bush shirt bore the three pips of a chief inspector. The rearmost runner tripped and sprawled on the tarmac. The leading runner did not pause but kept running, dragging the log behind him.

The bus staggered to a halt beside a whitewashed barrack block and an officious cadet inspector ordered us out. He was thin and had a sharp little voice. He chivvied us into three ranks and started to screech foot drill orders at us. He seemed to enjoy the authority but after a few minutes, his voice broke and he began to rasp. In a whisper, he marched us through the campus and brought us to a ragged halt next to a sign that read 'Officers' Mess.'

'Right, gentlemen.' A smirk twisted his lips. 'It's time for your induction interviews.'

We stumbled up a path that cut across a lawn bordered by broad-leafed plants. The mess was a single-storied building with a flat roof and walls of whitewashed concrete. Beside the main door, a duck bobbed in a small pond. Inside, sunlight streamed through large windows into a comfortable lounge. Air conditioners rattled at the windows and ceiling fans stirred the air. An inspector wearing an armband stamped with the word 'STAFF' stood inside the door. He held a plastic clipboard and had a leather-covered swagger cane thrust under his arm. The peak of his cap shielded his eyes. He had a voice like an angry Doberman. 'You will not look at any member of staff. You will stay silent unless spoken to. When I call your name, you will enter the room to the right.' He pointed his cane at a heavy mahogany door, checked his clipboard and snapped a name. '*Mister* Young.'

A dark mood spread among us. The door swung open and Jack Young, an ex-London −, went through it. He turned his head, a pleading look on his face as the door slammed behind him. No one spoke. We could hear muffled voices through the closed door but could make out nothing. After what seemed an age, the door banged open and to a roar of '*Leftrightleftrightleftright* ...' Young bulleted back into the lounge dressed only in his Y-fronts. His eyes were wide and he had the rest of his clothes clasped to his chest.

'*Mister* Emmett.' Call it instinct or call it telepathy, call it what you like but as I stepped through the door I knew as a crystal certainty someone large and noisy meant to ruin my day. The door slammed behind me. A row of uniformed officers sat behind a table at the far end of the room. There was a clock high on the wall behind the interview panel and as I entered the room, a menacing voice growled at me, 'Look at the clock. Keep your eyes on the clock.'

I had a brief impression of gold braided caps and crowned epaulettes then I stiffened to attention and fixed my eyes on the clock.

'Name, age, previous police experience?'

That seemed easy; I let myself relax. Next: 'sexual orientation; age of first sexual encounter?' Come on, I was as liberal as anyone but that was a bit much.

A musical voice introduced itself as the force padre. I began to believe in the power of prayer, but not for long. 'Can you sing? Know any carols?' The voice was a reassuring purr. 'We're a tad short of time, can you sing during the fitness test?'

Fitness test? What fitness test? I had not slept for two days, I was in no condition for a fitness test. The growling voice at the back of the room demanded twenty press-ups and as I dropped into position, the padre started to sing, 'Aw-ay in a manger, no-o crib for a bed ...'

From behind me came the count for the press-ups. 'One ... two ... two-and-a-half.' As I lowered my chest to the floor I heard myself croaking, 'The-e little Lord Jesus lay-ay down his sweet head ...'

I should have told them where to stick their fitness test and their Christmas carols but after a day cooped up in a Boeing 707, I did not have the will. So I did it, we all did. We followed every demeaning order; we sank to unplumbed depths of indignity and throughout it all, not one of us looked any member of staff in the eye. Our ex-journalist, fell into a sulk because the panel had referred him to the force psychologist. Our ex-draughtsman found himself scheduled for political re-education. We all have separate memories of that day, none of them pleasant but we finally reached a point beyond caring because we knew it could get no worse.

Then came the commandant's welcoming address.

We sat in the interview room on two rows of straight-backed

chairs, shoulders back, heads up and above all, silent. There was no escape from the whispering menace behind us. 'Look at the clock, keep your eyes on the bloody clock.' The training school staff banged to attention as a Chinese officer strode into the room. He threw his cap onto the table and started to harangue us in harsh Cantonese. We could not understand a word but there was no mistaking the distilled poison in his voice. It put me in mind of a grainy newscast of Chairman Mao's Red Guards waving their little red books and ranting at a defenceless old teacher. A British member of staff supplied a monotone translation. 'The commandant welcomes you to the police training school ...' The commandant's voice rose to a crescendo and a fleck of spittle splashed onto my cheek. The translation droned on, '... and he hopes you will be very happy here.'

How quickly we grow accustomed to the bizarre, nothing seemed odd any more. I wanted to see what the others made of all this but I dared not take my eyes from the clock.

'The commandant says we are one big family and his door is always open ...'

Biting cold water slammed against my head, neck and back. My shirt and jacket clung to my back. The water stung my eyes and plastered my hair against my scalp. Icy water filled my ears and drowned out all sounds except for -- laughter. Someone was having a laugh at my expense. I stood, turned and saw a line of grinning staff members, each clutching an empty bucket. Inside me, frustration, fear and anger merged into hot rage. As water dripped from my charcoal Terylene suit, one thought hammered at me like an old record with a nasty crack. 'Now, someone dies, *click* ..., now, someone dies, *click* ...'

I felt oddly self-possessed but I knew for sure I was going to give someone a good thumping. The staff were very senior, superintendents at least. Good, the bigger they are and all that. Who's first? I balled my fist and walked towards the laughing senior officers. With my eyes no longer fixed on the wall clock, I saw they were all ridiculously young, in fact, they were my age. An arm fell around my shoulder and a superintendent pushed a glass of beer into my hand. He was about twenty years old and his gold braided cap was a size too big.

'I think you could do with something wet and cold,' he chuckled.

I looked at him and then at the glass of beer. It was all perfectly clear, some time during the last twenty-four hours, I had gone crackers. Around the lounge, there was the sound of pennies dropping as young men stripped off their crowned epaulettes and other trappings of high rank. Someone pumped my hand. A white-jacketed steward passed amongst us with a tray loaded with dewed tankards of pilsner. An Ex-UK policemen who, a few minutes earlier had expressed horror at landing the role of Sleeping Beauty in the police Christmas pantomime, was now congratulating himself for having kept a vital secret.

'You really are a dull lot,' he crowed, 'I knew it was a send up, I knew it all along.'

'Sure you did,' I said. 'So now you can take off the wig.'

I wanted to be angry, I had been through a lot, I had the right to tear a strip off someone but I said nothing, I was too relieved it was over. I had always thought colonial policemen were pipe-smoking, Oxbridge types with pencil-line moustaches and *lah-de-dah* accents. I had dreaded the thought of weeks spent in polite verbal sparring just to earn grudging acceptance. Now here I was, drinking and laughing with a very unstuffy group who were doing their best to make me welcome.

On Monday, we became probationary inspector class number 62, or PI62 for short. A new batch of recruits arrived every two months but for now, we were the junior squad -- the babies. The senior and intermediate squads were PI60 and PI61. They were the ones who had organised our fake reception. Basic training would last six months. At the end of our junior stage, there would be an examination and only those who passed could move on to become part of the intermediate squad. There would be another exam at the end of the intermediate stage and a final exam to mark the end of basic training. To keep us focussed, there were informal tests every two weeks. In theory, anyone failing the main exams was supposed to move back a stage, 'back-squadding' they called it. In practice, failing the exams meant a one-way ticket back home. Looking on the positive side, passing our finals meant we could wear the single shoulder pip of an operational, probationary inspector. One-pip. It seemed a lowly badge for one with so much responsibility. During my job interview, I had asked about the duties of a probationary inspector and found they were the same as an inspector back home. In fact, Hong Kong police work seemed a lot like the job in England but with a rank structure similar to the army's. In the junior ranks, there were two grades of staff sergeant, the equivalent of sergeant major. Below the staff sergeants were sergeants and corporals. One-pip inspectors commanded units of between thirty and forty men and women, much like a one-pip subaltern in the army. In fact, our title had once been sub-inspector. At some point, the force decided that if a sub-inspector had not made the grade after three years, then he or she was out, finished, their services no longer required. In effect, sub-inspectors were on probation so in 1960, the force changed the title from sub-inspector to probationary inspector, or PI. For the first three years, our futures would be in the balance. We could be dismissed without notice and without any reason given.

That Monday morning, the barrack sergeant issued each man with three bush shirts, three pairs of enormous khaki shorts, a white, canvas-webbing belt with brass fasteners, a pair of clod-hopping ammo boots and a set of canvas gaiters. That day, three things happened that defined life in the training school.

First was the training school haircut. Our drill and musketry instructor, a gangling Chinese inspector with lungs of brass, marched us from the drill-square and halted us outside the school barbershop. 'I am kind and reasonable man,' he bellowed and we wilted under his unblinking stare. 'You may keep as much hair as you like, but don't let me see it.' This meant we could keep the hair that was under our caps but any hair showing below the capband belonged to the barber. We immediately split into two camps. I was in the group that went for the tough guy look. We wore our caps tipped forward with the peak low over the eyes. I figured there was no point in keeping much hair under the cap because once I took it off, I would look like an animated feather duster. The only answer was short on top, nothing back and sides. The other group decided to hide as much hair as they could. They did this by tilting their caps back and pulling down on the hatband with both hands whilst executing rapid clockwise and anti-clockwise twisting motions. This seemed to work best with the teeth gritted and eyes screwed shut. The result was a large bulge at the crown of the cap and ears that stuck out like matching teapot handles.

The second defining event was our meeting with PI62's Chinese inspectors. It took us by surprise; we thought they would be just like us except they would be -- well -- Chinese. They were friendly but a little too polite for easy conversation. When the youngest member of our squad, Eugene Tu, found I was from Northern England, he bubbled on about the North's principal cities as though it were a geography exam. Sammy Yip stunned our Irish squadmate by asking if he was Catholic or Christian. Curly Briggs took me aside. 'Ah think it's a language thing,' he confided. 'These here lads are going ta struggle with the exams, like.' He need not have worried. We would soon learn about the Chinese capacity for hard work and study. By the time of our first major examination, the Chinese PIs took most of the top twelve places. At the end of our training, one came within a whisker of winning the squad prize for academic achievement.

The third event was the commandant's welcoming address,

the real commandant, that is. He was tall and slim with a hook nose and eyes that could drill holes through steel plate. There was so much starch in his shorts, they could have stood to attention all by themselves. His shoes and Sam Browne were like black glass. We sat bright and attentive in our classroom as the commandant breezed in. He spoke in a resonant baritone. 'I want to welcome you to the police training school, I hope you will be very happy here. We are one big family. My door is always open.' I had heard this before somewhere. After a few minutes we were lost in our own thoughts but the commandant had an ace up his sleeve. In an instant twelve pairs of ears pricked up and we leaned forward, straining to catch every word. The trick was in two innocent little phrases: 'Cheap booze; loose women.'

Panic flashed through me, had I missed anything? He continued. 'I won't forbid you to visit these places.' He paused for effect and for a second I thought he would hand out maps. 'In fact, you should go to the Wanchai bar area. Just take a look and leave it at that. The beer might be cheap and the women are loose, but be warned, those women are expensive and not particularly good.' I guessed that as commandant, he was expert on both counts. He gave us a thin smile before continuing. 'So, what lies in your immediate future?' No one answered. 'Hard work,' he said, leaning forward for emphasis. 'Hard work and weeding. Here, we will weed out any who we think are not up to the job.' He ran his eyes over the squad as if already deciding which one of us would walk the plank. 'So far this year, we have trained sixty probationary inspectors,' he continued. 'PI62 will bring that number up to seventy-nine.'

I did a quick calculation. Six squads every year and a probationary period of three years. There must have been over two hundred probationary inspectors in the force. That was more than the entire strength of the Warrington Borough police force I had joined in 1967.

'To be precise,' the Commandant said. 'We will have trained

seventy-nine *if*, and only if, you all make it to graduation. But some of you won't.' He paused to let that sink in. 'Some of you will leave before the training is over. Others will graduate but will not make the grade. It's likely only half the expatriates will serve beyond three years.' He beamed at the Chinese recruits. 'Fortunately, most of the locals will make the force their life career.'

It is a good idea to have questions ready at the end of such talks; it flatters the speaker and tells him his audience was listening. A few hands went up and the commandant glanced at his seating plan. 'Yes, *er* ... Mister Briggs.'

Curly put on his most solemn expression. 'Sir, when we visit the Wanchai bars, can we wear these boots?'

The commandant rolled his eyes and decided we had asked enough questions. As he strode from the room, Curly bent his head close to mine. 'Take it from me, lad' he whispered, 'it's important to make a good first impression, like.'

On Tuesday, we met our course instructor. He was an amiable and quietly spoken man called Alan Wilson. He had greying hair and carried himself with an air of gentle reassurance. In uniform, he wore a lanyard of bright crimson that denoted a governor's commendation. The red lanyard was rare, it symbolized an act of unusual gallantry or outstanding professional achievement. When we quizzed him about it, he would only shrug and change the subject. He ordered us into plain clothes and told us to grab enough cash to open a bank account. We settled into the iron-hard seats of a police bus and within minutes were on a narrow road winding through the lush greenery of South Hong Kong Island. As we crested Wong Nai Chung Gap, the low-rise blocks of Happy Valley lay before us. Beyond it, the harbour sparkled under the autumn sun. We skirted the racecourse then it was along the tenement-lined roads of Wanchai and soon, we were in Hong Kong's business centre. The area's official name was 'Victoria,' but everyone knew it as 'Central.'

The bus dropped us at the steps of the Chartered Bank head-quarters and Alan Wilson ushered us into a banking hall with a vaulted ceiling and floors of polished stone. I had expected all the rigmarole that went with opening my first bank account back in Warrington but I had not counted on the way Hong Kong did business. Within an hour, PI62 left the bank with our life savings safely deposited and temporary cheque books tucked into our pockets.

'Have a look around,' Alan Wilson told us. 'Get a taste of the place and be back in an hour.'

We wandered, wide-eyed into what was fast becoming one of the world's premier financial centres. Buses, lorries and cars jammed the roads; there were Mercedes, BMWs, a Bentley or two and more than one Rolls Royce. So crowded were the sidewalks that some people stepped into the road, where the blare of car horns added to the clamour. We split into small groups and I found myself alone. I passed the bronze lions guarding the Hong Kong and Shanghai Bank headquarters. Next to it stood the Bank of China. Across the road from the Bank was that quintessential symbol of empire, the Hong Kong Cricket Club. I decided to explore the Hilton Hotel's shopping arcade. There were jewellers displaying the works of Gucci and Cartier. There were Rolex and Omega watches. A tailor's shop boasted it could deliver a Savile Row quality, bespoke suit within twenty-four hours. The window display included a bow tie with a price tag of ten dollars. That seemed reasonable so I went inside and offered one of my new, Chartered Bank ten-dollar bills.

The tailor looked at me as though I had handed him a used tissue. 'That would, of course, be ten *American* dollars, sir,' he purred.

'Of course,' I said and left.

I stepped back into the street and wandered to a grand colonial edifice that looked the very essence of permanence and probity. A discreet brass plaque by the main entrance announced I had found Hong Kong's supreme court building. Shaded colonnades ran the full length and breadth of the ground floor. Doric columns supported deep verandas on the upper floor. A dome sat on the roof like a crown.

Beyond the court building stood Chater Gardens. A few people wandered amongst its flowerbeds; a couple sat on one of the stone benches. A Chinese man wearing a sharp, three-piece suit stopped and placed his briefcase on the ground. He checked his watch then began to perform a fluid *tai-chi* exercise routine. I watched, mesmerised by the balance of power and grace as one movement flowed into the next. The routine over, he picked up his briefcase and strode off.

Elsewhere, Central district was a clamour of traffic and construction. Wreckers were busy razing the beautiful but inadequate buildings left over from the Edwardian era. Jackhammers pounded at huge steel piles that would make the foundations of the new Hong Kong. On the harbour front, Jardine Matheson's new fifty-plus storey Connaught Centre was set to become Hong Kong's tallest building, a title it would keep for eight years.

As our bus wound back to the training school, it buzzed with conversation but I heard none of it. I could not shake off images of a communist bank looming above a colonial cricket match; of stores brimming with luxury goods I had seen only in glossy, lifestyle magazines; of jackhammers, clamouring traffic and jammed sidewalks. But most of all, I could not forget the image of a city businessman taking time out of his day to conduct an ancient and elegant exercise ritual.

For the first time, I realised I was a very long way from Merseyside.

All through puberty, I daydreamed of the perfect woman. She had delicate cheekbones, long blue-black hair and almond shaped eyes. In my longest running fantasy, Nancy Kwan lured me into her boudoir and teased me to distraction with her oriental secrets of love. It was a thought uppermost in my mind as PI62's Brits sauntered, *en masse* down the Wanchai strip. Dotted along the kerb were signs that read, 'Welcome, USS *Kitty Hawk*, USS *Oklahoma City*, USS *Topeka*.' That first Friday night, Wanchai was a wall-to-wall assault on the senses. Red, blue and yellow neon signs invited us to try, 'The Neptune Bar,' 'Crazy Horse Twenty-Four Hour Tailor,' 'Pinky's Tattoo Parlour' and 'Bangkok Massage.' Behind every door and velvet curtain was a bar, a restaurant or other form of sensual diversion. The pavements were narrow and we had to sidestep barkers who called out to us: 'Cheapest beer. Prettiest girls. No cover charge. No clap.'

Curly Briggs strode along Lockhart Road with an invisible carpet roll under each arm. He found that if he thumped a parking meter hard enough, it gave an extra half-hour's credit. His face lit up like a toddler's birthday cake and before we could stop him, he ran down the road punching every parking meter he could lay his hand to.

It was a sultry, tropical evening. The Vietnam War was at its peak and the US Seventh Fleet was in town for a spot of R and R -- rest and recuperation. A door burst open and a band of carousing marines spilled into the street. Groups of uniformed Americans rolled along the pavements laughing and whooping like Texas rowdies after a cattle drive. The marines wore sharply creased slacks and medal ribboned shirts. The sailors wore tropical whites and Popeye the Sailorman hats. The strains of James Brown's 'Papa's Got a Brand New Bag' pumped from a neon lit storefront. Two rickshaws, each pulled by a uniformed sailor, raced down the middle of the street. From the passenger seats, the regular rickshaw pullers laughed whilst the sailors sprinted towards a finishing line marked by a length of string. The rickshaw pullers' laughter turned to cries of alarm as the sailors bounced the rickshaws over the kerb and pulled them through the open door of a bar. Back home, there had always been an air of menace on the streets, particularly when the pubs closed. In England, the rowdiness came from gangs of surly young men fuelled by alcohol and boredom. But Wanchai was different; in Wanchai there was no menace, only joyous carnival.

The *Seven Seas* was the regular jumping off point for PIs out for a night in the Wanch'. They do not make bars like the *Seven Seas* any more. Today's Wanchai bars have thumping music and flashing blue lights that highlight dandruff. On that magic evening however, the *Seven Seas* was every purist's vision of the perfect Hong Kong bar. Tasselled lanterns gave just enough light for customers to navigate across the floor. Nestled around the walls were booths, their occupants shielded by ornate wooden screens. A beaded curtain hung at a darkened doorway that led to the office and the staff quarters. Cigarette smoke fogged the air, musky incense burned at a little altar behind the bar, tinny Chinese music drifted from an old record player. And who could forget the ladies?

The *cheong-saam* is the most sensuous garment ever designed for the human form. In a passing nod to modesty, its brocaded silk covers the body from jaw to knee. Modesty, of course, is not what the *cheong-saam* is about. The dress clings so tight to the body that there is a slit from hem to hip to allow any kind of movement. Nancy Kwan's film portrayal of Susie Wong, showed a bar girl who was a subtle mix of sensitivity, sexuality and vulnerability. When I set eyes on the ladies of the *Seven Seas*, I saw nothing subtle about their smiles or the unblinking gaze of their almond shaped eyes. For years, my teenage fantasies had done reality a grave disservice.

An older woman with a lapel badge that read *Mamasan* ushered us to the bar where a barman with oiled hair and a white tuxedo poured the beers two glasses at a time. 'You sit here. No, not there, here. You sit here.' *Mamasan* had a voice like a squeaky door and she guided us onto alternate barstools with a skill that would have done a border collie proud. I wanted to talk to my new mates but as soon as the glass of San Miguel appeared on the bar in front of me, I felt a soft hand on mine.

'Hello, how are you today?' The girl was slender; long black hair framed a heart shaped face. A soft fringe covered her forehead. She smiled, revealing even white teeth and I felt my pulse quicken. It was really happening; my teenage dreams were coming true. There was a rustle of silk as she eased herself onto the barstool next to mine. The slit down the side of her *cheong-saam* parted to reveal a perfectly formed thigh. She leaned closer, her voice was sweet and musical, 'What's your name?'

I tried to answer and managed a squeak. She stroked the nape of my neck and walked her fingers up the inside of my thigh. She rested her chin on my shoulder. Her breath was warm and perfumed on my cheek. She spoke in a throaty half-whisper, 'Now you buy me one little drink, okay?'

A hostess drink was five times the price of a beer and payday was not for two weeks. Not wanting to offend, I explained that although she was very pretty and I would love to buy her a drink, I was short of funds. At least that is what I would have said but in the middle of my speech, she yawned, slipped from her stool and latched onto a man who stood swaying, further down the bar.

A braying laugh told me Curly had tired of beating up the Lockhart Road parking meters. He had some catching up to do and the beers disappeared as fast as the bartender could pour them. After beer number five, Curly put his arm around my shoulder. 'Hey, Yanks,' he shouted. I tried to twist away but Curly's grip was too strong. 'This 'ere bonnie lad is the canniest bleedin' policeman in the whole bleedin' world.'

At the end of the bar, a knot of combat-hardened Marines stopped their conversation and gave us a flat stare.

'And,' Curly continued, 'he'll buy a beer for any bleedin' yank what knows the chorus to "Rule Britannia."'

The Marines placed their drinks on the bar-top and fanned

out in a line to face us. I shrugged my apologies but their eyes glistened like polished flint. In the shadows, a grizzled master sergeant said something and they went back to their drinks, muttering like sports fans turned away at the turnstiles.

Beer number twelve did for Curly. His eyes went glassy and he slumped forward with his chin resting on the bar-top. He reached for beer number thirteen but he could see two of them and kept grabbing at the wrong one. He closed his eyes. His arms dropped to his sides. The barstool became his bed and the bar-top his pillow.

With Curly out of the picture, the evening drifted by on a cloud of boozy companionship until a group of uniformed sailors swaggered in from the street. A taut hush descended on the *Seven Seas* as the sailors and the marines spotted each other. The sailors drank in grim-faced silence, their backs to the bar and their little caps angled forward. The marines, under the glare of their sergeant, also drank quietly, their eyes glued to the sailors. The silence seemed to go on forever until the largest sailor, a brawny giant with the biceps of a Cunard stoker banged his glass on the bar, passed a remark about his ship's departure time and headed for the door.

To this day, I do not know why I did it. There is inside me a little voice that works like a conscience, only in reverse. It is always getting me into trouble but I have never learned to control it. As the sailors headed for the door, I just opened my mouth and my little voice did the rest. 'Whoa. What about this guy? Shore patrol'll crucify him for bein' outa uniform.'

The huge sailor stopped and turned. He looked around for the person who had spoken so I hunched my shoulders and stared into my beer. PI62 watched with a mixture of eye-popping horror and buttock-clenching glee as the big sailor ambled back to the bar, and prodded Curly in the ribs.

'Hey, buddy. Hey, time to go.'

Curly gave a gentle snore.

'Okay buddy, take it easy. Up we go.' The sailor hefted Curly over his shoulder like a floppy hearthrug and carried him to the door. Not one of us spoke; nobody rushed into the street to explain that Curly was not his shipmate. There was not a single protest as the US Navy disappeared into the night carrying with it the limp form of Curly Briggs.

The next afternoon we paused in our game of football as a buzzing dot appeared in the sky. The dot grew into a Sikorsky helicopter with a five-pointed star and the word, 'NAVY' emblazoned on its tail. The buzz turned into a staccato clatter as the Sikorsky circled then hovered over the parade ground. With a massive, 'Whumpwhumpwhump,' it dropped onto the square, throwing up a cloud of stinging grit. The door slid open and a helmeted crewman leapt to the ground followed by a sheepish Curly Briggs. Curly shook the crewman's hand. The crewman clambered aboard and the Sikorski's engine roared as the helicopter climbed then banked towards the South China Sea. Curly was not alone on the square; in the shade of the drill shed stood the commandant.

And he looked rather vexed.

CHAPTER 2
THE DUCK IS GO FOR LANDING

Basic training lasted six months during which we lived with Police General Orders and the two-volume General Duties Manual. Each was the size of a small doorstep and written in language that looked like English but, on close examination, bore no relation to any language. Police General Orders gave clear instructions on 'tonsorial standards.' I did not know what that meant but felt sure it was important. A clue came in a sentence directing that sideburns should not extend below the tragus. So, definitely something to do with haircuts. But what's a tragus?

On our first day of training, we filed into an airy classroom and took our place at desks arranged in a rough horseshoe. Alan Wilson greeted us with a genuine smile of welcome and we spent the next hour wading through the mass of paperwork needed to embed us into the force and the wider community. Paperwork done and shuffled aside, we settled down to our first lecture, which was force history.

Back in 1843, Sir Henry Pottinger, Hong Kong's first governor, realised there was more to the job than gymkhanas and garden parties. Hong Kong was an unruly corner of empire and among Pottinger's many headaches was the alarming number of murders, robberies, kidnappings, child stealing and pirate attacks. This being bad for business, the good burghers of Hong Kong demanded that Pottinger do something about it. In spring the following year, he authorised the formation of a properly appointed police force. Coming just fifteen years after Britain's Sir Robert Peel had set up the world's first police force, this was a radical move. Policing was a new science and Pottinger asked Charles May to be Hong Kong's first captain superintendent of police. May was a good choice, he had served as an inspector in Peel's police force. May did not have an easy time but to be fair, he did not have a lot to work with. The force was woefully underfunded and most of his recruits were drunks and ne'er do wells.

May soldiered on for seventeen years but his pleas for better funding went unheeded. Then, in 1859, Sir Hercules Robinson stepped into the governor's post. Robinson increased police pay, brought in a better rank structure, improved uniform and equipment, and introduced a pension scheme. He cast the recruiting net further and took on a contingent of Indian ex-soldiers. Robinson did a lot to improve morale and standards but sadly, the rot was too deep. The situation was so bad that when Sir Richard MacDonnell took over as governor in 1866, he claimed to have never seen a body so inefficient or corrupt as the Hong Kong Police. He set about purging the force and in short order, a quarter of its members found themselves out of a job.

Over the following decades, funding improved and so did the calibre of its officers. In 1941, the Japanese occupied Hong Kong. They rounded up the force's British officers and interred them with the other civilian detainees at Stanley Camp. Under the command of police commissioner John Pennefather-Evans, the interned police officers gave unflinching service to the camp community. With hostilities over, there came Pennefather-Evans' final legacy, which was to be even more profound than his wartime leadership. He realised Britain's place in the world had changed forever; the days of Empire were over. Among Pennefather-Evans' far-reaching recommendations was that Chinese police officers should have the same status as their British colleagues. The very idea met strident opposition from die-hard colonials. However, wiser counsel prevailed in the shape of Hong Kong's post-war governor, Sir Mark Young. Young accepted most of Pennefather-Evans' recommendations and put in place policies that, in time, would lead to Chinese officers filling the highest ranks of the force.

In 1949, China's communist party came to power and Hong Kong's population exploded. This brought fresh challenges for the force. In 1956, pro-Taiwan riots left more than fifty dead and at least five hundred injured. In 1966, an increase in ferry fares fed simmering frustrations and led to four days of rioting. Then, in 1967, China's Cultural Revolution hit Hong Kong like a coastal hurricane. Beginning in May, red guard activists organised a campaign of rioting, bombings and intimidation that shook Hong Kong to the core. A fearful public rallied behind the force in a way never before seen. The police received widespread praise for their steadfastness and restraint. Officers on normal day-to-day duty found strangers pressing small gifts into their hands. Thousands contributed to a fund set up to pay for the education of police children. In December, the rioters melted away and the bombings ended. The force had stood firm and returned the streets of Hong Kong to its people.

In 1969, in recognition of the police courage and steadfastness, Her Majesty the Queen declared that henceforth, the force would become, 'The *Royal* Hong Kong Police.'

Over the following weeks, we settled into a routine of lectures, physical training, and drill. Of all this training, it is the drill that stayed with me the longest. We marched from our quarters to the classroom and from the classroom to the drill-square where we marched some more. Then it was a short march back to the classroom, or the gymnasium, or the firing range, then back to the drill-square. The Training School developed us in mind and body. The constant drill and physical training hardened our bodies; regular classroom tests kept our minds focussed.

In the second week, came our first lesson in the use of firearms. Our drill and musketry instructor was waiting for us in the classroom and on his desk was a muscular box with heavy snap fastenings.

'Today, I introduce you to the Colt Police Positive revolver,' he said. He unsnapped the box and told us to line up. Inside the box, two rows of oiled pistols nestled in purpose-made brackets. The DMI took a pistol from the box and held it up so we could see it. 'When I hand you a service revolver, I will open the cylinder, thus.' He thumbed back the cylinder catch and the cylinder swung away from the frame. He turned the pistol end on, showing us it was not loaded. 'First rule,' he continued, 'always display empty cylinder when you take revolver from someone or when you hand it to someone.' He fixed us with a glare. 'Treat it with respect,' he said. 'Never do this.' He flicked the pistol to the side and the cylinder snapped shut. 'This is not Hawaii Five-O,' he growled. 'If you break cylinder lock you will pay cost of repair. Also, you will look bloody stupid picking bullets up from ground while the bad guy is shooting at you.'

We filed past the DMI and each took a pistol, making sure the cylinder was open and devoid of cartridges. It was heavier than it looked. The wooden grip was hatch-cut and felt rough in my hand. I returned to my desk and wondered if this particular revolver had seen action. I sighted it at a fly on the wall and squeezed the trigger. There was an oily click. Around me, there were more. *Clickclickclickclickclick.*

'No random snapping,' the DMI barked.

'But it's empty,' someone answered.

'Tell it to the coroner,' the DMI growled. 'There are no accidental discharges, only negligent discharges.'

Behind me, there was a snigger. My little voice wanted to say something but I bit my lip and fought it down.

Over the next hour, the DMI talked us through the specifications of the Colt Police Positive: its weight, its range, the correct way to carry it, the right way to sight and fire it. He stressed the safety precautions: safety on the range, safety in the armoury, safety in the police station and safety on the street. 'Never draw your revolver unless you mean to use it,' he said. 'If you ever open fire, many people will spend weeks looking at decision you made in split second.' He looked around the room. 'Are there questions?'

I raised my hand.

The DMI raised an eyebrow.

'The UK police manage fine without guns,' I said. 'In fact, it's a matter of pride. Why carry them here?'

The DMI looked at me as though I had suggested we strip down to our jockstraps. 'What force were you?' he asked.

'Warrington,' I answered.

One of the ex-London coppers gave a quiet chuckle.

The DMI put his hands on his hips. 'How many Warrington police officers murdered in the last ten years?'

'*Er* ... none, I think.'

How many in Hong Kong?'

I could only shrug.

'Fifteen,' the DMI said. 'In ten years, fifteen Hong Kong Police officers were murdered on duty.' His eyes burned. 'They were shot, stabbed, two were blown up with bombs and one was hacked to death with a cargo hook.' He looked around the class. There was complete silence. 'All were armed,' he continued. 'Still, they could not defend themselves.' He turned to Eugene Tu. 'Would you patrol Mong Kok without a gun?'

Eugene lowered his eyes and shook his head.

'How about Yau Ma Tei? How about Kwun Tong housing estates? How about bloody arse end of Causeway Bay?'

All the Chinese inspectors shook their heads. The DMI turned to me. 'Forget Warrington,' he said. 'This is Hong Kong. In Hong Kong the triads and the street corner toughs would cut you up just to earn themselves some face. But they won't cut you up.

They will act tough and they will curse you behind your back but they will think hard before pulling a weapon on you. Why? Because you carry a gun and they know this DMI has trained you very well.' For a moment, he was silent. 'Any more questions?' he asked.

There were none.

The training regimen did not suit everyone. Within a few weeks of our arrival, the commandant's prediction started to come true. Three members of the intermediate squad left. Shortly afterwards, two clever and popular members of PI62 returned to England.

Mind you, it was not all work. The officers' mess was our retreat, a place to right the ills of the day over a cold beer. At least it was for the British inspectors. We began to wonder how our Chinese colleagues whiled away their spare time. The answer came when our course instructor read out the fortnightly test results. At first, the Chinese lagged behind but test by test, their grades improved. By the time we neared the end of our junior stage, their results were in the stratosphere. The Chinese inspectors pursued academic excellence with a vigour that left us Brits bewildered, which was probably the start of the problem. Of course, there was more to it than that. Culture shock: the words conjure images of stunned Westerners lost in a blizzard of all things oriental but believe me, it is not nearly so simple.

We British are a strange lot. Who else would travel thousands of miles in search of a new life then complain it is not like home? The expatriate Briton has a talent for creating a world that looks British but is nothing at all like Britain. Back home I knew Englishmen who never celebrated Saint George's day, Scotsmen who never danced a reel, Welshmen who never ate a leek and Irishmen who until they left the emerald shore, could stomach neither Guinness nor plaintive ballads. There are, however, Welsh male voice choirs in the Canadian wilderness, Burns' societies on the Argentine pampas and morris dancers locked away in Antarctic science stations. Only when he finds himself on foreign soil does the British expatriate get dewy-eyed about his roots. This probably explains why nineteenth-century empire builders were such a dull lot. With few exceptions, they were either dowdy bureaucrats or fugitive scoundrels. Suddenly, thanks to the imperial foreign policy of the day, they found themselves members of the governing classes. They lived in airy villas served by cooks and houseboys. For the first time in their lives, they had *status*. But still something was missing, namely that never-really-existed Britain of endless summers, punts on the river and croquet parties on sun-dappled lawns. So, the old colonials had no choice but to fill in the gaps as best they could. There were beachside picnics, country clubs and cricket matches on whatever bit of green they could find.

And that was part of our problem; the British inspectors expected everything to be just like home and of course, it was not. PI62 divided into two camps. In one camp were the Brits who did not understand the Chinese; in the other, were the Chinese who knew nothing about Westerners. It was only a matter of style but one thing was clear, we annoyed the hell out of each other. The Chinese never queued and they all seemed to talk at the same time. The Brits queued for everything and instead of complaining, we muttered darkly to ourselves. As a result, we thought the Chinese brash and unruly; the Chinese thought us pompous and unfriendly.

Garry Mak was different. He was cool and streetwise and the whole squad, British and Chinese latched onto him. He had a foot in both camps and worked harder than anyone to bring us together. He organised a five-a-side football match and called it the PI62 International. The Chinese won four-nil and celebrated in a way we thought brash and unruly. They thought our subdued congratulations were pompous and unfriendly. We were getting nowhere. Then the answer to our problem came from a Chinese proverb: if it has its back to heaven, you can eat it.

Back in England, my only experience of Chinese cuisine had been the number five banquet served in my local Ming Palace Restaurant. I expected Hong Kong eateries to have flock wallpaper and passable meals served by helpful waiters wearing dark suits. Instead, Garry led us into a place lit by stark neon. Paint peeled from the walls and wads of grey lint blocked the ventilation vents. The tables were crammed so close together, there was hardly room to move between them. Nothing can describe the noise, it was like a wall. There were clattering pots and blaring Chinese music. The place was packed, all conversations were shouted. Garry led us to two tables covered in plastic sheeting. A cheerful waiter greeted us. He wore shorts, rubber sandals and a grimy singlet. Garry oversaw the seating, ensuring that the Chinese and Brits were evenly distributed, then he scurried off to arrange the meal.

'Fancy a beer?' Eugene Tu asked me. He waved to the waiter, who came forward, grinning and bobbing his head. 'You order,' Eugene suggested. 'A half-dozen, large San Miguels will do.'

I beckoned the waiter. 'Six large San Miguel, please,' I said.

'*Gong m'yeh*?' he answered.

'SIX-LARGE-SAN-MIGUEL-PLEASE,' I shouted. We English have a knack for languages.

The waiter turned to Eugene and shrugged. '*Ni goh gwailo gong m'yeh?*' (What did the foreigner say?) Eugene put his head close to mine. 'Try: *luk booi dai san lik*,' he suggested.

I gave it a try and a grin split the waiter's face. '*Dak, dak, dak*,' he said, which I guessed meant, '*OK, OK, OK*.' He scuttled off chuckling to himself and saying something that sounded like, '*Aiyah. Gwailo sik gong. Ho siu.*'

'He thinks it's great a foreign devil knows how to talk,' Eugene translated for me.

Within a minute the waiter was back with a tray of beers. I was astounded. I had spoken Chinese, communicated in an Asian tongue. After just a few weeks, I had become a proper colonial. Like they say, I had got my knees brown.

Garry passed out menu sheets, which were in Chinese and English. I ran my finger down a list of delights that included: 'sir's groin of beef in ginger,' and 'pigeon balls in black beings sauce (special chilli beings on request).' As it turned out, Garry had already ordered and a course of cold cuts appeared on the table. There were bite-sized portions of pork cracking, slivers of beef and something that looked like elastic bands. 'Jellyfish,' Garry said. 'Try it. You'll like it.'

Somebody called out, '*Yam booi!*' and raised a glass. We toasted the food, and the Chinese dived in with their chopsticks. And that was when the evening became interesting. Eugene was ever helpful. 'Should I tell the waiter to bring knives and forks?' he asked. He smiled and raised an eyebrow. Everyone at the table fell silent. It was as if a motorcycle salesman had asked, 'And would sir like training wheels with that?' The British inspectors swapped, 'I will if you will,' looks and decided to stay with the chopsticks.

Eugene talked me through the basics, which are really quite simple. First, anchor one chopstick between the tips of the second and third fingers and rest it on the hollow where the thumb joins the hand. Next, hold the second chopstick like a pencil. *Voila*, what could be easier? I tried it on a matchbox. It worked. I grinned; everyone grinned back. I reached for some pork crackling. The Chinese PIs were perfect examples of Asian courtesy. Not one of them laughed as the morsel of pork went cartwheeling across the table. They chewed their lips, their faces turned crimson and the veins in their necks stood out like mooring hawsers but they did not laugh. My British comrades were not so discreet and a few nearly fell off their chairs. Then, one by one, the laughter died as they realised, they were next.

By now, we had ordered a second round of beers and had become adventurous. We suggested different chopstick techniques to the Chinese PIs and, God bless them, they were game for anything. The two-handed method was slow and messy. A single chopstick made an effective skewer. Now, we were all laughing. One wonderful dish followed another: beef in ginger, fish steamed to perfection, crab and sweetcorn soup, *baak choi* in black bean sauce. There were more beers, more food. The conversation became louder; the banter more hearty. At some point, it hit me: the Chinese were not brash and unruly, rather they had a joy for life that made Italians seem as dour as Scottish weather forecasters. It was a joy for life that proved infectious. On that night, the antipathy between Chinese and British PIs ended. Yes, there were differences and yes, we sometimes annoyed each other but our differences no longer divided us. We became like family and like a family, we sometimes got on each other's nerves. However, everything had changed; in the years to come, it was all right for me to have the occasional moan about my Chinese colleagues and it was fine for them to moan about me, but God help any outsider who did the same.

This unspoken deal was set for life and it cut both ways.

There are two types of expatriate in a place like Hong Kong: there is the majority who are hard-working, get-the-job done, respect-the-local-culture type of expatriate and there is the type I call the old colonials. The old colonials are every bit as hard-working. They can be decent and honourable people, but they believe it is their destiny to bring good governance to the outposts of empire. There is a tendency for the colonials to forget their roots. If he is not careful, plain Joe Smith will break out in hyphens and become Joe Thingummy-Smith. He will lose his regional accent, forget the council estate where he grew up and in his own mind, become part of the ruling elite.

I quickly realised the importance of staying grounded, but one item of colonial accoutrement came close to being my downfall.

For my money, the formal dress uniform known as the 'mess kit,' was the height of colonial *chic*. One look and I was hooked. The waist-length mess jacket was white linen, silver buttons adorned the cuffs and there were miniature officer's pips at the epaulettes. The force insignia graced elegant lapels. The trousers were black with a buff stripe down each leg. A black cummerbund and a bow tie completed the outfit.

Do not let the formality put you off, functions in the officers' mess were a blast. The band decked itself out in their dress uniforms and mess members drank far more than was good for them. The food was good, the company better and the speeches were witty. During training school mess nights, the youngest mess member, dubbed Mister Vice, had several duties. He called the toasts and at some stage would parade the mess duck around the dining table. Before parading the duck, he had first to catch the thing, climb up onto the table then pick his way around the table ornaments and port glasses. If he could present the duck to each mess member without falling from the table or without the duck disgracing itself, then his part of the evening was a success.

The senior squad, PI60, would soon graduate from the training school and that called for a formal mess dinner. Our problem was that we did not yet have our mess kits. Mess rules were perfectly reasonable, if our mess kits were not ready, we could wear dark trousers, a white shirt and a dark tie. But damn it, I had become Thingummy-Smith, I wanted my little officer's pips and my white linen jacket. How could I face the mess without a buff stripe on my trousers? A few others felt the same way and we found our way to a Wanchai tailor who could make police mess kits at half the price charged by the police contractor. You might think that here lurked disaster, but as far as quality is concerned, the world has given Hong Kong tailors a bum rap. Most came from Shanghai after the communist takeover and many of Hong Kong's swishest tailor shops contracted out to these old Shanghai craftsmen. Our tailors smiled and plied us with beer as they took our measurements. Maybe it was the beer, but at some point it dawned on us that the poor little mess duck had no mess kit at all. 'There's ... *um* ... just one more, small but rather special order,' one of our ex-coppers said. 'I do hope you can help.'

The tailors beamed and nodded. Of course, they could help, there was no order they could not fill. Emboldened by the beer, we told them that not only did we want mess kits for ourselves but also one for the duck. The shop went quiet. The tailors looked first at each other and then at us before erupting into a tirade that consisted of arm waving and rapid-fire dialogue interwoven with the phrase, '*Chee-sin gwailo,*' -- Crazy white devils.

I do not know if it was our powers of persuasion or our offer to pay in advance, but they calmed and agreed to design a mess kit just for the duck. The tailors extracted one more price. 'After party, we come to training school and bring photographer from South China Morning Post, yes?'

The SCMP's readership was mainly Westerners who formed only a tiny part of Hong Kong society. Why not, I asked, invite the Chinese press?

'Ah, not good idea. British think duck in dress uniform very jolly. Chinese are smart; they think whole idea bloody nonsense.'

Even on the first fitting, the duck looked great. We promoted him to superintendent and fixed him up with a full winter mess kit. He had a little opera cape of black worsted faced with buff lapels and decorated with the marine police insignia. On the big night, the duck passed muster but as we humans entered the mess, a senior PI stopped us at the door. 'Non-standard mess kits I'm afraid, gentlemen,' he said, all pomp and officiousness. He snapped open a tape measure and held it to the front of my mess jacket. The senior PIs gathered round him. Their grins told me they had been planning this for days.

'Lapels: three-and-a-half inches.' The senior flashed a smile. 'So far, so good, Mister Emmett.' He moved behind me and I felt a light touch on my shoulder. 'Epaulettes: five-and-a-half by two-and-a-quarter. He went down on one knee. 'Buff stripe along outer seam; oh dear, oh dear.' Another senior PI pushed his way through the crowd. He was holding a brimming yard of ale glass. The PI who had inspected me showed the tape measure to the other seniors. 'I make that one and fifteen-sixteenth inches,' he said. He turned to me, a look of mock sympathy on his face. 'Sorry, it's supposed to be two inches.'

The seniors began to chant, '*Up, up, up.*' As the chanting grew louder, hands grabbed my arms and legs. I demanded a re-inspection but felt myself hoisted onto a tabletop. The room went quiet and a laughing senior handed up the yard of ale. The yard is an elegant glass, three feet long with a small bulb at the end. It carries three pints of beer and the first thing I noticed was how heavy it felt. As soon as I took hold of the glass, the chant became one of, '*Down, down, down.*' There was no mercy in their voices, even my squadmates joined in, shouting and clapping in unison. I lifted the yard to my lips and it struck me that not only was it very heavy, it was also very long. On my first gulp, the cold beer hit my pallet like a block of ice and my eyes filled with tears. I slowed the pace and tipped back the yard. I saw the level falling away. I was going to do it. The rhythmic call of, '*Down, down, down,*' turned into applause. The stem was nearly empty; all that remained was the contents of the bulb at the end of the glass.

The knack, of course, is to pause before proceeding to the bulb. This allows the drinker to control the flow of beer. I know that -- now. I was triumphant as I tipped back the yard to finish my penance. Everyone fell silent. Eyes were wide and expectant. There was a small '*ploot*' noise from somewhere inside the glass and I saw a wall of lager charging towards me like an amber *tsunami*. Amidst applause, cheers and laughter, the contents of the bulb smacked into my face and cascaded down my neck, drenching my shirt and the front of my mess jacket. I stood on the table, gaping in horror at my jacket. It was soaked. Beer dripped from my face. My hair was slick with the stuff. The mess went quiet. A booming voice broke the silence.

'Gentlemen, pray stand to welcome our commandant and his guest.'

The commandant's mess jacket was whiter than any white I had seen, the trousers blacker, and the buff stripe brighter. The silver crowns and bath stars of a chief superintendent adorned each of his epaulettes. Miniature medals decorated his lapels. His guest, another chief superintendent, was equally resplendent. I snapped to attention; perhaps they would not notice a beer soaked junior PI, standing on a table in the middle of the mess. The commandant turned to the assembled mess members. 'Carry on gentlemen.' He gave me a light smile and arched an eyebrow, 'that is, Mister Emmett, if you've finished with the *aperitifs.*'

I tidied myself up as best I could. I washed out the jacket and although it was soaking wet, it showed no traces of the beer. The rest of the evening filled my every expectation, the food and companionship were excellent, the wine plentiful. After the mess stewards took away the cheese boards and passed out the port decanters, the mess president called upon Mister Vice to propose the formal toasts. By the time I started on the port, I was floating on a fuzzy cloud of contentment. The yard of ale and the wine, I was not used to it. Mister Vice paraded the duck then, as was mess tradition, the guest clambered onto the table and delivered the after dinner speech. He used no notes and regaled us with stories from his time as a probationary inspector. I thought him the funniest and perhaps the cleverest man I had ever met. I was sure I would hear more of him. I was not wrong; his name was Peter Fitzroy Godber and his legacy is one still felt today.

The speeches over, it was time for the mess games. I never saw the point to those games unless it was to make complete idiots of us all. The rocking horse races were too much like hard work and high cockalurum involved seeing how many people it is possible to leapfrog in one leap. Great fun for the leaper but not for the poor frog he lands on. The mess jousting was harmless but we had to abandon the indoor rugby when the brick we used as a ball smashed into the mouth of one of our squad members, breaking three of his teeth.

Some time after midnight, Curly Briggs appeared at the bar with the duck held in the crook of his arm. 'Hey, lads, watch this,' he called. He trapped some vodka in a drinking straw then transferred the straw into the duck's beak. The duck's bill clattered and with the straw empty, it clamoured for more like a hungry nestling.

The science of aeronautics missed a great chance that night. Until then, it had ignored the flight mechanism of drunken ducks wearing full mess uniform. If we include Curly in the equation, then science blew it twice. Dealing with drunks can be tricky, handle them right and they are as sweet as pie; one wrong word and they want to rip out your heart. I do not know what Curly said to the duck but later that night, on the roof of the officer's mess, the bird turned downright cantankerous. Curly swore he never meant to launch the duck from the roof but he never explained what he was doing up there. He said the duck had writhed, kicked and pecked itself loose. Whatever the truth, the duck had no chance; it was in no state to walk let alone fly and its little opera cape could not have helped. Luckily, the duck had only ten feet to fall and it landed on its back, an angry quacking ball of feathers and black worsted, robbed of dignity but still in one piece. Meanwhile, Curly, who was in the same condition as the duck, peered over the edge to see what had happened. He swayed forward, teetered for a second then, arms flailing, he followed the duck down onto the patio.

I was taking some air when first the duck, then Curly hit the ground and I am not sure which squawked the loudest. We were not having a good night, first a poor squadmate carted off for emergency dental treatment and now Curly, lying face down on the patio, cursing and groaning as though he had damaged an important bit. I rushed to Curly's side and told him not to move. He lay on his stomach, his face twisted with shock and pain.

'Ah'm dead, ah'm fookin' dead.'

I told him he was no such thing but he kept groaning as I ran my hands down all four limbs, checking for broken bones. If the gods take care of drunks and madmen, then fate had Curly covered twice. I rolled him over but apart from a clump of turf and a few feathers stuck to his mess jacket, he seemed fine. He raised himself onto his elbows and shook his head. I looked around but there was no sign of the duck and for a moment, I thought it had staggered off into the night. Then, a dreadful realisation made my neck hairs tingle. I looked closer at the clod on Curly's mess jacket and a knot of panic grew in my stomach. What I had dismissed as a clump of turf was wearing a black worsted opera cape with buff facings. A marine police badge winked in the light from the mess window.

Some people swear by black coffee, others believe that more alcohol is the perfect cure. A raw egg with Worcester sauce sometimes does the trick, but I have always preferred a long lie down in a dark room. Mess night hangovers were doozies.

Maurice Brown revelled in the glorious title of Chief Drill and Musketry Instructor. A retired sergeant major, he was a giant of a man with a heart to match his physique. He swore his personal hangover cure never failed, although I never saw him drunk enough to need one. He was a humorous and sociable character with just one flaw: when it came to hangovers and sloppy drill, he was not one to see the other chap's point of view. As the mess night yawned and spluttered to a close, Maurice suggested that at six o'clock the next morning, we all put on our PT kit and join him on the drill-square. We were horrified, but when the CDMI made a suggestion, it was best not to disappoint him.

The next morning, in the muggy half-light before dawn, all

members of PI60, PI61 and PI62 gathered on the parade ground. I suppose I looked like everyone else: round-shouldered, red-eyed, tousle-haired and in no mood for conversation. Even the normally temperate Chinese inspectors were looking worse for wear. Maurice Brown on the other hand was all cheer and good humour. He rubbed his hands together. 'Good morning, good morning gentlemen; and isn't this the very best part of the day?' There were a few grunts. Maurice smiled and continued. 'We'll just have a little stroll over Brick Hill to put us in the mood for breakfast.' He nodded to the physical training sergeant who flashed a malicious smile and punched his stopwatch. Maurice hung back long enough to make sure nobody sneaked back to our quarters and as soon as we were all on the path to the hill's summit, he stormed past us like a mountain goat on a promise.

Brick Hill did not look imposing until the first time I had to run to the top. Then I knew how Mallory felt when he looked up at Everest's peak and noticed the weather had taken a turn for the worse. We have seen the TV shows where a fearless police-man chases the bad guy across rooftops, hangs from fire escapes and vaults over car bonnets. In truth, the only exercise I got as an English Bobby was to open the door of my little patrol car. I have met manicurists fitter than most policemen. In the United Kingdom, the days of the super fit policeman disappeared along with the police bicycle. PI62's ex-UK coppers were the products of years of alcohol and nicotine abuse. For the first part of the run, the incline was so steep that I had to grab tufts of grass to stop myself from toppling backwards. At the half way point, a ridge ran along the north face of the hill. From the lower slopes, this ridge looked like the summit and no matter how many times I made the run, my heart always sank when I got there and re-alised I was nowhere near the top.

Maurice Brown meant to get back to the training school first so he could count us all in. The plan would have worked had the path leading down the other side not been damp and slippery.

Curly Briggs reached the top just a few yards behind Maurice. He jogged across the flattened summit and on towards a gap in the foliage that marked the downward path. The downhill part was easy enough, but in the pre-dawn gloom and with the after-effects of the night before nagging at him, Curly lost his footing. He skidded into a patch of brush and reached out his arm to steady himself. His arm disappeared up to the shoulder and his hand connected with what felt like a sturdy branch. Curly took a tight grip but to his dismay, the branch moved. A dry, hissing noise came from the depths of the bush and in the shadows, Curly saw two spots of reflected light.

Some people know what to do when faced with a snake but Curly Briggs was not one of them. Most of us would say something like, 'Oh golly, a snake,' then leave the area. Curly did neither. He let out a strangled gurgle and froze. The snake, finding something static and warm, freed itself from the bush and wrapped itself around Curly's forearm. Curly's eyes widened to the size of silver dollars and keeping his arm stiff in front of him, he backed away. This, of course, confirmed Curly's fears that the snake had indeed abandoned the bush in favour of his forearm. He began to wail and started to trot down the path, his arm stretched out before him in an attempt to keep the snake as far away as possible. As the enormity of his plight seeped through Curly's hangover, he picked up speed and began to howl like an air raid siren. He must have lapsed into automatic pilot because he did not notice when the snake grew tired of his company, dropped onto the path and slithered into the undergrowth. By the time Curly reached the training school, he had left the rest of us far behind. If Maurice Brown had qualms about being passed by a screeching PI, running like an Olympic miler with one arm thrust forward like a crusader's lance, then he was too polite to mention it.

That morning, Curly clocked the fastest ever Brick Hill run and his record stood for years.

They built us up slowly. The first few weeks, we slept in barracks and every Saturday we had a parade followed by something called the School Hygiene Inspection. The inspection involved a staff inspector checking the barracks for the smallest trace of dust. Wearing a white glove, he would run a finger along the tops of the barrack doors. He would pull lockers away from walls and check behind them. He would open toilet cisterns and *tut tut*, if the ball cocks had not been cleaned.

Then, little by little, effort received reward. The week after we passed inspection, we moved to single room accommodation in the officers' mess. Still, we could not wear the force badge in our caps until judged smart enough to give a proper salute. It was a grudging process but somehow, we got there. Six months after stepping onto the griddle-hot apron of Kai Tak airport, PI62 marched from the training school's drill-square for the last time. We were done with the class work, the leadership modules, sessions on the firing range, the physical training, the square bashing and the examinations.

Graduating with us were more than two hundred Chinese constables, divided into nine squads. For weeks, constables and inspectors drilled together, preparing for our graduation parade. With two inspectors leading each squad, we practiced the march-past, the complex manoeuvre of forming squads on the move and finally, the advance in review order. A few days before the parade, we learned that the Governor, Sir David Trench, would take the salute. This drove the training staff into a fury of activity and there were extra drill sessions all round.

The day arrived. We wore buff-coloured, dress uniforms and gleaming Sam Browne belts. The uniform buttons were silver and pinned to our collars was the force insignia. On each epaulette was a single bath star and a plate bearing the letters 'RHKP'- - Royal Hong Kong Police. My good friend, Martin Samson and I were in charge of 'T' squad and we joined them in the shade of the junior ranks canteen. They were immaculate in starched, olive-green uniforms and spit-polished leather. There was a smile on every face. Out on the square, the police band struck up. There was a single *crunch*, as 'T' squad stamped to attention. We led our squads onto the drill-square, halted and faced front. Then we waited, stock-still and tried not to wilt under the May sun. Sir David's limousine whispered onto the drill-square and he stepped onto the saluting dais. He was a dour individual in a crumpled suit. However, his aide-de-camp, a police chief inspector, was dazzling in an exquisitely tailored, dress uniform, adorned with gold braid and topped off with a white solar helmet. The CDMI led Sir David and his aide along the ranks and he stopped from time to time to chat with one of the constables. Finally, he resumed his place on the dais for the march past and as the band's pipes and drums played 'The Black Bear,' then 'The Happy Wanderer,' I floated past the saluting dais on a cloud of pride.

But now it was time to face the real world. In the training school, the pass mark was fifty percent, but the ex-coppers among us knew that out on the streets, everyone demanded perfection. When a police officer puts on a uniform, the pass mark jumps to one hundred percent and the hardest critics are our colleagues. Our non-police veterans were bouncing with excitement but amongst the ex-coppers, there was only creeping expectation that the biggest tests were yet to come.

CHAPTER 3
SCRATCHING THE SURFACE

EVERYONE THINKS OF Hong Kong as a glitzy, Asian city with big-city policing problems. That is true up to a point but there is far more to the place than that. The biggest challenge to the police commissioner was the sheer diversity of the task facing him.

Beyond the urban city limits, the New Territories and the Sai Kung peninsular were green hinterlands of rolling hills and isolated coastline. Policing the rural communities needed skills that drew less on street-wise coppering and more on tact and community engagement. Give or take the occasional feud, the villagers were very law abiding but in the 1970s, many villages were so isolated that the police rural patrol teams were their only direct contact with government. Rural patrol officers were special: they had their roots in the community, they spoke the local dialects and were in tune with rural issues.

Policing Hong Kong's waters and outlying islands was something else again. The marine police covered more than 630 square miles of water and 263 islands. In addition to marine licensing and safety concerns there were problems with smugglers, people traffickers and pirates. To combat this, the Hong Kong police had, and still have, the world's largest marine police unit.

Even the different urban areas were unique. Within the force, the men and women working on Hong Kong Island were known as, 'The Hong Kong Police.' Those working the tougher areas across the harbour were, 'The Kowloon Cops.' To manage all this diversity, the commissioner had to act like a coachman with a team of strong-willed horses. All must pull in the same direction but the coachman must allow each to use its full strength.

Below the commissioner, there were four districts, each commanded by an assistant commissioner. These districts were: Hong Kong Island, Kowloon, New Territories and Marine. The assistant commissioners in charge of the land districts had problems similar to those of the commissioner. They commanded several police divisions, each led by a senior superintendent and each one unique.

At the bottom of the pile, under the divisions, came the sub-divisions and this was where the real work was done. The person in charge of the sub-division's uniform duties was a chief inspector dubbed the sub-divisional inspector, or SDI. The SDI was the most important man in the probationary inspector's world. I could talk at length about his responsibilities and the downright myth that surrounded him. He assigned duties, granted leave, bestowed career advancing compliments, wrote our staff reports, and dispensed character-building bollockings. When he yelled 'jump,' we jumped, when he yelled 'go,' we went and when he invited us into the mess, we grabbed a cold beer and told him what a great time we were having.

I was to take command of a patrol subunit in Tsuenwan, a new town in the rural New Territories district. It may have been in the New Territories, but Tsuenwan division was just north of the Kowloon boundary and there was nothing rural about it. Once, it had been a sleepy fishing village with a small market. Now, there were high-rise, public housing projects that served as dormitories for the Kowloon factories. With the influx of new residents, the little market had grown into a bustling commercial centre. There were restaurants, banks, cinemas and all manner of shops. In Tai Ho Road, a courthouse served the southern New Territories. Street hawkers had taken over the lanes and side streets. Drawn by lower office rents, commercial traders had relocated from Kowloon and Hong Kong Island. Tsuenwan was a town on the move.

The gate guard threw me a casual salute as the Bedford J3 truck turned into the compound of Tsuenwan police station. The sun had faded his bush jacket and shorts to pale green. His leatherwork was dull. The oiled butt of a revolver poked from under the flap of his holster. The Bedford squealed to a halt beside a line of blue and white Landrovers. The tailgate crashed open and a dozen tanned and crew-cut constables vaulted to the ground. I told the driver to wait, but as soon as a constable secured the tailgate, he threw the truck into gear and accelerated towards the gate. The gate guard waved him onto the main road and laughed at some remark I did not catch. The constables dumped their kit bags and fell into three ranks. One of them, an athletic young man, broke ranks and walked towards me. He wore a strip of red flannel behind his shoulder numerals, identifying him as an English speaker. 'What are your instructions, sir?' he asked, and twelve pairs of eyes fixed me in disciplined anticipation. They did not know what to do; neither did I, but I was the inspector and I was supposed to know. I sent them off to the canteen and did what all good inspectors do when faced with a tough decision: I went looking for a sergeant.

The station duty officer should have been an inspector, but in some stations, he was an experienced sergeant. Assisted by an English speaking constable called the *tailau*, the duty officer ruled an empire that started at the public enquiry desk and ended at the station transport office. His biggest worry was the cells. If a prisoner escaped or injured himself, then the duty officer had a lot of explaining to do. He had a safe for bail money, petty cash and valuable property. Heaven help him if the tally did not match the safe register during one of the frequent snap checks. He was responsible for the station armoury and always carried a few spare rounds of .38 ammunition in case some clown handed in five rounds instead of six at the end of shift. If anyone waltzed out of the station compound with a cart from the street hawker's exhibit store, then the duty officer's head was on the block. If the gate guard did not salute the divisional superintendent, the duty officer got the bollocking.

That Saturday afternoon, the Tsuenwan duty officer was a sergeant known as *Daibanjeung*, which meant, 'The Elephant.' He was a man of enormous girth and legendary wisdom who had been a sergeant for as long as anyone could remember. The report room was a large, open plan office and it was bubbling with activity. A red-tabbed constable sat at a desk, sorting a pile of minor summonses into some kind of order. A group of unlicensed street hawkers urged another weary constable to hurry with the bail so they could return to their unlicensed pitches. A telephone jangled and a constable scuttled to answer it. A constable led a handcuffed man to a door marked 'Charge Office.' On a bench against the far wall, people waited their turn at a public enquiry counter.

Behind the enquiry counter, The Elephant had squeezed himself into a roundback chair and was making a hand written entry in the miscellaneous report book. The MRB was a ledger somewhat bigger than Merlin's spell book and into it went all the lost property, holes in the road, missing grannies, neighbour disputes and every type of street drama. I was in plain clothes so I clipped my glossy new warrant card to my shirt pocket and gave him a cheery, 'Good morning, sergeant.'

The Elephant glanced up and sighed. He replaced the top of his fountain pen and laid it on the desk. He scraped the chair around to face me, leaned back and folded his hands across his ample belly. He looked me up and down up and smiled. 'Good morning, sir,' he said. 'How may I help?'

I told him there were twelve new constables in the station canteen and he barked orders to the *tailau*. Within half an hour, each constable had a locker, a duty assignment and was on his way home secure and happy about his immediate future. If I had expected similar treatment for a *bongban-jai*, literally, a boy inspector, I was to be disappointed. Whilst The Elephant treated the new constables like visiting royalty, I learned about the one-pip inspector's place in the sub-division's pecking order. I thanked The Elephant for his help.

'You're very welcome, sir.' He waited in smiling anticipation of any other request I might make.

'*Er* ... can I have transport to my quarters?'

The *tailau* stifled a snigger. The Elephant inclined his head as though he had misheard. 'Pardon me, did you say "transport?"'

'Yes sergeant, *transport*.' I may have sounded tetchy, it had been a long day.

The Elephant looked at me as though I had asked him for a vanilla ice cream with chocolate topping. 'Transport?' he said, shaking his head. 'Transport? No, no, no. No transport at all.'

Of course there was transport, I told him, I had just been in the compound and it was jammed with transport.

'That is true,' he said, 'but there is none available.' The Elephant then talked me through a list of woes that included breakdowns, shortages of drivers, impending prisoner escort trips and patrol car meal times. He reinforced each point by shaking his head and counting off each problem on an extended finger.

There was a minibus stop outside the station so, feeling a bit glum, I hefted my trunk and was about to head into the street when the divisional staff sergeant came into the report room. The staff sergeant was the station's senior non-commissioned officer and his unofficial title was 'major.' A silver crown adorned the sleeve of his bush shirt and a crimson sash hung across his shoulder. The report room lapsed into awed silence. The Elephant grabbed the arms of his roundback chair and struggled to lever himself from its grip. The major graced him with a smile and waved him back into the chair. The Elephant collapsed into his seat, a look of relief on his face. The major spoke in quiet Chinese and the Elephant snapped at the *tailau* who scuttled through the door leading to the station compound. Seconds later, a Landrover crunched to a halt outside the report room and with the *tailau* holding open the passenger door like a Savoy footman, the major boarded.

I watched, aghast. 'You said there was no transport,' I complained.

The Elephant looked up from his paperwork. 'Correct,' he said. 'There is no transport.' He seemed so sure, that for a few seconds I thought I had imagined it all.

'So, what was that?'

'That was transport for the major,' he answered.

'How come there's transport for him and none for me?'

The Elephant blinked at me and for a moment, seemed lost for words. 'Because he is the *major*,' he said at last.

'What's so special about the bloody major?'

Everyone in the report room gawked as though I had asked why the number three follows the number two. The Elephant's jaw dropped and he struggled for an answer. 'He ... he is the *major*.'

'So, there's transport for a staff sergeant but not for an inspector?'

The Elephant grinned, 'That is right, sir,' he said, then bent back over his paperwork.

I was not going to let him off that easily. 'Why?'

The Elephant again replaced the top on his pen and lay it on the desk. He was the model of decorum. 'Why what, sir?'

'Why does the staff sergeant get transport when an inspector can't?'

'Ah ... why indeed, sir?' The Elephant smiled like a wise old Buddha. 'That is because he is the major.'

I sighed, grabbed my little tin trunk and headed for the inspectors' quarters.

Hong Kong police officers were an insular lot, but not by

choice. The sad fact was, no one really wanted to know us. The Chinese say good iron will not become nails and a good man will not be a soldier. By soldier, that means anyone in uniform, including policemen. Westerners were not so direct but the same rules applied. The swanky Hong Kong club had an unspoken ban on admitting policemen as members. In 1984, a long-serving chief inspector got round this ban by listing his occupation as, 'second-hand car salesman.' To this day, he is still a member.

We tried not to let our lowly social status bother us. Instead, we took solace in the officers' mess. Most British inspectors lived in police stations. The accommodation was nothing special, just a single room with a toilet/shower shared with the room next door. There was a communal lounge, a dining room and a well-stocked bar. Each mess had a resident cook and a roomboy to keep things tidy. Mess life did not come cheap, everything was on signed chits and monthly mess bills accounted for half our pay. From the divisional superintendent to the lowliest, one-pip inspector, everyone could use the mess. Fortunately, the bosses were savvy enough to know when it was time to leave the young inspectors alone so they could enjoy a good old moan about the job.

Most resident members worked shifts, so the messes were generally quiet places. The parties however, were legend. Famously, a resident member of a Hong Kong Island mess decided to spark up a party with a surprise floorshow. He booked what must have been Hong Kong's only dancing bear act. However, while bringing the bear up to the mess, the station lift became stuck between floors. As time passed, the bear became more agitated. On the mess floor, the party guests could hear it grunting and banging around in the lift. With each passing minute, the handler's attempt to placate the bear became more plaintive. An hour or so later, an engineer fixed the problem. The lift ascended to the mess floor, the doors opened and a very pissed-off bear barrelled out of the lift and set about destroying the mess furnishings and fixtures. The incident did not go down well with the guests, particularly the ladies. For many weeks, the mess residents suffered a severe state of collective celibacy.

General Orders were clear. No female guests allowed in the inspectors' quarters. Never was an order so widely disobeyed and so blithely ignored by the bosses. A procession of young women passed through the officers' messes. There were cheery bar workers, cool airhostesses, haughty socialites, teachers, nurses and the occasional bright-eyed tourist. They were of all races and from all points north, south, east and west. I do not know what attracted these ladies to policemen but I will forever thank whatever God made it so.

I say, *most* British inspectors lived on station, but there were a few exceptions. At Tsuenwan, I was one of them. Tsuenwan's British inspectors lived at Fung Chik Sen Villa, a shabby art deco building about two miles west of Tsuenwan police station. It had broad verandas that faced west, overlooking a channel between the New Territories' shoreline and Tsing Yi Island. Six inspectors shared the house but when I arrived, there was no one home but Ah Wan, the housekeeper. He greeted me with a smile and a bobbing head. He was a cheerful, middle-aged man with a startling resemblance to the Chinese Premier at the time, Zhou Enlai. He showed me around my new home. There were two self-contained apartments, one on each floor. The upstairs kitchen had a small cooking range and an enormous refrigerator full of San Miguel beer. The six resident inspectors treated the upper floor living room as a communal lounge, but it was an impersonal place. The furniture was government issue and the walls were bare. I followed Ah Wan to a gloomy bedroom at the back of the house. It was nothing much: just a bed, a battered wardrobe and an electric fan. A grassy embankment filled the view from the window and there were no curtains. The floor was scuffed linoleum and the ceiling light had no shade.

Summer was well on the way and my shirt clung damp to my

skin. A mosquito buzzed past my ear and a small lizard scuttled across the ceiling. I dumped my trunk on the floor and sat on the bed. The door swung shut and I stared at the bare walls. The inspector's quarters of the recruiting brochures had clubby bars and neat, *en suite* bedrooms. Had I travelled thousands of miles for *this?* I wandered back to the lounge and stepped onto the veranda where there were two rattan loungers and a scuffed coffee table. The loungers had peeling varnish and their bindings were starting to unravel. A small cargo ship passed through the channel below, black smoke billowing from its funnel. In the distance, the hills of Lantau Island were soft and green. I guessed sunsets would be spectacular.

But who were the other five inspectors? Back at the training school, I could always find someone I knew. Fung Chik Sen felt like a deserted waiting room. I was still worried about what the job might hold. I missed home. I missed my family and friends. I missed my mates from PI62. I never thought it possible, I even missed the training school.

In ones and twos, the other residents returned but it was a few days before I met them all. There were two subunit commanders, already old sweats with three months operational experience. There was a wisecracking detective, a Yorkshireman who ran the New Territories' district vice squad, and the inspector in charge of the division's general nuisance team. They were an agreeable group and we were to spend many happy evenings sitting on the upstairs veranda, sipping cold beer and watching the sun go down over Lantau Island. Off duty, we often took the mountain road over Taimoshan and spent a few relaxing hours in the bars at Kamtin. They were rustic places but the beer was cheap and the waitresses were pretty. They were decent, country girls and for the price of a Coca-Cola, would sit and chat for a while. There were no *Mamasans*, instead, the bars had matronly overseers who tried, not too successfully, to make sure the girls got up to no hanky-panky with the customers.

Breakfast at Fung Chik Sen Villas shamed any British transport cafe. Lunches were simple but enormous and I could have sworn Ah Wan's dinners came straight from the Ritz. I had never eaten Chicken *Mozambique* and Ah Wan's special recipe spoiled me for any other. Fung Chik Sen was to be my country haven from the rigours of the day. A few weeks after I moved in, one of the other residents transferred out of the division and I graduated to that most wonderful of luxuries, a room with a sea view.

The divisional superintendent's morning conference, dubbed 'morning prayers,' started at eight a.m. and on a bad day, lasted more than an hour. During this hour, the DS and his chief inspectors pored over the crime reports for the last twenty-four hours. If the crime rate went up or the detection rate went down, then all three caught flak from New Territories district headquarters.

By nine o'clock, morning prayers were over but this was never a good time for a chat with the new boss.

On my first day at Tsuenwan, I stood to rigid attention before the sub-divisional inspector's desk, saluted and told him I was probationary inspector Emmett, newly transferred from Police Training School. The SDI had an open bottle of aspirin on his desk. He waved me to a chair, rifled through his in-tray and retrieved a memo headed 'Staff -- In Confidence.' It was the transfer list. My name was on it but it was the first time the SDI had looked at it. We talked for a while. Actually, the SDI talked and I listened. 'I want to welcome you to Tsuenwan. I hope you will be very happy here. We are one big family and my door is always open.' He waved me away and my next stop was the assistant SDI's office. The ASDI peered at me over a mountain of files and sent me along to the subunit commander's office.

The subunit is the very core of police work. Be it Hong Kong, New York or Bolton, it is the subunit constable who pounds the beat, night and day and in all weathers. He is the unthanked foot soldier who keeps us safe. For his reward, he must suffer low pay, long hours and daily abuse. That day, the duty sub-unit commander was a cheerful probationary inspector called Jason Woo. He was my age and had left the training school six months earlier. He was talking to a competent looking sergeant. He waved me into the office, which was the size of a cupboard. Jason suggested we tour the sub-division and told the sergeant to arrange transport. 'And, if the duty officer gives you crap,' he snapped, 'tell him my cousin in Marine Outer Islands division is looking for a smart sergeant.' I liked him instantly. Jason would soon move to a nine-to-five job in divisional headquarters and I was to take over his subunit. 'No one stays in subunits for long.' he said. 'It's the front line but all subunit commanders are fresh from training school.' He shrugged. 'Don't worry, you'll pick it up.' He stood and moved to the door. 'Right,' he snapped. 'First, we go to the armoury.'

It felt odd taking a revolver from the station armoury. It was as routine as drawing a beat radio from the comm's store back in England. Jason rapped on the armoury's serving hatch and with a groan, it swung open. The armoury constable checked the duty list then squeezed a dog-eared register through the hatch. I signed it and he handed me a lightly oiled Colt revolver, butt first with the empty chamber open for my inspection. Next came six rounds of .38 ammunition. With six rounds in the chamber, the revolver felt heavy as I slipped it into the cross-draw holster at my belt. I had done the training and knew the Colt Police Positive backwards but still, it felt strange to feel it tugging at my belt.

The threat of Outer Islands division did the trick. We boarded a Landrover, rolled through the gate and within minutes, arrived in Tsuenwan's town centre.

Hong Kong is a vibrant place, but chip at the surface and you will find old Asia hiding below the veneer. All through the 1970s and well into the 1980s, I saw computerised cash registers lying idle while cashiers clicked up the bill with an abacus. Even in the twenty-first century, the only scaffolding to adorn Hong Kong buildings is a bamboo lattice held together with knotted raffia.

Tsuenwan was new and growing. The high-rise office blocks lining its main streets hid the small market town that was the real Tsuenwan. Jason abandoned the Landrover in Sha Tsui Road and with dire warnings for the driver to stay put, we set off on foot. The sun was like a hammer and damp patches formed under the arms of my bush shirt. The Sam Browne bit into my waist and the revolver banged against my hip. My cap band seemed to shrink. I removed the cap to mop my forehead and winced as the sun hit my eyes. We stepped into one of many alleys and pushed through crowds that jammed the lanes and plazas. The calls of market hawkers enveloped us. A hawker had a stall piled high with cheap looking T-shirts bearing labels like *Adidas, Nike and Slazenger*. '*Yau leng, yau peng,*' he called -- Best quality, cheapest prices. A butcher swatted at flies buzzing around pork and chicken hanging from hooks above his stall. With a massive cleaver, he cut the meat on a scarred chopping block then weighed purchases on a spindly balance with a brass pan at one end and a small weight at the other. Two dogs, their ribs showing, snarled and snapped at each other over scraps lying discarded in the gutter. On another stall, live fish splashed in shallow metal tanks. In a bucket, crabs squirmed against raffia bindings. A street chef worked at a wheeled cart fitted with a hissing gas burner. He deep-fried sweet smelling bean curd to golden crispness. Beside him, a woman hawker splashed water onto piles of *choi sam,* thick leafed *baak choi* and pale *wong nga baak*. The noise and heat were like a blanket and soon I found myself gasping as though I had just finished the Brick Hill run.

We shouldered through the crowd. Behind me, someone said, '*Wah, yau goh gwai jai.*'-- Wow, it's a devil boy. Another answered, '*Mo gam cho, kui wooi lau ge la.*'-- Not so loud, he'll be angry. As we moved through the market, the street hawkers made a show of moving their pitches a few inches to clear a path. Jason spread his arms and turned full circle. 'Headquarters want all this controlled. The best we can manage is to keep the main roads clear and stop the triads squeezing the hawkers dry.'

A constable appeared from a doorway and snapped off a salute. Jason wrote a line in the constable's notebook and we went back to the Landrover. I slumped onto the back seat, drained. In the short time we had been in the market, the heat had sucked the strength from me. How did anyone manage a whole shift?

Jason ordered the driver to take us to a public housing project called Kwaishek Estate. As we ground our way through the traffic, he gave me the lowdown on the subunit's characters. 'Most are dependable,' he said and seemed sorry to be leaving. 'Watch out for the *sui-jais*, the bad boys. They are awkward and they know every trick.' He gave a rueful frown. 'But they bring in most of the good arrests and you can always count on them when there's a tough job.'

We left the town centre and headed for a cluster of high-rise blocks that stood stark against the skyline. Their sheer scale was awesome. Kwaishek's twenty-two blocks had an official population of thirty-five thousand but Jason guessed the real population was far higher. Next to one of the blocks, a group of men lounged in a small sitting-out area. They had skeletal faces; their eyes were hollow and dull. Their clothes were threadbare and unwashed. '*Do yaus* -- drug addicts,' Jason growled. 'They're all over the estate. There would be next to no crime if it wasn't for the bloody *do yaus*.'

'We should get the beat constable onto it,' I suggested.

Jason gave a small laugh. 'Four beat constables for the whole estate,' he said. 'If a constable makes a drug arrest, he's tied up for the rest of the shift. That gives these other bastards a free hand. Best we can do is to show them who is boss.' He ordered the driver to pull in. As we approached them, the addicts regarded us with mild amusement. 'They're not running,' Jason said. 'They're clean.'

Scorched tin foils littered the sitting out area. The addicts went through a practiced routine. They stood, grinned at each other and raised their hands. I searched the one nearest to me and in one of his pockets, found a folded tin foil. I waved it like a trophy. 'Hey Jason,' I crowed. 'My first case. Possession of drug paraphernalia.'

'You're not at the training school,' Jason scoffed. 'The magistrate will send you off with a bollocking for wasting his time.'

The addict grinned at me. '*Mo yeh, bongban,*' he said. '*Ngoh dei ho gon jeng.*' --Nothing here, inspector. We're all clean.

Jason and I went through the pantomime of a full search. We rummaged in their pockets, we made them take of their shoes and open their mouths, we lifted their shirts and checked their waistbands. Nothing. I took out my notebook. 'We should take their details,' I said. 'One of them might complain.'

Jason waved away the suggestion. 'Forget it,' he said. 'There won't be any complaint.' He glowered at the addicts. '*Jau,*' he snapped. '*Fai di jau.*'-- Go. Go quickly. He pointed his finger just inches from the face of one of the addicts. '*Ngoh giu nei jau, nei m jau?*'-- I tell you to go and you don't go? His voice rose to a shout. '*Ham gar chan, fai di jau!*'-- Death to all your family, get out of here. The addict glared back, sullen and defiant then he turned and moved to the exit, muttering to himself. The others followed and left in separate directions.

We went back to the Landrover and returned to the station. The air-conditioning in the sub-unit commander's office was bliss. Jason had already prepared a detailed handover report, which I read and signed. He wished me luck and went off duty early.

I had done the sub-divisional tour. I had gone through the handover report.

Now I was on my own.

At first glance, Hong Kong policing looked much like the job back in England. Laws about theft, burglary, violence against the person, public order and road traffic were almost identical to British law. Arrest procedures were the same. At Police Training School, the staff had drilled into us that famous chant, 'You are not obliged to say anything unless you wish to do so ...' Rules on the use of force were the same as back home -- minimum force to achieve the desired aim.

Then I began to notice the differences. Like many things in Hong Kong, the police relied on the British system but gave it an Asian tweak. The Hong Kong police set its working strength as a proportion of the total population. However, because Hong Kong was more crowded than Britain, the police beats were more compact than those back home. Anyone walking along a busy Hong Kong street would see policemen everywhere.

Hong Kong policing methods were about five years behind the United Kingdom. This was no bad thing because it meant fewer constables in cars and more on the beat. In Hong Kong's urban areas, British style personal radios were useless so, every half-hour, constables had to attend pre-scheduled meetings with their sergeants. That made policemen even more visible. Back in England, police had no authority to arrest for minor offences and dealt with day-to-day mischief by way of court summons. In Hong Kong, people moved home so often, it was impossible to deliver a summons. As a result, Hong Kong police had the authority to arrest for every offence, be it homicide or jaywalking. Station duty officers quickly processed minor cases then bailed the offender to attend court. Cash bail always equalled the likely court-ordered fine. If offenders did not show up at court, they lost their bail money. And that was that: no bench warrants, no early morning knock on the door to dig out bail jumpers.

The working shift at Tsuenwan started with a fifteen-minute briefing in the station compound. As soon as I appeared, the senior sergeant brought the subunit to attention and saluted. Next, he went through the crime reports for the last twenty-four hours then assigned the constables to their beats. I could add nothing to what was a well-practiced system and after the first week, I started to feel redundant.

Apart from some swear words and an ability to order a beer, my Cantonese was non-existent. For me, this divided the subunit into two parts: red-tab officers and black-tab officers. Sergeants and constables who spoke English wore a strip of red felt behind their shoulder numerals. Those who spoke no English wore black felt backing. This was a time when Hong Kong offered free education only at primary or elementary level. All sergeants and constables were literate in Chinese but to wear the red tab, they had to study English up to the third year of secondary school. The force offered training to anyone prepared to study in their spare time and many took advantage of it. Those wanting to take things further could study up to the British General Certificate of Education, which qualified them for promotion to inspector. Quality of English varied and it was common to see reports like, 'Cause of death -- lack of breath,' and, 'Illegal Immigrant came to Hong Kong by swam.'

We native English speakers were slow to criticise. No matter how quirky the English of our sergeants and constables, it was often better than our Cantonese. So long as we were communicating, there was no problem. Luckily for me, we had a language unique to the police force. No language school taught it. The only way to learn it was by day-to-day use. It was a blend of English, Chinese, useful acronyms, and police jargon. There were stock phrases for all sorts of police odds and ends. Minor cases were, '*M R-oh B casee*,' named for the miscellaneous report book, or MRB, where they were recorded. Time off taken to compensate for extra duty was, '*Time Off-oo*.' Landrovers were, '*Jeep-jai*,' literally, little jeep.' The question, 'Do you have the crime report on the assault occasioning actual bodily harm case?' became, '*Yau mo* AOBH *CR-oh?*' That is, '*Yau mo* (Have you) AOBH (assault occasioning actual bodily harm) *CR-oh* (crime report)?' Outsiders could only sit in dazed amazement as they tried to fathom any sense from it.

Police jargon aside, without any Cantonese training under my belt, I had to take an English-speaking sergeant with me everywhere. Sergeants being sergeants, they did everything needed to keep the constables on their toes. They meant only to help, but it left me feeling like a passive observer. Then I became *Ah Sir*, and it all changed.

Everyone knows how Chinese names work. The family name comes first and the given names come next. So, when you meet a gentleman called Wong Ka-ming, the correct address is Mister Wong. So far, so good. Then you have a few drinks with Mister Wong and as you become more familiar, you may be tempted to call him Ka-ming. Now it is a case of so far, *not* so good. Ka-ming was fine when Mister Wong was at elementary school or if he is one of your best friends but it will not do for an exchange of pleasantries at a business lunch. When you get to know Mister Wong better, he will be delighted if you call him K.M. It is friendly but has a businesslike ring about it. When you become good friends, you might call him *Ah* Ming but until then, you are best sticking to *Ah* Wong. The term, '*Ah*,' is a bit like Mister or Madam, but far less formal.

When I first joined my subunit, I was 'Sir.' Then, on my third week, I approached a constable in the street. He grinned, snapped up a salute and said, 'Good morning, *Ah Sir*.' This time, the constable handed the notebook to me, not the sergeant. He had written it up in neat Chinese and for all I knew, it could have been the form guide for Saturday's meet at the Happy Valley racecourse. I signed it anyway and handed it back. The constable saluted, said, 'Thank you, *Ah Sir*,' and went back on patrol. I realised I liked being '*Ah Sir*.' It implied acceptance while at the same time recognising I was in charge. For now, I still needed an English-speaking sergeant but I felt more a part of the subunit. I was starting to fit in.

We rotated through three shifts: nights were from midnight to eight; lates were from four to midnight; and earlies were from eight in the morning until four in the afternoon. Briefing started fifteen minutes before shift. Debrief and statistical reports went on for fifteen minutes after shift ended. The working week was Sunday to Saturday with one day off midweek. Every Sunday, we changed shifts and there was just seven and a half hours between going off duty and coming back on again. On these fast changeovers, most junior officers did not bother going home, preferring to rest up in the station barracks. The change from night shift to late shift was particularly hard.

After pre-shift briefing, the constables boarded transport out to their beats. I would catch up on general administration before heading out myself. My main job was to make sure the constables did not spend too much time in some cosy teahouse. Each officer had to appear at a designated conference point every half hour. This raised the police profile on the street and it allowed me to meet my constables. On the downside, it introduced some predictability into an otherwise flexible patrol system. By way of extra supervision, constables had to sign visiting books placed at high risk premises like banks and goldsmith shops. This offered a sense of security to people working at high risk businesses but it never worked. Intelligent villains simply waited until beat constables signed the visiting book then moved in when they left the area.

The job turned into a check list of the mundane: morning briefing, general admin, out on patrol, visit the conference points, countersign the constables' notebooks, check the visiting books, then back to the station for more administration. Occasionally, the SDI sent out enquiry files on low-key issues like licensing or broken traffic lights. But where were the triad street battles and the war against international dope smuggling?

The subunit constables were reliable enough. They never missed a conference point and the beat visiting books were crammed with signatures. They brought in a steady stream of minor cases and made some good arrests. They were smart and always graced me with a snappy salute. All, that is, except Ah Ban. It was hard to fault Ah Ban, he knew exactly where the line was and he never crossed it. His leatherwork was dull but clean. His hair was almost, but not quite, too long. His salute was leisurely but not insubordinate. He turned up for every beat conference but at any other time, he was the devil to find. 'Good afternoon, *Ah Sir*,' he would say in a dull monotone as he handed me his notebook. 'Thank you, *Ah Sir*,' he would say in the same monotone as I signed it and handed it back.

'*Bei lai*,' the sergeant would growl and Ah Ban would give me a half-hearted salute.

'Watch him,' my sergeants cautioned. And I did, if I could find him. He was one of Jason's *sui-jais*, one of the bad boys. My sergeants saw him as a disruption to good order and discipline. I should have tried to chase him out of the subunit but there was a problem, Ah Ban was a superb copper. His arrest record was second to none. His cases were high quality: burglaries, pickpockets and street intimidation. He had a reputation for robust prisoner handling but the householders, shopkeepers and street hawkers who lived and worked on his beat, thought he was a hero. His cases were solid and always stood up in court. He was a surly bugger but I knew he was special. Later that year, he would prove me right.

There was no escape, all overseas Inspectors had to do it. There was no point in trying to avoid it; it was essential. It was the language course. I have nothing against language courses; I looked forward to going beyond, 'six large beers please,' but having said that, I did not relish the prospect of twelve weeks cooped up in a classroom. They say things are never as bad as you fear but whoever coined that phrase never attended the Hong Kong government's elementary Cantonese course.

The government language school was in the Lee Gardens Centre in Hysan Avenue, next door to the Lee Gardens Hotel. It was in a stylish but quiet corner of Causeway Bay. Nearby, there were reasonably price restaurants and understated shops selling everything from fashion to furniture. The school comprised a suite of offices and classrooms. There was a language laboratory where students could record and play back set phrases then compare their efforts to those of a native speaker. On our arrival, the laboratory door bore a notice declaring, 'Out of Order.' Three months later, the notice was still there.

In Cantonese, you can say each word with six different inflections. Different inflection, different meaning. Get it wrong and you can land yourself in big trouble. Take the word for 'buy,' that is, '*maai.*' Now consider the word for 'sell,' that is also '*maai.*' The difference is in the way you say it. Inflect upwards whilst speaking and you are a buyer. Keep the tone flat and you are a seller. Needless to say, there were no white faces on the floor of Hong Kong's stock exchange.

We spent the first day chanting the different tones. It was, *wei* (high level even), *wei* (mid level rising), *wei* (mid level flat) and so on. From the street we must have sounded like the world's worst choir. Then came essential phrases such as, '*Nei gwai sing ah? --* What is your honourable surname? I wondered how that would go down in Kwaishek Estate. There was the phrase we never forgot: *Saam goh wo seung mo sui sik --* Three Buddhist monks will have no water to consume. In quiet moments, I thumbed through the text book searching for useful phrases like: 'You are very pretty, may I have your telephone number,' but no luck. By week two, I knew how to buy an umbrella and could probably manage a cinema ticket. I would not understand much about the film, but at least I would be dry.

Not everyone in the class was moving at my stellar pace. Jack Ridge was not a natural linguist and neither was Toby Staynes. Staynes would use only two words, *mah fan*, meaning, 'trouble.' For his part, Ridge knew just one phrase: *m sik teng gwong dung wah* -- 'I don't understand Cantonese.' He swore it was the only phrase he ever needed. Our language teacher was a long-suffering gentleman called Mister Woon. He tried every trick to coax some learning into Ridge and Staynes but it was like trying to spoon-feed babies who will have none of it. The mildest rebuke to Staynes was met by, 'sorry to give so much *mah fan*.' Any attempt to include Ridge in class discussions received a stock response: '*m sik teng gwong dung wah.*' Desperate, Mister Woon invited Staynes to use the words *mah fan* in a sentence. Staynes chewed his lip, cleared his throat and furrowed his brow. '*Mah fan*,' he said and Mister Woon's eyes brightened. '*Mah fan* has two speeds: slow and fuckin' fast.'

Ridge looked perplexed. 'What does *mah fan* mean?' he asked.

Autumn was sneaking up on us but at the language school, the air conditioning was still set for high summer. By now, I was getting somewhere. I knew how to buy a pound of fresh *baak choi* and to ask if my bus went to Causeway Bay. But still, we were not a happy bunch. Outside, the skies were clear, the humidity had abated and the temperature was like England in late spring. Indoors, we shivered in Arctic misery.

'I'm cold,' Ridge declared.

Mister Woon seized his chance. '*Gong gwong dung wah*,' he fired back. 'Say it in Cantonese.'

'I'm bloody cold,' Ridge said.

'Say it in Chinese,' Mr Woon insisted. 'It's easy. Just say, "*ngor ho dung*."'

'I can't,' Ridge answered. 'I'm too cold to think.'

Mister Woon's eyes became hooded. He spoke through clenched teeth. '*Gong gwong dung wah*,' he growled.

Ridge folded his arms and stared at the ceiling. 'Can't,' he said.

66

Staynes shook his head. 'I *do* hope there won't be any *mah fan*,' he sighed.

Mister Woon placed both his fists on his table. 'I shall report this to your Director of Personnel and Training,' he snapped.

'Tell him to fix the bloody air conditioning while you're at it,' Ridge shot back.

The rest of us watched with mixed feelings. Ridge's conduct was outrageous, but it relieved weeks of crushing boredom.

'I shall do it now,' said Mister Woon, half-rising from his seat.

Ridge sat with his arms folded, eyes on the ceiling.

Mr Woon stood and walked towards the door.

Ridge rummaged in his pocket and a smile played on his lips. He opened his copy of Sidney Lau's Elementary Cantonese textbook. There was a *click* and a flash of flame. Ridge played the cigarette lighter on the textbook and within seconds, it was alight. He dropped it onto his desk and made a show of warming his hands. Mister Woon let out a shriek and dashed from the room. He returned in an instant carrying a CO_2 fire extinguisher. With clenched teeth, Mr Woon aimed the extinguisher at the blazing text book. There was a metallic roar as Jack Ridge, the textbook, the desk, and half the classroom disappeared in a fog of carbon dioxide vapour. We staggered from the room, spluttering and coughing. A thin mist hung in the corridor and there was a smell of burnt paper. Ridge was last out, there was a dusting of frost in his hair and eyebrows but he was still smiling.

The following week, all was back to normal except for an empty chair. Jack Ridge was no more. A composed and I believe happier Mister Woon spoke to Toby Staynes. 'Mister Staynes, please use the phrase *mah fan* in a sentence.'

Staynes did not hesitate. '*Wan foh, ho mah fan.*'

And he was right, playing with fire can be very troublesome indeed.

CHAPTER 4
A ROSE BY ANY OTHER NAME

THINGS LOOKED UP AFTER the language course. All right, I could communicate only at the level of a three-year-old, but it was a start. The Chinese are delighted to find a *gwailo* ready to have a stab at their language. They will happily advise on the best word or phrase for any given situation. Slowly, my spoken Chinese became more street savvy. *Nei gwai sing ah?* -- 'What is your honourable surname?' gave way to, *'nei giu m'yeh meng ah?'* -- 'what's your name?' There were peals of laughter when my poor pronunciation produced something odd or downright obscene. Night shift was a good time to practice. The restaurant workers and street cleaners were chatty and openhearted. As my Cantonese became stronger, I grew into the job. I found the confidence to patrol on my own and enjoyed exercising my limited vocabulary with shopkeepers and others on the street. At least once a shift, I commandeered the sub-divisional mobile patrol and went to one of Tsuewan's housing estates. I would order the crew out of the Landrover and we performed what we called 'high-rise patrol.' I never got used to the scale of the Hong Kong government housing blocks. They were like vertical towns. There were high street shops and teahouses on the ground floor but the upper floors were bleak suburbs. There were featureless corridors marked only by row after row of iron-grilled doors. We chased the *do yaus* from the corridors, staircases and public sitting areas but they came back as soon as we left. Sometimes we would get lucky and catch one with a packet of heroin or, more importantly, a knife.

Through no fault of their own, most of my constables had only basic schooling. This put them at the bottom of the pecking order in a Chinese society that places so much value on education. I have seen educated Chinese refuse to speak to constables in anything but English. Triad slang for a policeman is *fohgei*, literally an unskilled worker just one step up from a coolie. Hong Kong coppers turned the insult around by adopting the word as their own. They use the phrase, *ngoh hai fohgei* -- I'm a *fohgei*, as a statement of pride.

I grew closer to the men and women in my subunit, particularly the black-tab officers, who supposedly spoke no English. Now I could speak directly with them, I found many spoke English quite well. When caught out, they would shrug and admit they wore the black numeral backing because it kept the *gwailos* off their backs. I began to spend more time with the less educated constables. Uneducated maybe, but they were streetwise and sharp. Hong Kong was a society that valued education above strength of character but soon, I would learn that when your back is against the wall, character beats education every time.

Nestled in a hollow at the foot of a mountain called Taimoshan, was the village of Tai On. The buildings were dark granite, they had glazed roof tiles and hooked eaves. The houses huddled so close together, there was just enough room for two men to pass in the narrow lanes. Children dared each other to jump from one rooftop to another. Tsuenwan's bustling town centre was just a short walk from the village and the busy Castle Peak Road passed close by. Above the village, stunted trees and dense scrub covered Taimoshan's slopes; concrete storm drains scarred its contours. During the rainy season, the storm drains overflowed and Tai On's narrow alleys became coursing streams.

Miles to the north, electric generating stations pumped out

power for the factories and apartment blocks of Kowloon. High-tension pylons bracketed Tai On and sagging cables passed over the village. When China Light and Power built the pylons, the villagers mounted noisy protests about damage to the local *feng shui*. Like most *feng shui* disputes, all was resolved the day the power company handed over the compensation cheques.

Feng shui disputes aside, Tai On was a decent place. In Tai On, people looked after each other. A problem for one family was a problem for the whole village. For the children, every adult was an aunt or an uncle. But fate was to test this village spirit when, at the tail end of summer, thunderclouds gathered to the south-east and the winds turned gusty.

A China Seas typhoon is not child's play but it does work like a child's top. The storm rotates around its centre and the whole system drifts across open ocean at about ten knots, kicking up lots of water in the process. Eventually it makes landfall where it rattles around for a bit before losing all power. Trying to figure where a typhoon will land is not easy, but Hong Kong is a small dot on a long coastline and there were few direct hits.

Our first warning of the typhoon came from the Philippines. TV newscasts showed waves crashing over sea walls and palm trees flailing around like a demented Hydra. There were close-ups of the distraught homeless. Sombre voice-overs warned that the storm had moved northwest into the South China Sea. In a less politically correct time, all tropical storms had female names and this one was named 'Rose.' I had a private smile about that, I knew a girl back home called Rose, a real sweetheart: pretty, open hearted and full of fun. I had never been outside during a typhoon and I looked forward to some action.

The airport warned of flight delays, TV stations aired typhoon precautions and the harbour's storm moorings began to fill with ships.

Rose packed centre winds of more than ninety miles per hour but she could not decide where to go. For days, she staggered around the South China Sea like a drunk looking for a fight. Then, one morning in August, just before eight o'clock, Rose stepped over an invisible line, four hundred nautical miles to the southeast. The Royal Observatory hoisted the tropical cyclone warning, known as 'the number one.' By five that evening, Rose had moved closer and the number three -- the strong wind signal -- went up. For the next three days, Rose stalked around to the South but the skies over Hong Kong stayed clear and the winds remained gentle. The Observatory reported she had veered away and life returned to normal. In a few days, I would be twenty-three years old and I had important things on my mind, like ordering the beer for my party.

Rose lurked outside the four hundred nautical mile mark, beyond the threshold but still in view like a beggar at a wedding. The Observatory kept the number one signal up for two more days and then, on the third morning I woke to find the skies dark and the wind rattling the veranda doors. The number three signal was back up. By nine that morning, it was so dark, the streetlights came on. A grape-sized raindrop hit Fung Chik Sen's patio with a heavy 'swapt.' At ten, the duty officer telephoned to say that the number eight -- gale force warning had just gone up. This meant we were in for some serious weather. By law, employers had to shut up shop and send everyone home. With the number eight signal hoisted, Hong Kong ground to a halt, much to the disgust of the local chamber of commerce. A chamber executive once raised a storm of his own by suggesting a lost life or two did not justify the cost of closing everything down. Other chamber members distanced themselves from him but secret ballots kept him in office for years afterwards.

When the number eight went up, most shops, factories and offices closed. Public transport stopped and car owners parked their vehicles under cover. Anyone slow off the mark could find themselves stranded, but that was not so bad. At the first hint of a strong gust, any club manager worth his Chinese New Year bonus laid in enough booze to keep a panel of appeal court judges happy. For those not part of the clubbing scene there were plenty of typhoon parties. Except, of course, for dedicated public servants like policemen; when the number eight went up, we went to work.

I arrived back at the station and found two hundred constables trying to find somewhere to spend the night. The barrack rooms were overflowing and there were crowds five deep at the canteen counter. It was the same in the officers' mess. There were damp patches on the carpet where the duty inspector had entered to a chorus of jeers. The barrack sergeant issued folding camp beds and his assistants crisscrossed the windows with masking tape. At the bar, I jostled with other subunit, traffic and CID inspectors but the SDI decreed soft drinks only. There was nowhere to sit, so most of us just milled around waiting for orders.

There was usually a twelve-hour gap between the number eight signal going up and the full force of the storm hitting the city, but Rose was not a normal storm. By late afternoon, clouds were scudding over the station at incredible speeds. They blocked out the daylight and outside it was like night. I stood at a taped window and watched a constable battle his way across the compound, his helmeted head bowed and his rubber poncho flapping like a loose sail in a Nor'Wester. The door of the hawker's exhibit store banged open and broke a hinge. A wicker basket tumbled across the compound. As evening drew on, the SDI collared me. 'Get your gear, Mister Emmett, we'll take a look at the town.'

I grabbed my riot helmet and rain gear. I unlatched the report room door and it exploded inwards, knocking me back. The *tailau* made a grab at a pile of papers as they billowed around him. I stepped through the door, and with me pulling from the outside and the *tailau* pushing from the inside, we got it shut. The SDI sat hunched in the front seat of a Landrover parked by the armoury. The transport sergeant had fixed iron grilles over the windscreen and side windows. I clambered into the back and powered up the radio. Even in the compound, the Landrover was bouncing from side to side on its springs. The driver gunned the engine and accelerated in a wide arc across the compound. I pressed the radio's transmit button and reported SDI on mobile patrol. The vehicle shuddered as it passed the lee of the station wall and the driver blanched. A wall of rain hit the windscreen and for all the good our wipers did, we might have had none. The Landrover shuddered as the wind caught it head on. For a moment, I thought the engine would stall. The SDI hunched forward and wiped the inside of the windscreen. He shook his head. 'I've never seen it like this,' he said. 'Even Wanda wasn't this bad.' He turned to me, the corners of his mouth pulled down. 'Killed a hundred and forty, did Wanda. Have you cancelled beat duties?' I told him I had.

The driver double-declutched into first gear, and with his nose almost touching the windscreen, drove along Castle Peak Road at walking pace. Tsuenwan town centre was empty. There were no pedestrians, no workers and apart from us, no traffic. Roller-shutters blocked the entrance to every shop and office block. In Sha Tsui Road, the buildings funnelled the storm, turning the main street into a giant wind tunnel. The shutters rattled and banged. Signboards swung insanely from their hanging chains. We ducked as a rubbish bin bounded down the middle of the road and whacked the front of Landrover like an angry rhino. It bounced onto the bonnet, smashed against the mesh screens and tumbled over the top, taking the Landrovers' blue flashing beacon with it. The topmost section of a ten-storey lattice of bamboo scaffolding swung away from a building and swayed above us. A fifteen-foot bamboo pole came loose from its fastenings, tumbled down into the street and clattered like a spent javelin on the pavement next to us. The scaffolding groaned and buckled as the wind tore at it like a child with a paper doily. Another length of bamboo twisted loose and we watched, frozen by its grace as it fell towards the Landrover like a dart. It arced towards us, gathering speed. All I could think was, *'oh shit ...'* Then the wind seized it and whipped it away. It bounced off the road with a hollow *'tonk,'* then cartwheeled into a roller-shutter, which crumpled like tinfoil. The driver slammed the Landrover into reverse and floored the accelerator as ten storeys of bamboo scaffolding wrenched itself from the building and tumbled into the street, filling it with a crashing, splintering, tangled mass of wood, raffia, canvas and chandler's rope. Razor-like slivers of bamboo *pinged* against the Landrover's bodywork and shredded a shop's canvas awning. The driver braked to a halt and rested his forehead on the steering wheel. The SDI touched the driver's shoulder then turned back to me. 'Tell control I'm cancelling mobile patrols,' he said. His lips were white but he forced a grin. 'That includes us.'

I tried to raise the control room but the radio was dead. The Landrover's aerials were back in Sha Tsui Road, along with our blue beacon.

The compound was a pocket of calm. I found the patrol cars all under cover next to the station transport office and my beat constables drying off in the canteen. The SDI disappeared into his office and sent me to the divisional operations room for an update.

We used the DOR for special operations and most of the time, it lay empty. It was a windowless chamber. Maps, aerial photographs and PVC whiteboards covered the walls. The headings of the boards read, 'Floods,' 'Landslides,' 'Houses Collapsed.' Other boards, unused for years, told of more violent times. 'Major Disturbances,' 'Company Deployment,' 'Ammunition Expended.' One whiteboard was good for all emergencies; printed at its top was the word, 'CASUALTIES' and below that, in smaller letters, 'Dead,' 'Serious' and 'Minor.' Booths of wood and glass housed telephones and radios tuned to divisional and headquarter networks. A green baize table stood in the middle of the room. Air conditioning hummed through the ceiling vents. Two constables moved around the walls, updating information on the whiteboards. There was a constant crackle from the radios and the telephones rang in jangling relay. I checked the figures. Not bad, in Tsuenwan at least, dead -- nil, serious -- nil, minor -- three.

Jason Woo, my predecessor on the subunit was in charge of the DOR. He had a telephone lodged between his ear and his shoulder and he scrabbled around for a notepad. I hovered near the door but he waved me forward. His brow, normally smooth, was lined and his mouth was a thin line. He scribbled me a note and I read it twice. A Hong Kong-Macao ferry had capsized in heavy seas off the Pearl River estuary and many people were missing feared drowned. Jason put down the telephone, closed his eyes and massaged his temples. He nodded to a storm map propped on an easel next to him. The China coast bisected the map in a diagonal line. The landmass of Guangdong province filled the top left-hand section; the South China Sea filled the rest. Radiating outwards were concentric rings marked from one hundred to four hundred nautical miles. The map looked like a target and bang in the middle, like a bull's eye, was Hong Kong. A red line marked the course of typhoon Rose. It meandered around the edge of the outer circle then curled inwards. At three hundred nautical miles, the line became arrow straight and it pointed right at us. Jason tapped the map with his forefinger, 'That was one hour ago. The Observatory reports centre winds gusting one hundred knots *and* getting stronger. Observatory says we will take direct hit. Number ten signal may go up any time.' He sighed. 'Number ten. Hurricane.'

'*Ah Woo Sir.*' The constable held a telephone towards Jason.

Jason took the phone. 'DOR,' he snapped, grabbing his notepad, '*Jesus* ...' he motioned me to stay, '... the subunit commander's here, I'll get him onto it.' He hung up. 'There's a landslide behind block twelve of Kwaishek estate. If any more of the slope goes, we'll be digging out bodies for days. You've a sergeant,

75

goes by the nickname Iron-man Tan.' I nodded. Jason continued. 'He's up there with some constables. I know him. He will be on top of things but it is a good idea if you get up there.' He grabbed the emergency telephone directory. 'Social Welfare Department has opened their storm shelters. I'll tell them you have customers for them.'

I headed for the report room and told the duty officer I needed transport. For once, there was no argument. He winkled out a driver who looked through the window and weighed up which was the scariest, the storm or the DO. No contest, he grabbed a set of keys.

I went upstairs to the canteen and cornered two constables as they tucked into bowls of steaming noodles. The bigger of the two was Ah Ban, our subunit maverick. The other was Peter; he had joined us from another subunit where his commander had been glad to see the back of him.

'You and you, station compound, now,' I ordered.

They eyed me up and down. This was not the time for a test of wills so I turned and walked to the door. They followed, sullen and complaining. I stepped into the compound, brought my poncho under control and bent my head against sheeting rain. Ah Ban and Peter raided the emergency store and loaded rope, crowbars and torches into the back of the Landrover. I had been back in the station just thirty minutes but already the wind was stronger. We boarded the Landrover and headed back to Castle Peak Road, which was now axle-deep in water. The rain was a horizontal torrent. The Landrover bounced and jigged as we crawled along the road. The windscreen looked as though someone was playing a power-hose on it. The constables sat on the rear bench seat with their shoulders hunched and their riot helmets pulled low over their eyes. The radio crackled and Ah Ban reached for the handset. It crackled again and Ah Ban shouted to make himself heard. '*Joi gong.* -- Say again. *M ching choh.* -- Not clear.' The storm beat at the Landrover like an angry mob.

The rain *tackatacktacked* against the doors, bonnet and windows. Ah Ban made shushing motions with his hands and put his ear against the radio speaker. Then he sat back, muttering and shaking his head. He leaned forward and cupped his hand to my ear. It was the first time he had spoken English to me. 'DOR says now we have number ten signal.' His brow furrowed in concentration. 'Hu-rric-ane,' he said, pronouncing it slowly. 'Is it the right word?'

Yes it was. I checked the time: twenty-two fifty-five hours; five to eleven in the evening.

Off to our right, there was a flash of blue-white light and a crack like a snapping tree trunk. The sour smell of ozone seeped into the Landrover. For a second, I thought we had been hit by lightning but then I made out the shape of electricity pylons. The high-tension cables were swinging in undulating waves. We had come no further than Tai On village. At this rate, we would not reach Kwaishek in time to do any good. There was another flash and I saw a figure clawing up the embankment towards us. He was bare-chested and caked in mud. His hair thrashed against his cheeks. He clawed at the ground to stop himself from sliding back towards the village. At the top of the embankment, the wind's full force hit him and I thought it would blow him clear off the road. He shielded his eyes with his forearm then inched towards the Landrover. He beat against the window's wire mesh with a clenched fist. Ah Ban opened his door and Peter cursed as the rain flooded in. Ah Ban dragged the man into the rear compartment where he slumped onto the bench seat, gasping. He was babbling and I could not understand what he was saying.

Ah Ban grabbed the man's shoulders, thrust his face closer and shouted, '*Gong mat yeh? Gong m'yeh?*'-- What are you saying? What?

'*Jaam sei. Jaam sei.*'-- Drowning. Drowning. The man's chest heaved and he began to sob. '*Chuen bo dou jaam sei.*' -- They're all going to drown.

77

I opened the door and the wind ripped it from my grip, buckling the hinge mountings. I stepped into the road and water tugged at my legs. The poncho whipped at my body and I grabbed the Landrover's door pillar to steady myself. There was a nudge in my back and Ah Ban handed me a torch. We trained our torches down the slope. Rain and spray gleamed in the beams, obscuring the view. I squinted and saw water running off the road and gushing into the village. I remembered how the storm drains cut into Taimoshan's slopes. I pictured them now, filled with rain, the overflow pouring into the hollow below. Tai On village lay in that hollow. And now, Tai On village was drowning.

I played the torch on the power lines swinging above me. They slammed together with a blue-white flash and a scalp prickling *BAZZZT*. My skin tingled in the charged air. Ah Ban opened the Landrover's rear door, grabbed armfuls of rope and stuffed a tyre-iron into his belt. The three of us scrambled down the bank into blackness and I found myself knee-deep in water. We ducked as the power lines arced again, showering us with sparks and illuminating the area with strobing light. I had a fleeting picture of a village house, the ground floor underwater. A face peered at us from behind a barred window. Even above the howl of the wind, I heard a shout of '*Gau meng!*'-- Save life.

Ah Ban was gone. Peter had his feet planted in the embankment above the waterline. He had the rope looped around his waist and over his shoulder. He paid it out into the dark. I swung my torch across black floodwater and made out Ah Ban's head as he swam towards the nearest house. I shone the light back on Peter. The water now lapped his ankles. Either he was slipping down the embankment or the flood was rising. A sudden torrent washed down the embankment, hit me in the back and knocked me full length into the flood. My shoes and sodden uniform carried me down. The rubber poncho tangled my arms so I could not swim. I tore at the button fastening it to my throat and it drifted away. I broke the surface, coughing water.

'*Ah Sir*. Here! Over here!' The voice was Ah Ban's and I swam towards it. Now, I could see a faint glow of yellow light flickering from a window above me. A quavering voice called, '*gau meng!*'

Ah Ban turned to me. Above the shriek of the wind, his voice was just audible. '*Ah Sir*, I find a way to roof.'

I told him to wait but he swam off into the darkness. I could see the top of a door jamb just a few inches above the water. I took a breath, gripped the doorframe then pulled myself down and through the open door. I surfaced and my helmet banged against something hard. I tipped back my head and a wedge of panic blocked my throat. The ceiling was just inches from my face. My breath came in sobs. I grabbed for the doorframe and the feel of the wood was reassuring. I thanked my private angel for a dim light that seeped into my airspace. As my eyes grew accustomed to the gloom, I saw I had surfaced under a half-loft. What I had thought was the ceiling was the underside of the loft's floor. In the dim light, I could just make out where it ended.

'*Gau meng. Ngoh ho geng*,' -- Save me. I'm afraid.

I pushed myself hand over hand towards the sound of the voice. I ducked out from under the floor and saw terracotta roof tiles, ten feet above me. A rickety staircase led from the water to the half-loft where an old man knelt on all fours, searching the water's surface. Despite the claustrophobic heat, he was shivering. He spoke in a whisper, as though afraid the storm might find him. '*Ho geng*.' -- I'm very afraid.

I grabbed onto the staircase and dragged myself into the loft. The old man took my arm and pulled me up. The cockloft was small and lit by a hurricane lamp that threw hard shadows. My uniform was sodden and water slopped around my shoes. The old man's name was Grandfather Wong. He said he was less afraid now someone was with him. He held on to my arm with both his hands. If we stayed put, he said, we would be safe.

Security bars blocked the windows. I grabbed one and gave it a shake but the window frame held it tight. I tried them all with the same result. I did not like the alternative, which was to take the old man out through the front door. With a mix of sign language and simple Cantonese, I told Grandfather Wong we should swim to safety. I slipped back into the water. It had crept nearer to the top of the ladder. I beckoned to the old man but he repeated that he was no longer afraid and would understand if I decided to go back to my duties. He chatted about his neighbours and the weather as though making small talk with a favourite nephew. I tried again, but I was getting nowhere. I considered dragging him out through the front door but one look at that frail old man convinced me it would not work. I climbed back into the cockloft and took off my helmet. I could not leave the old man; I could not stay. I stared at the window, if only I could get it open. Grandfather Wong kept up a continuous stream of chitchat as I searched for something to rip out the window frames. There was nothing. I tore drawers from their cabinets and scattered their contents across the floor. There was another blue-white flash and a heart-stopping *chunk* of breaking roof tiles. I froze in a half crouch, eyes fixed on the ceiling. I pictured the power lines snapping under the battering of the winds. I imagined them flailing into the village, smashing roof tiles and turning the floodwater into fountains of exploding steam. Now I had something new to worry about: electrocution. I felt giddy and almost laughed. Hi folks, do you want the good news or the bad news? The old man stopped talking. His confidence snapped and he began to wail. There was another bang and a hole appeared in the ceiling. Metal glinted in the glow of the hurricane lamp and a stiletto-like shadow angled across the ceiling. I waited for the roof to collapse; waited for live cables to come snaking into the room. There were more thumps. A shower of terracotta stung my face. The hole became bigger. Rain and wind swirled into the room. A picture frame hit the floor and shattered. A face appeared at the hole and a voice called, '*Ah Sir*, hurry, hurry.' It was Ah Ban and he was hacking at the hole with his tyre-iron. I jammed on my helmet, pushed a table to the middle of the room and man-handled Grandfather Wong onto it. With me pushing his back-side and Ah Ban pulling on his arms, we forced him through the hole. As I dragged myself after him, the wind stung my face and tried to batter me off the roof. I flattened myself against the tiles and turned my face from the wind. A group of villagers had joined Ah Ban. They formed a protective knot around Grandfather Wong and led him to safety across the nearby roofs.

The three of us, Ah Ban, Peter and I, lay on a slick, wind-battered rooftop as the rain hammered at us. Then it was as if someone had turned off a giant spigot. The rain ceased and the wind fell away to a whisper. For a moment, I thought I had gone deaf. I rolled onto my back and looked up at a sweep of stars in a velvet sky. Water gurgled through flood courses but there was not another sound. The moon shone down from a clear sky. Ah Ban's sleeve hung by a shred. Blood seeped from a gash on his cheek. I felt bruised inside and out. Our uniforms were soaked but now, there was not even a breeze. It was a clear tropical evening. Seconds earlier, we could see only a few feet; now the village lay clear before us, rooftops shining silver under a full moon. A fallen tree lay across the main road. Our driver seemed not to notice the calf-deep water as he stood by the Landrover, his face to the sky. Grandfather Wong and his rescuers crouched on a nearby rooftop, motionless like dancers frozen in a spotlight. All was peaceful. For a full minute, no one spoke; no one moved.

The eye of the hurricane gave us time to make our way back to the Landrover. In a daze, we packed up our equipment and did not notice another Landrover pulling up next to ours.

'Busy night, Mister Emmett.' The divisional superintendent stepped from the passenger seat and frowned as the water soaked his shoes. The major joined him, immaculate and as calm as ever. 'The major tells me your boys and girls have done us proud tonight.' I had long since given up trying to figure how the major got his information. This time, he had excelled himself. 'Your canny old sergeant did a marvellous job at Kwaishek. I expect you'll be pestering me for commendations.' The DS shot a sideways look at the major who replied with a sage smile. They climbed back into the Landrover and as it pulled away, the DS called through the half-open window. 'Looks like you've got some paperwork to take care of.' I saluted the Landrover's tail lights and went back to packing up our kit. Ah Ban would need treatment for that gash and I hoped we could get him to a clinic. As I stowed the last rope, I heard a roar like a convoy of trucks lumbering up Castle Peak Road. I peered into the dark but some kind of mist had sprung up a few hundred yards away. As the noise grew closer, an amorphous wall emerged from the dark and edged closer. A gust ruffled the floodwater and a sheet of corrugated iron wafted towards us like an unmanned magic carpet. I ducked and it *whooshed* overhead. The roar became louder. I stared into the mass that advanced on us and saw it was a swirling mix of rain and debris whipped up by furious winds. We stood paralysed and appalled then we scrambled back aboard the Landrover. In this little part of Tsuenwan, Typhoon Rose had given us a small breathing space, but now she was back.

It is not true that the worst part of a hurricane lies behind the eye, but I forgive anyone who thinks it does. The wind hits from the opposite direction, which is a surprise, but the worst part is its sudden impact. During the storm's initial approach, wind and rain increases over hours or even days but there is no such luxury when the eye passes. There are no *pitter-patter* warning drops of rain, no gradual increase in wind strength. The tail end of Typhoon Rose hit us like a baseball bat. The driver swung the Landrover round in a U-turn and the suspension groaned as the wind caught us broadside. The driver gasped and I thought we were going over. We inched our way back to safety, passing an abandoned fire engine on the way. Back at the station, the compound was awash. The hawker exhibits store door was gone;

smashed trolleys and baskets were strewn about the compound. From behind a steel door next to the report room came the throb of the station generator. We parked the Landrover under cover and battled our way back to the main building, bruised and soaked to the bone.

One hundred and thirty people died during Typhoon Rose, including eighty who drowned when the Hong Kong-Macao ferry capsized. Hundreds more were injured. The typhoon left five thousand people homeless. Sergeant 'Iron-man' Tan managed perfectly well without my help. In appalling conditions, he and four constables evacuated over one hundred people from the lower floors of a housing block in Kwaishek. Half an hour later, the earthen slope behind the block collapsed. Thousands of tons of water-sodden soil battered through doors and windows, swamping ground and first storey apartments with stinking ooze. I was writing for a week, but with a push from the SDI and the DS, we got the awards through. Ah Ban and Peter each received the Colonial Police Medal for gallantry. Sergeant Tan received the commissioner's high commendation for leadership and his four constables each received commendations for gallantry. At first, I thought only my subunit had distinguished itself, but in the following weeks, I heard tales of heroism from all over the force. The stories were all similar, at the height of the typhoon, sergeants and constables regarded as troublemakers had behaved with outstanding courage. I mentally filed that away. A little forbearance costs nothing, and one day I might need someone to help me out of a jam.

Typhoon Rose crossed into China where she weakened into scattered showers and the occasional whisper of wind. However, the cleared skies did not mean we could relax. There were fallen trees, blocked roads, abandoned cars and when the power came back on, all Tsuenwan's burglar alarms went off. People returned to work to find shattered windows and waterlogged offices. It was a hectic time and the last thing I needed was trouble from the Imperial Japanese Air Force.

Factories and offices got back to the serious business of making money. On a Sha Tsui Road building site, a worker fired up his mechanical digger, but when its claw bit into the earth, there was a loud *clunk* and it grated against what seemed like a boulder. The worker called his foreman and together they scraped away the mud. They uncovered part of a rusty cylinder and at first, thought it was an old water main. The foreman ordered a gang to dig it out but soon found it was something very different. It was about six feet long, pointed at one end and had a battered fin at the other. The site manager cursed. The typhoon had knocked his schedule back days and the lump of iron sitting in the middle of his site meant even more delay. By the time I arrived, the site workers were lounging around the perimeter, smoking and chatting. A constable stood guard over the object, which lay half-exposed in a shallow trench. Even to my untrained eye, there was no mistaking the shape of a Second World War bomb. Its casing was rusty and crusted with hardened mud.

The constable gave the tailfin a nudge with his toe. 'Don't be worry *Ah Sir*,' he said, 'bomb's not gone off yet.'

Funny things, bombs. They are weapons of terror but mention the words 'unexploded bomb' and people will travel miles to see it. I should have been afraid; no, I should have been terrified, but instead I gave the casing a gentle kick. 'No,' I said, 'I don't think it has.' We nodded wisely at each other.

I got on the radio and asked New Territories control to turn out an explosive ordinance disposal team then gave some thought to evacuating every shop, office block and apartment in Tsuenwan town centre. The NT controller ordered a para-military Police Tactical Unit platoon to provide assistance and within half an hour, forty-one policemen arrived in two Bedford trucks. The PTU men wore standard police uniforms but instead of peaked caps, they wore navy blue berets. They were quiet and tough looking. Their commander was a laconic young Chinese inspector. He acknowledged my briefing with a nod and then started setting up road diversions and arranging the evacuation of nearby buildings. Shortly afterwards a Landrover arrived and a bereted superintendent climbed out. He returned my salute with a half-hearted wave. His voice was a lazy drawl, 'Blinkard. Victor company commander. What's the damned panic?'

I told him about the bomb and assured him there was no panic.

'So, what are you doing about it?'

'There's not much to do,' I said. 'EOD's on the way and your platoon commander has a grip on everything else.'

'So, I suppose you're just going to sit here scratching your arse.' The wail of a siren spared me the task of answering. EOD -- the bomb squad, had arrived.

The EOD team leader was a slim European in his late twenties. He had a sharp, animated face dominated by a thicket of ginger hair. His handshake was firm and he spoke like someone eager to get on with the job. 'Dennis Flambers. EOD. Where is it?'

'Hang on, Flambers,' Superintendent Blinkard's voice was petulant. 'You'll report to me if you don't mind. Where's the bloody Force Bomb Disposal Officer?'

Flambers did not answer right away. He scanned the building site noting loose chains, piles of lumber, iron pipes, rubble and other debris that would become lethal if the bomb exploded. He replied without a glance at Blinkard. ' FBDO's on a beach in Sarawak, lucky sod.'

Blinkard fixed Flambers with a hard stare. 'Sir.' he snapped.

'Pardon?' There was a splinter of irritation in Flambers' voice.

'That's a crown on my shoulder,' Blinkard tapped his epaulette.

'Yes, of course. Sorry.' Flambers walked around the bomb, pausing to examine it more closely.

Blinkard spoke through clenched teeth. 'That's sorry, "Sir."'

'Indeed. *Sir.*' Flambers' tone was dismissive. 'Now, if you'll kindly give me some bloody elbow room, I'll get on with it.'

Flambers' number two was a cheery sergeant called Aap Jai, literally meaning little duck. Aap Jai fussed around the EOD team as they dug earth from around the bomb and lined the deepening pit with timber. Straddling the pit, they erected a tripod from which they hung chains and a pulley. They shovelled earth into sandbags and laid a telephone line to a temporary command post outside the construction site. Flambers ordered everyone not part of his team to leave. I went back to the command post but noticed Blinkard had not joined me. I waited a few minutes then headed back to the site entrance so I could see what was going on.

Blinkard had refused to leave the area and was making a complete nuisance of himself. He stared into the pit until Aap Jai complained he was blocking the light. He inspected the EOD equipment and railed at its chipped paint and dull finish. When he realised the EOD team was ignoring him, he prodded Flambers' shoulder. 'Well Flambers, what's the score? Come on man, you've been frigging about all morning. Let's have a situation appraisal. Now, *dammit.*'

Flambers squinted into the pit and stoked his chin. 'Well, if I'm pushed for an urgent appraisal, *Sir,* I'd say it's a fucking bomb.'

Blinkard's face flushed crimson. He choked and seemed about to speak when Aap Jai emerged from pit, his face and clothes spattered with mud. 'Water's filling pit, boss. You come now.'

To Blinkard, the deference shown to rank was vital to good order and discipline. Once that was lost, everything else was gone. '*Boss?*' he choked. '*You come now?* Who's in charge of this unit, Flambers, you or your sergeant?'

Aap Jai turned and walked back to the pit, muttering under his breath.

Flambers called after him, 'I heard that Aap Jai,' he chastened. 'You will *not* refer to the superintendent as "a wanker."' He cupped his hands to his mouth and bawled, *'especially if he is one.'*

Blinkard spluttered and harrumphed but, lost for words, he retreated to his Landrover and spent the rest of the morning plotting his revenge. Flambers inspected the bomb's fuse and found it rusted solid. He declared there was no immediate danger and decided to take the bomb to the army's tank range at Ma Cho Lung. There, he would remove most of the charge then destroy the shell with a controlled explosion.

'Bloody great bang,' he cackled. 'World's best hangover cure.'

Flambers had the bomb winched from the pit and loaded onto a flat-bed truck. As the truck pulled out of the site, he clambered aboard, straddled the bomb and fished a briar pipe from his pocket. He knocked the pipe's bowl against the bomb's casing and filled up with tobacco. As the truck rolled into Sha Tsui Road, onlookers behind the police cordon broke into applause. Flambers stood and with the poise of a regency dandy, bowed from the waist.

Nothing is simple. Small problems tend to cause bigger problems and if they are not dealt with, everything ends in a mess. One such problem was a haulage garage in Texaco Road. With depot space at a premium, the drivers parked overnight on the street. This caused problems for the early shift who, until the drivers went off on their deliveries, had to deal with a traffic block that affected the whole town centre. I spoke to the subdivisional traffic inspector. He promised to deal with it but the problem continued. I had a word with my sector sergeant and told him to start issuing tickets. He raised an eyebrow. 'Haulage firm has traffic inspector's special permission for night parking,' he told me.

Frankly, I did not care; the Texaco Road traffic block had become daily routine and I was sick of it. 'After tomorrow morning's briefing, take two constables and ticket everything in Texaco Road,' I ordered.

'Yes sir,' he said. But he never did.

There were no licensed taxis in Tsuenwan and this opened the market to illegal hire cars, known as *paak pais*. The *paak pais* had become so bold, they worked from an unofficial taxi rank in Sha Tsui Road. This was embarrassing so I told the beat constables to move them on.

'Yes sir,' they said. But they never did.

On night shift, a restaurant worker signalled for me to join him in a nearby alley for a quiet word. There was an illegal casino above his restaurant, he told me. It was a big one, he had lost a month's pay there two nights earlier and was keen to see some payback. I spoke to the divisional crime collator. He wrote down the address and made a big show of thanking me. Nothing happened.

I had a good old moan to a couple of my fellow inspectors. They made sympathetic noises and changed the subject. The next evening, all became clear.

I was on afternoon shift and took my break in the tiny divisional officers' mess. I was chatting to some nine to fivers who were enjoying a beer before shooting off home. The divisional planning officer put his head round the door and the room went quiet. He came in, nodded to the others and in an instant, the mess emptied. That was odd, the DPO was a sociable sort but that evening he seemed tense. He was around thirty years old and had eight years service under his belt. We PIs liked him and often sought his advice. He slipped behind the bar, signed for two beers and invited me to join him. 'You seem to be settling in well,' he said. 'How's it all going? Any personal problems ...' He paused. 'Any money problems?'

I got on well with the DPO, he was good-natured and sociable but that evening, there was something odd about him. His smile was tight, his voice was a little too loud.

'You're getting yourself known around the division,' he said then fell silent as though expecting me to say something.

I sensed not all was right so I said nothing.

The DPO's face took on a pained expression. 'The problem with you ex-UK coppers is that you think everything has to be the same as back home.'

Again, I stayed silent.

'Well it's not,' he declared.

Still, I said nothing.

The DPO cleared his throat and shifted on his bar stool. 'Look at it this way,' he said, speaking in a rush. 'There are no licensed taxis in the New Territories so we tolerate the *paak pais*. We tolerate overnight parking because there isn't enough depot space ...'

'And do we tolerate gambling divans because TV's rubbish?' I asked. I started to feel uneasy.

He fluttered his hands. 'No, no, no. Look, I'll get to the point.' He glanced at the door, pulled an envelope from his pocket and laid it on the bar. I picked it up; inside were two, one hundred dollar bills. He leaned closer and lowered his voice. 'Play the game and you'll get one of those every week,' he said.

I took a deep breath. My pay was just one thousand, four hundred a month. I put the envelope back on the bar-top and for long moments there was silence. 'I should report this to Anti Corruption Branch,' I said at last.

'Go ahead,' he said with a shrug. 'I'll say we had a falling out and you made it up. AC deals with reports like that every week.'

'What if I tell the SDI?'

'Who would he believe? A one-pip trouble maker or the DPO? The bosses like things peaceful.' He tapped his nose. 'Enough said?' He relaxed and became his old, affable self. 'It's not just this division,' he said. 'It's the same everywhere.' He fixed me with an earnest look. 'The Hong Kong government has no idea how much it costs to run this police force,' he said. 'Consider this: who pays for crime information? The detective staff sergeant, that's who. Does he claim it back? Does he buggery. Does the vice squad have transport? No. The boys use their own cars.

Who pays for that? They do.'

'And if I decide not to play your game?'

'That's your choice,' he said. 'It's a bit like a bus,' he added. 'You can climb aboard and ride in comfort or you can run alongside and sweat your bollocks off just getting to the same place.'

'My choice?' I asked. 'So, there's no problem if I raid the gambling divan above the Hoi Tin Restaurant?'

'None whatsoever,' he said. 'Someone will pay the gamblers' bail and cover their fines. The arrests will count to our case statistics. Everyone's happy; everything's peaceful.'

'What about the *paak pais*?'

'Ticket away,' he said. 'Fines will be paid; life will go on.'

'So, who else is on board?' I asked.

He shot me a reproving look. 'You'll find out,' he said. 'But take it from me, there's more than you think.' He picked up the envelope and put it back in his pocket. 'Think about it,' he said. 'It won't affect your work, it'll just make life a bit easier.' He stepped from behind the bar. 'Remember, it's like a bus,' he said. 'You can get on board or you can run alongside. But whatever you do, don't stand in front of it.' Then he left, shutting the door behind him.

This was my darkest time. I spoke to colleagues that I knew and trusted but got the same answers: don't worry about it; it's just the way things work; it helps us keep a lid on things.

I wondered how far it went. Who was in? Who was out? In my mind, I wrote my resignation letter over and over. A few days later, I found myself alone in the mess when the divisional detective inspector joined me. The DDI was the detective equivalent of my boss, the SDI and we held him in something akin to awe. 'Ah, glad I caught you alone,' he said. He beckoned me to the bar. 'Step up here young man. You and me need a word.'

I looked at my watch and made for the door.

'No you don't,' he said. He jammed his index finger down

onto the bar. 'Get yourself here, now. There's something we need to sort out.'

With some reluctance, I took a seat at the bar.

'I know you've had "the talk,"' he said. 'And I can see you're troubled.'

I stayed silent but the DDI would have none of it. 'Don't give me that old sulk,' he said. 'Talk to me.'

I shrugged. 'I'm going to put my ticket in,' I answered.

'*Resign?*' the DDI scoffed. '*Resign?* Not clever, young man,' he said. 'Not clever at all.'

'What choice do I have?'

'Stick it for a year,' he said. 'There's a new bribery law coming and it'll change everything.'

I must have looked dubious so the DDI went into detail. He told me that within a year, it would be illegal for any government officers to own assets or enjoy a lifestyle that did not match their official pay. 'My mates in Anti Corruption Branch are already drawing up a target list,' he said. 'And between you and me, there's some pretty high-flyers on it.' He stood and headed for door. 'You sit tight, my lad,' he said. 'Give it a year. In a year, everything will change.'

We left it at that but for days, I was torn. Should I go or stay? Finally, I decided to take the DDI at his word and give it a year.

As things turned out, it was the best advice I would ever get.

In December, northerly winds replaced the Pacific monsoon and for a week, Hong Kong policemen shivered in their bush shirts and shorts. At police headquarters, staff officers consulted the Royal Observatory, drafted and redrafted orders then issued urgent instructions for the force to change into winter blues. That gave us just twelve hours to dig out our winter uniforms, brush away the summer mildew and get them smart enough to wear in public. With the change of uniform complete, the clouds parted, the sun shone and the public headed for the beach. I sweltered in my blues until January then just as the cool weather set in, a testy SDI met me in the subunit office. He waved a postings memo at me and demanded to know why I had not reported for duty on the Hong Kong-China border.

I was moving to Frontier division.

CHAPTER 5
HIGH TIDE MARK

WHAT'S IN A NAME? Quite a lot, actually. Why must we British endure place names like Grewelthorpe and Chipping Sodbury when Ireland has towns like Limerick and Tralee? American cities rejoice in names like Kalamazoo and Chattanooga. In Hong Kong too, place names have resonance. The swanky residential area on Hong Kong Island is Victoria Peak; parts of Kowloon twist the tongue with names like Shamshuipo and Tsimshatsui. I like place names that make a statement and the name 'Frontier Division,' said it all. It conjured up images of Caruthers of the Khyber and Davy Crockett. Soon, I would stand at the high tide mark of empire. Sobering thought, that.

Before my posting to Frontier, I did not give China much thought. I was not alone in that; Hong Kong life was complicated enough, so most people just got on with it. This was despite China's presence being everywhere. China's Sin Hwa News Agency had a Hong Kong office that doubled as an unofficial consulate. China's central bank had a branch next door to the Hong Kong and Shanghai Bank's international headquarters. There were communist schools, trade unions, and newspapers like *Ta Kung Pao*. Well-stocked China Products Emporiums graced main streets from Yuen Long in the New Territories to Queens Road in Hong Kong Island's business district. Most of our food came from China. A network of communist delivery companies operated lorries that, apart from discreet yellow squares painted on the tailgate corners, were indistinguishable from other goods vehicles. Police officers issuing tickets to these lorries would find themselves surrounded by workmen shouting *'KONG YEE -- PROTEST.'* Any police action against leftists met a barrage of abuse. For police officers, it was all part of the job. They became inured to it all and shrugged it off with comments like, 'Bloody *jaw-jais* -- bloody commies.'

Come first of May, Chinese flags sprouted at every left wing business. There were portraits of Mao and big character posters declaring, 'Sailing the seas depends on the helmsman,' and, 'Boundlessly loyal to the great leader.' Across the road from the Bank of China was that classic symbol of empire, the Hong Kong cricket club. During leftist celebrations, a portrait of the Great Helmsman sometimes hung from the bank's balustrade and served as backdrop to men in cricket whites, stroking willow against leather.

China's view of Hong Kong was hard to fathom. She condemned as unequal the treaties that ceded Hong Kong to Britain, but continued to honour them. Many believed China tolerated the British presence because Hong Kong was a source of much needed foreign currency. This was true to a point but people underestimated the strength of Chinese nationalism. It is more likely that behind the red guard's rhetoric, wiser heads knew that for China to take her rightful place in the world, she had to honour her treaties, equal or unequal.

China was emerging slowly from Chairman Mao's Cultural Revolution but just four and a half years after the 1967 disturbances, Hong Konger's were still wary. China was like a bad-tempered tough guy sulking in the barroom corner; certainly not someone to ignore, but you had best tread carefully. No one knew what China had in store for Hong Kong, so most tried not to let it worry them. At social gatherings, talk of China was brief and usually ended with the phrase, 'China could take back Hong Kong with a single phone call.' A local wag suggested that if London ever received the phone call, Her Majesty's foreign secretary would call first for a brandy and then for an atlas.

The simple fact was that Hong Kong was all about business and so long as business was good, nothing else really mattered.

I was sorry to leave Tsuenwan. With the language course under my belt, I had grown into the job. I was fond of my subunit and would miss the easy camaraderie of the Fung Chik Sen crowd. I was sorry to leave Ah Wan's wonderful meals and the glorious sunsets over Lantau Island. I was half way through writing my handover report when the telephone rang. It was the barrack sergeant telling me his assistant, the barrack-*jai*, was on his way to me with my New Territories kit. Within minutes, the barrack-*jai* struggled into the office carrying a large cardboard carton.

'NT kit,' he said and dumped the carton on my desk. 'All year round, same uniform. Make bloody sense, yes?' I checked the contents: three bush shirts, an itchy looking khaki pullover, one black webbing belt and holster, canvas jungle boots and glory glory be, long trousers. All in my size too, the barrack sergeant must have known about my transfer for weeks.

This was quite a move. Border policing meant paddling in the murky pond of international diplomacy. Policemen are pretty versatile and usually everything worked out fine. I say 'usually' because as I bade my farewells, word of what we called 'a border event' filtered down from the Frontier.

At a small border post called Lowu, an iron-latticed railway bridge spanned the Sumchun River. Lowu was a quiet place with only one interesting feature, it was where the Chinese and Hong Kong rail systems met. There was not much passenger traffic and both the Chinese and Hong Kong railheads were sleepy little places. Policemen at Lowu had little to do except affirm sovereignty by patrolling their side of the bridge. On the other side of the border, the People's Liberation Army did the same. At a personal level, relations were good. Chinese soldiers gave a discreet nod to the constables when they saw an inspector coming and whenever possible, the constables returned the favour.

It was the tail end of Chairman Mao's Cultural Revolution. Banners bearing bold but meaningless slogans adorned every public area in China and Mao's Red Guards still brought turmoil to a few isolated pockets of countryside. But Lowu was different; apart from some fiery billboards, the Chinese side was an oasis of pragmatic calm. On the British side, common sense and tolerance ruled, or at least it did until inspector Danny Sanders happened on the scene.

Danny was a typical probationary inspector, young and full of energy, but at Lowu there was not much to challenge him. After a few days of bluster and bullying, he had the smartest, shiniest constables on the border. The police post gleamed, there was always someone to answer the telephone and the administration had never been so slick. There was only one problem, Danny was bored out of his skull. Then one morning, he noticed the post's flag. It was nothing special, just an ordinary six feet by two feet, government issue, British flag . For all Danny knew, it could have been the very flag planted by Captain Elliot back in 1841, it was certainly grubby enough. And that annoyed Danny Sanders, who thought a grubby flag was downright unpatriotic. He ordered it hauled down and given to the Frontier barrack sergeant for cleaning.

Lowu post now had no Union Jack, and that would not do at all. The barrack sergeant hunted around his store and came up with a spare flag left over from a long forgotten parade. The replacement was in perfect condition and it was clean but instead of the usual six by two, this flag was twelve feet by four. Danny accepted the barrack sergeant's promise to have the regular flag back within a few days and he hoisted its replacement.

None of this went unnoticed by the Chinese side. Danny's Chinese counterpart matched Danny in energy, but I suspect his meagre workload left him feeling equally brain-dead. So the premature lowering of the British flag on the Hong Kong side of the border stirred up a lot of interest on the Chinese side. A group of Chinese officials bustled onto the bridge and despite it being only a few yards away, they trained powerful binoculars onto Danny's naked flagpole. Danny was blithely unaware of their attention, but as soon as his new, much larger flag unfurled, there was a collective gasp from the Chinese. They huddled in urgent conference then scuttled back across the bridge.

Next morning the loudspeaker outside the Chinese post erupted with scratchy bugle music and a Chinese soldier hoisted the five-starred Chinese banner. There was a decent breeze but the flag hardly stirred. Danny watched through his binoculars and reckoned the Chinese flag measured at least twenty feet by six. This drew some laughter from the Hong Kong immigration officers, not to mention Danny's own men. Danny silenced them with a glare and thrust out his chest. If the Chinese wanted war, then war it would be.

Danny Sanders was an enterprising chap but the problem with the flag kept him on the phone all morning. Eventually, he got hold of an amateur operatic group who had just finished a run of 'Last Night at the Proms.' Before the day was out, they delivered to Danny their main backdrop: a British flag no less than thirty feet along the fly and ten feet high. With a triumphant grin, Danny ordered it run up the flagpole.

From the Chinese post, a group of hatchet-faced cadres watched in silence.

The next day broke still and clear. Danny stood on the roof of his post and through his binoculars, watched the Chinese officials watching him through their binoculars. Danny nodded to a constable who for the second day running hoisted the enormous theatrical backdrop up the flagpole. Danny watched the faces of the Chinese and to his surprise, each cadre lowered his binoculars and broke into a curious smile.

Two PLA soldiers struggled through the door of the Chinese

post. Between them they wrestled with a mountain of crimson fabric. The soldiers each braced a foot against the Chinese flagpole and grunted on the halyards as they raised the five-starred banner. The wind whistled through the bridge's iron latticework but the Chinese flag did not give the slightest flutter. Its crimson folds clung to the Chinese post's balustrade, its drape covered the south facing wall and its hem trailed across a neat flowerbed at the wall's base.

Danny felt the crushing weight of defeat drag at his heart. He lowered his binoculars and sighed. He could not guess the Chinese flag's size but he knew he was beaten. Later that day, the barrack sergeant returned the post's original flag, cleaned and ironed. Danny immediately reinstated it. The group on the roof of the Chinese post pumped one another's hands and slapped each other's backs. Within minutes, a two metre by half metre, five-starred banner flew gaily on the Chinese side of the border.

Two great nations stepped back from the abyss. For now, world peace was secure.

The road to the border meandered through the craggy hills and soft farmland of the rural New Territories. It was a pleasant drive and the weather was unseasonably warm. No one can just drive to the Hong Kong-Chinese border, first they must cross a strip of land called the Frontier Closed Area and no one may enter that without a permit from the police commissioner.

Shataukok main police station stood on a hill just outside the closed area. On the road below the station stood a concrete checkpoint where the police turned back tourists, lost travellers and the just plain curious. I gunned my old Ford Cortina up a short driveway to the station and nearly knocked over a cheerful man dressed in rumpled NT kit. I was about to comment upon the state of his eyesight when I noticed three pips on his epaulettes. He was the sub-divisional inspector and his name was Stanley Watts. He always insisted I call him 'Stanley' but there was never any doubt about who was the boss. He waved aside my salute and gave me a bone-crushing handshake. He took me through a tiny report room and into his office. 'Caught me on a busy day,' he said, waving a memo at me. 'I've written one whole memo today. All this paperwork will see me off.' He slid the memo into his out-tray. 'Sod the admin, get yourself into uniform and I'll take you to meet the *bing*.' He saw the question in my eyes. 'The *bing*; the army. Don't worry, they're on our side; or so they tell us.'

The report room *tailau* showed me to the inspector's quarters and I let myself into an airy bedroom. The window was open and the air smelt sweet and clear. There were no diesel fumes; no sound of traffic. All I could hear was the trill of a bird and wind rustling through the leaves outside my window. I changed into uniform and felt quite grown-up in my long trousers. Without starch, the NT kit felt soft against my skin. I rolled up the sleeves of my bush shirt and fastened the laces of my calf-high jungle boots, their rubber soles squeaked on the polished floorboards.

The border village of Shataukok was a short drive from the main station. Once through the checkpoint, we travelled along a narrow road with paddy fields to our left and the shallow waters of Starling Inlet to our right. Beyond Starling Inlet was Mirs Bay where, during the summer months, young Chinese braved sharks and Chinese patrol boats to make the swim to Hong Kong's golden streets. Occasionally, a body washed up on a stony beach, a reminder of the dangers the swimmers faced.

There were two police posts in the village, one a modern concrete structure, the other an empty shell with bullet-pocked outer walls. In the troubled summer of 1967, disciplined gunfire from the Chinese side of the border killed five policemen and took out the post's radio aerials. Police headquarters called out the army and in short order, a company of battle-ready Ghurkhas appeared at the closed area checkpoint. After some wrangling with the defence ministry in London, the Ghurkhas moved forward. They advanced at a steady walk, strung out in line abreast across the fields and paddies. Their commander, in full view of bewildered Chinese machinegun crews, ambled down the middle of the road, swatting imaginary toadstools with his walking stick. The shooting stopped the moment the Ghurkhas appeared and the guns have remained silent ever since.

The army stayed on after the attack but they considered the old police post indefensible. The Royal Engineers strengthened and fortified a nearby building and it became the new police post. Five years on and the old post still stood, a reminder of a hot and crazy summer.

We stopped in a small plaza where a bored British soldier pretended not to notice the arrival of Shataukok's senior police officer. A few yards away, a cluster of scruffy buildings huddled around a 'T' junction. Facing us across the junction was an open-fronted general store, its entrance shaded by a candy-striped awning. And standing in the awning's shade was a Chinese soldier. I did a double-take but there was no mistaking the soft Mao cap with its red star above the peak or the baggy green tunic with scarlet tabs at the collar. There was no mistaking the curved magazine of a Kalashnikov assault rifle strapped at the high port across the soldier's chest.

Stanley's mouth was a bloodless line. 'We're not supposed to get too close without the army,' he said. 'But I won't tell if you don't.' He walked to the T-junction and I followed. We were just feet from the Chinese soldier. *Christ*, where was the border? The plaza and the police post were behind us, the general store directly in front and to our left was a narrow street, lined with ramshackle houses. We stopped next to a knee-high concrete post. Stanley nodded to the street to our left. 'Chung-Ying Street,' he said. 'It translates as "China-England Street."' He nudged the post with his toe. 'That's the Chinese border,' he said. 'Doesn't look much, does it?'

The Chinese soldier was so close that to a casual observer, the three of us would have looked like a huddle of old friends. He was heavyset and over six feet tall. He fixed me with an unblinking stare and I could see him working through a mental checklist. New boy: rank, approximate age, height, weight, general description.

Stanley winked at me. 'Relax, this time tomorrow they'll know your hat size and your mum's maiden name.' I tried to come up with a flippant reply but did not feel at all flippant. Stanley continued. 'In East Germany, the *Vopos* patrol in pairs. If one does a runner, the other lets him have it.' He made shooting motions with his fingers then jerked his thumb at the Chinese soldier. 'This lad's all alone. One step and he's in Hong Kong.' There was grudging admiration in his voice. 'It's never happened. Don't let the Charlie Chaplin trousers fool you, he's one of the most disciplined soldiers in the world.'

It felt unreal. Then, China was a great closed empire but here I was just inches from its border. There was no bamboo curtain, no graffiti-covered wall, no slavering dogs, no observation towers bristling with searchlights; just two Hong Kong policemen and a Chinese soldier standing in a dusty street in a run-down little village.

In a fit of 1960s revolutionary zeal, the People's Liberation Army abolished all ranks. Great for a workers' struggle committee, not so smart for the world's biggest army. However, when the PLA officers threw away their shoulderboards, the rank structure just moved underground. There were always signs: sentries would come to attention or tug their tunics straight on the approach of an officer. Also, the officers' tunics had two breast and two hip pockets. Ordinary soldiers had breast pockets only.

We turned back to the village post. Behind me, the Chinese soldier hawked and spat on the ground.

The village post's main door was steel plate and it swung heavily on greased hinges. We stepped into a small report room manned by a constable. He snapped to attention and grinned at us. He had a mouthful of gold teeth and I noticed the felt backing to his shoulder numerals was black, not red. This meant he spoke no English. I asked Stanley how he managed.

'That's Kiang and he speaks better English than me.' Stanley lowered his voice. 'He doesn't let on about his English; it makes life easier, particularly when the *bing* are about.'

We shared the post with a platoon from the Royal 15th/21st Something or Other. It was the kind of regiment with chain mail epaulettes on their dress uniforms and officers named *Wupert*. Their billets, stores and orderly rooms took up the top two floors of our post and they had a sandbagged observation post on the roof. We headed for the stairs and on the first floor landing, found a red-faced lieutenant colonel voicing some strident opinions to a slender young subaltern. The subaltern had smooth skin and fair hair. He looked like he would be happier back home, neck deep in horse manure. Stanley cleared his throat and the senior officer turned on us.

'*What?* Oh, it's you.' He looked at his watch. 'Will this take long?' He had a voice like a Sheffield rasp and I was to learn that his men called him Tank. He thought he had earned the nickname by being an unstoppable military force. However, it was all down to his personality: noisy, thick-skinned and slow.

A small muscle twitched in Stanley's lower jaw and his voice took on a brittle edge. He introduced me as the new inspector in charge of the village post. He stressed the words, '*in charge.*'

Tank scowled and offered a cursory handshake. 'Civil bloody power's always in bloody charge but I hope you realise, young man, that without the army you wouldn't be *in charge* of anything.' Although he was speaking to me, Tank was looking at Stanley.

I decided to broker a truce. 'I'm glad you're here,' I said. 'Those PLA troops look a real handful.' It was just an offhand remark but I should have kept quiet.

Tank's eyes hardened and the subaltern took a step back. 'A

handful, young man, a bloody handful?' he growled and I wanted to melt into the shadows. 'The Chinese infantryman is scruffy, ill-equipped, badly trained, poorly led and what's more, he's got *Gawd*-awful manners.'

Instantly, the words 'Singapore' and 'Imperial Japanese Army' sprang to mind but I thought it best to keep such thoughts to myself.

Tank glared at the subaltern, who gave a dutiful laugh. He turned his attention back to me. 'Give me a company of *British* troops.' He jabbed a finger at my chest. 'And I don't mean, Johnny "please don't shout at me," bloody, Ghurkha, I mean proper, *British* troops. Give me that and I'll be in Peking by Friday.' He turned away with a dismissive sniff.

There was no point arguing, in fact I agreed with him. I pictured Tank's company of about one hundred British soldiers taking on three million carbon copies of the Chinese soldier I had just seen in Chung Ying Street. If we included time spent chained to the floor of a Peking-bound PLA train, then Friday seemed about right.

My working hours were two days on, two days off. On duty, I was supposed to stay at the village post but usually I slept and took my meals at the main station. Frontier SDIs like Stanley worked from 8:45 in the morning until 5:15 in the evening but they had to live on station and stay in contact twenty-four hours a day. They could leave the New Territories only on their days off. The restrictions were not for everyone and Frontier was not a popular posting.

From day one, I loved it. The Frontier closed area was a time capsule untouched by developers. There was always a police Landrover available for the short trip to the village, but if there was time, I preferred to walk. The January air was crisp. To my right, the waters of Starling Inlet were like glass and in the early mornings, a gauzy mist clung to the surface. To my left, and standing back from the road, a few farmhouses nestled in the trees. They had granite walls, glazed roofs and hooked eaves. In the paddies, water buffaloes with backswept horns stood belly deep in the ooze. Sometimes, they lumbered onto the road. Then, a young boy would guide the beast back to the paddy with sharp cries and blows on the rump with a leafy twig. The air was sweet and clear. There was hardly any traffic. Life was slower.

First business of the day was the seven o'clock, police-military patrol along Chung-Ying Street. We did the patrol at exactly seven in the morning and seven in the evening. It served no purpose other than to reinforce British sovereignty over our part of the village. In short, we walked along our side of Chung-Ying Street because we could. This irked the Chinese and a sense of tension always overshadowed the patrol. It was something to which I never grew accustomed. As soon as we formed up outside the police post, hard-faced workers gathered on the Chinese side and glared at us. The PLA soldier would hitch his Kalashnikov into a more comfortable position and a hush would fall over the village. To ease tension, the British army kept the magazines of their weapons in their fatigue pockets and we stuck to rigid schedules of time and patrol route.

I arrived at the village post at oh-six forty-five. The sun was bright but I shivered in a morning mist that loitered around the village lanes. A few chickens pecked at the plaza's asphalt and the air smelled of wood smoke. Loudspeakers on the Chinese side played the sweet voice of a woman singing. I have always thought of Mandarin as a language more suited to lovemaking than revolution, and I imagined a dewy-eyed peasant girl singing just for me.

'She sings for you.' It was Kiang. He saluted and flashed me a gold plated smile. He mimicked the girl's voice with an exaggerated falsetto. 'Grind bones of imperialist pigs.'

'Grind ...?'

'The song.' He pointed to the loudspeakers. 'Chinese army play it for new *bongban-jai*.'

Kiang may have had black tabs on his shoulders but his English was fine. He had resisted every offer of promotion and he remained a vital member of the Shataukok police contingent. In addition to Cantonese, he spoke Mandarin, the official language of China, and Hakka, a dialect common along the border. He had cousins living in both the Hong Kong and the Chinese parts of the village. Kiang had eyes and ears everywhere; he could get things done; he was a man of influence. Stanley half-joked that he was probably a full colonel in China's Public Security Bureau.

The police post door swung open and six British soldiers filed out. In silence, they spread themselves in a wide arc across the plaza. They checked rooftops, doors and windows, searching out possible dangers and making a mental note of useful cover. Each carried an SLR semi-automatic rifle and seemed to know instinctively his arc of responsibility. Within seconds, there was a one-eighty-degree sweep of firepower in front of the post. A radio operator whispered a transmission check into his mouthpiece. A sergeant passed among them, checking weapons and equipment. This was the first time I had seen British soldiers at work and it struck me that Tank might not be as loopy as he seemed.

'*Hairlairthere*.'

The pale young subaltern had joined his men in front of the post and he headed towards me, hand outstretched.

Hairlairthere? It took a second to sink in. 'Oh ... hello there.' I stuck out my hand and introduced myself. The subaltern had a firm grip and an open face.

'Glad to meet you, old thing. Browne, Julian, Lieutenant. Do *please* call me Jools.' The single pip on his shoulder was even shinier than mine. He turned to Kiang, and spoke like a Victorian botanist befriending a native. 'AND-HOW-ARE-YOU-MY-STOUT-FELLOW?'

Kiang turned to me and rolled his eyes.

'Right, old man.' Jools was talking to me. 'With your kind permission, let's show the jolly old flag to the Mongol horde.'

The soldiers fell in behind us and as we moved away from post. I felt the soldiers gauging the range to every darkened window and shadowed doorway. We approached the border stone in front of the general store and the PLA sentry came to meet us. We stopped, his face was just feet from mine, eyes unblinking. I glared back at him but it was like trying to stare down a block of concrete. As I looked away, the Chinese sentry gave a snort and adjusted the shoulder strap of his Kalashnikov.

I told Jools to stay close. We turned and walked into Chung-Ying Street; us on our side of the street, the PLA sentry on his. The street was just a few feet wide and we walked almost shoulder to shoulder down the narrow strip of tarmac. It was cracked and potholed on the British side; smooth and well maintained on the Chinese side. I tried to ignore the Kalashnikov's muzzle, just inches from my right cheek. I could smell the armourer's oil that glistened on its barrel. Civilians watched in silence. A man stepped across the border from the Chinese side and stood in my path. He had a seamed face and spiky hair. He wore a cotton tunic unbuttoned to reveal a grubby singlet. His trousers were loose and rolled up to the knee. On his feet were rubber sandals. He planted his feet wide apart and put his fists on his hips. His lips curled and he spoke with a nasal accent.

'Wei, baak pei jue, jo m'yeh?'-- Hey, white skinned pig, what are you up to?

Humourless laughter mocked me from the Chinese side. I looked dead ahead and walked around him. My heart nearly stopped when a child skipped from the shadows and threw a firework at my feet. It went off like a pistol shot and the Chinese soldier smiled.

On our side of the border, the British soldiers did not even blink. Jools was unruffled. 'This is frightfully jolly, don't you think?' he said.

'What?' I said, giving him a withering look.

'All this. Jolly. *Frightfully.*'

I looked away and shook my head but the gesture was lost on him.

'So tell me,' he asked, 'what would happen if I pinched that Chinese soldier chappy's hat and scooted back to the post? Cause a stir in the mess, I can tell you.'

'It would be a pinch between who shot you first,' I said. 'Him.' I jerked my thumb at the Chinese sentry. 'Or me.'

Jools guffawed and slapped me on the shoulder. 'That's what I like about you police fellows,' he chortled. 'Always good for a laugh.'

I had a premonition of tomorrow's headlines:

'CRAZED BORDER COP BLUDGEONS YOUNG ARMY OF-FICER.'

We reached the end of Chung-Ying Street and the patrol stopped. Jools beamed like a boy scout who had just earned his housekeeping badge.

'Right chaps, far enough. Well done everyone. Any questions before we go back?'

A soldier raised his hand. The sergeant flashed him a bayonet-hard glare, the others bit their lips and looked away. Jools was oblivious to it all.

'Yes Tomkins. Speak up man.'

Tomkins blinked in feigned stupidity. 'Well, sir ... you know how we ...er... kept to the left coming down the street ...?' His voice tailed off and he looked at his boots.

The sergeant made a fist and gave Tomkins a, 'one more word and you're dead,' look. The rest of the patrol pretended to be interested in other parts of Chung Ying Street.

Jools smiled like a country vicar. 'Spit out, Tomkins, there's a good fellow. Don't be shy.'

'Um ... I was just wondering, like ... when we go back, Sir, should we keep to the right?' The wide-eyed choirboy look did not slip from his face.

'I say, that *is* a good question, Tomkins.' Jools answered. He turned to me, his brow furrowed. He lowered his voice. 'Well inspector, what do you suggest?'

That afternoon, cloud rolled in from Mirs Bay. It clung to the hillsides and lay heavy over Shataukok village. Stanley came into the village post and signed the visits and inspection register. 'Fancy a walk in the hills?' he asked. 'You've not been to the Pak Kung Au Post, have you?'

I was not overly keen. I had heard of the Pak Kung Au police post, it overlooked the border about a mile west of Shataukok village. There were stunning views along the Linmahang Road, which made it a perfect observation post. The problem was that to get there meant climbing nearly eight hundred steps, concreted into the hillside. The keep-fit types vied to see who could climb them the fastest. The record holder was the aptly named Tarzan Wong, who had done it in a shade over four minutes. We boarded the Landrover and set off along the Linmahang Road. Normally, I would have reported our movement to the Frontier control room but this particular Landrover had no radio.

Five minutes later, we were slogging up the steps to the post, which was lost in mist. We seemed to be climbing forever and as we entered the low cloud, our clothes became damp and chilled. After what seemed an age, I could see the post perimeter and at last, we neared the top of the steps. The post sergeant stood at the gate, concern written on his face. He waved us to hurry.

'*Ah Sir*. Orders from divisional superintendent. Call Frontier control room immediately.'

The post was a concrete blockhouse with everything needed to sustain its crew for a week. We headed inside and while Stanley signed the visits and inspection book, I telephoned the control room.

'Where the hell have you been?' the duty inspector demanded. 'The DS is going bonkers.'

I put on my best calming drawl, told him we were at Pak Kung Au Post and asked what the panic was.

'Army's reported a Chinese armed incursion below Pak Kung Au,' he said. 'They've withdrawn their forward observation post. Their last sitrep said something about the intruders approaching a police Landrover on the Linmahang Road.'

Oh bugger, I thought. 'We'll assess the situation and get back to you,' I said.

'Is it your Landrover?' he asked.

'Yes it is,' I answered. 'And it hasn't a radio.'

'Oh bugger,' the duty inspector said.

'Probably illegal border crossers from China,' I suggested, praying I was right.

'Hope you're right,' he said. 'DS has authorised the army to meet you there.'

I hung up the phone and briefed Stanley.

'Probably illegals,' he said.

'Probably,' I answered. I paused for a moment. 'Or maybe it's Chinese army.'

'Maybe,' Stanley said.

'Or some trigger happy farmer from the commune bloody militia looking for glory,' I added, hoping he would dismiss the idea.

'Could be,' Stanley said. 'Only one way to find out.'

'Some one had best go and check,' I said in a small voice.

'Indeed,' Stanley answered. 'Some one had best go and check.'

So that is what we did.

As we made our way down the steps, the cloud enveloped us, giving the whole situation an unreal sense. Were there armed Chinese troops on the road below? It seemed unlikely, but the army was not easily rattled. Suddenly, we were beneath the cloud and the vista of the border opened up below us. Never have I felt so exposed, so vulnerable. I pictured how clearly two Hong Kong

coppers in khaki uniform would show up against the grey concrete of the steps. Now I could see the Landrover parked on the
Linmahang Road. Dense bush bordered the road. Further back, a
strip of scrubby flatland lay between us and the hills of southern
China. Cutting across the flatland, a chain link fence marked the
border. Beyond the fence stood a concrete pillbox where a Chinese soldier watched us, his Kalashnikov ready at the high port.
Was anyone watching from our side of the border? All seemed
still. Were they waiting for us to get closer? My mouth dried. My
heart pounded. I scanned the road, the brush, the fence. Nothing
moved. Wait, what was that? There was a flicker of movement
in the undergrowth. Was it the wind? I unclipped the flap of my
holster. We were closer to the road. The driver lounged by the
Landrover. He looked bored, unconcerned. Now we were on the
road. I ran my eyes along the roadside. There was movement.
There was a flash of green cotton and with no warning, three
men stepped onto the road. They wore ill-fitting tunics and baggy trousers of dull green. Their faces were grimed and careworn.
They stepped forward, walking in a half crouch. They held out
their hands, palms forward. One spoke but I could not understand him. The others joined in, gabbling in God-knows-what-
dialect. Their voices were pleading and fearful.

'*M'sai geng,*'-- Don't be afraid, I said.

They fell silent and looked at me, uncomprehending.

'*M'sai geng,*' I said again and made calming motions with my
hands.

In an instant, they squatted on their haunches and put their
hands on their heads. They stared up at me, silent, eyes wide.

There was a squeal of brakes. An army Landrover stopped beside ours. A corporal stepped from the front and three soldiers
carrying SLR rifles clambered from the back. They ran forward
and formed a line in front of the three Chinese, their rifles level.

One of the Chinese hunched down as if wanting to become
smaller. He began to wail. The others extended their arms as if

trying to stop an attack. They began to plead in words I did not understand.

'For God's sake, lower your rifles,' I snapped.

The soldiers looked to their corporal. He paused for a moment then nodded. The soldiers stepped back.

I took the hand of one of the Chinese. It was thick with calluses. I saw he was just a boy, probably in his mid-teens. Gently, I pulled him to his feet. I smiled and softened my voice. 'It's Okay,' I said. '*M'sai geng.*'

His eyes were wide but now there was understanding there. He gave a short nod and spoke to his companions. I felt his hand tighten on mine. Then he was grinning and pumping my hand like a long lost brother. Tears cut through the grime on his cheeks. He laughed. They all laughed.

I guided them to our Landrover and as we drove back to the main station they were all speaking at the same time, their voices excited and joyous. As we passed the Chung-Ying Street sentry, they fell silent and ducked down behind the door panel. At the main station, we placed them under guard and brought food from the canteen. The duty officer called transport to take them to a holding centre where immigration officers would document them and eventually grant them permission to stay in Hong Kong.

I often wonder what became of them. Many of Hong Kong's business and community leaders had arrived just like these three young men: afraid, hungry and with no possessions other than their clothes. Once, we had called them refugees but now they were just illegal immigrants; bloody IIs. Scorned by many, ignored by most, but human for all that.

A few years later, Government policy changed. Only those illegal immigrants who reached the urban areas were allowed to stay. This was the so-called 'Touch Base' policy and it turned the rural New Territories into a giant game of British Bulldog, where a team must rush from one side of a gymnasium to the other, whilst another team tries to catch them. Then, in 1980, everything changed again. With Hong Kong's public services stretched and the emergence of a more liberal China, all illegals were sent back across the border.

Frontier headquarters was the division's engine but the officers' mess was its social heart. The mess was a sounding board where we bounced ideas around. An hour in the mess was worth a week of management meetings, tasking conferences and steering groups. It was also more fun. The mess was the perfect place to meet the division's other officers, but with a room full of chief inspectors and superintendents, we one-pippers were supposed to keep our heads down. On my first visit, Stanley introduced me to the other members and they gave me a comradely welcome. That is, with the exception of a morose individual from New Territories headquarters. He gave me a look designed to leave me nailed to the far wall. He scowled and thrust out his hand. 'Brethers. CI - NTHQ.'

Okay, I thought, last name and a string of letters that defined his rank and job title. His meaning was clear, 'That's sir to you boy.' Without warning, my wicked little voice took over. I grinned and pumped his hand, 'How d'you do,' I said. 'Emmett. E-M-M-E-T-T.' There was an icy silence, he knew I was taking the piss but could not prove it.

A cultured baritone rescued me, 'And I would be Tynan, T-Y-N-A-N. At least, I think that's how I spell it.'

Pat Tynan was a bouncy, six-foot-two, Irishman who was also a one-pip PI. Pat was incapable of keeping his head down but so good was his nature, he never offended anyone. He put his arm across my shoulder and guided me to safety at the other end of the bar. There I met the only mess member who was more popular than Pat. Bob Wilkinson was in his thirties and was a proper two-pip inspector. This made him a rare commodity in a front line division. Usually, anyone with experience would be whisked out of divisions and put into a headquarter staff post. Bob Wilkinson was the very picture of an English gentleman. He had a round, apple-cheeked face, was full of hearty cheer and never had a bad word for anyone. For Bob and Pat, good manners were an obsession and everyone defined deadlock as Bob and Pat trying to get through the same door.

'After you, my dear fellow.'

'Wouldn't dream of it old chap, please, after you.'

'No, no, I must insist.'

If British colonialism ever needed ambassadors, there were none better than Bob and Pat. Constable or commissioner; councillor or coolie, Bob and Pat treated all with equal courtesy. Bob's many qualities included an overwhelming concern for the feelings of others and he was forever apologising on the off-chance he may have caused offence. 'Is it my round? So sorry, let me get them in.' 'Am I in your chair? I'm dreadfully sorry, please take a seat.' One evening, a chief inspector known as 'The Hatchet,' cornered Bob at the bar and gave him an ear bashing.

'What do you mean, sorry? That's all you've said all bloody night. "Sorry this, sorry bloody that." For God's sake, man, get a backbone. If I hear you say "sorry" one more time, I shall go bloody bonkers.'

This took Bob aback. 'Oh dear, I didn't know it upset you. I'm most *dreadfully* sorry.'

The Hatchet knocked his head against the bar and never mentioned it again.

For his part, Pat Tynan had not an enemy in the world. However, on a bright and chilly New Year's Day, Pat's good nature landed him and his best mate, Roy Nicholls, in deep and very hot water. Having spent the previous evening in serious celebration, Pat and Roy decided to do their bit for cross border harmony. Early on New Year's morning, they met at Shataukok main station, changed into their smartest NT kit and tied red kerchiefs around their necks. They took the morning transport to Shataukok village then marched up to Chung-Ying Street, where the PLA sentry scowled and stepped forward to meet them. Pat produced a bottle of Johnny Walker and three glasses. He placed the glasses on the border stone, filled them to the brim then he and Roy each raised a glass. Pat called the toast. '*Kai Fong Kwan, maan sui.*' -- Long live the People's Liberation Army.

The sentry watched all this with his bottom jaw resting somewhere near his ankles. As Pat and Roy raised their glasses, the sentry shook off his astonishment and unslung his Kalashnikov. He uttered something in Mandarin that sounded unutterable in any language then swept bottle and glass from the border stone with his gun butt, splattering whisky and broken glass several yards along Chung-Ying Street.

Pat tried a placatory smile but the solid click of a Kalashnikov cocking mechanism ended any festive plans. Pat and Roy beat as dignified a retreat as they could and stayed quiet about the episode.

Like most Royal Hong Kong Police secrets, it was common knowledge within days and they both found themselves on the carpet. They stood to rigid attention before the divisional superintendent's desk, their eyes fixed on the wall behind him. The boss had a reputation for fairness and unflappability. 'Before I say anything,' he said, 'I will give you the chance to explain why you thought it a good idea to offer a glass of Scotch whisky to a Chinese sentry.'

Pat did not hesitate. 'It was all a dreadful miscalculation, Sir. You see, I couldn't lay hands on any of the Irish stuff.'

Legend has it you could hear the bollocking at the main gate.

CHAPTER 6
FEUD FOR THOUGHT

ONCE, THE PHRASE 'access to foreign markets' meant British traders could take what they wanted and keep what they could defend. So, in 1814, the Honourable East India Company decided to take the Kingdom of Nepal. Sadly, the Honourable Company did not count on Nepal's Ghurkha tribesmen being pretty adept at keeping what was theirs. Stumped for ideas, the East India Company called upon the smarter people on its payroll to come up with a plan. A year later, the company formed its first Ghurkha regiment, which, all things considered was a smart move.

In March, the Royal 15th/21st moved on and the Ghurkhas came to the Frontier. They spilled from their transport and without fuss, fanned out to the observation posts, communication centre, armoury, orderly room and barracks. Within an hour, they were at home. They moved into the post in silence. Orders were rare and delivered in hushed tones. The only immodestly loud voices were those raised in laughter.

The platoon commander was a no-nonsense Scot named Baz. That first afternoon, Baz had to attend a briefing so he could not come with me on the evening patrol. At nineteen hundred hours, I joined a group of Ghurkha soldiers who stood chatting in the plaza outside the post. With the exception of wickedly curved knives, called *kukris*, that hung from their belts, each man carried the same arms and equipment as his British counterpart. Their sergeant was a stocky man with a face of creased leather. I knew enough about the army to realise I had to assert myself so I gave it my cheerful, parade ground best. '*Good evening, gentlemen.*'

The plaza went quiet and five pairs of eyes took aim at me. Obviously, 'Good evening gentlemen,' meant something rude in Ghurkhali. The sergeant threw me a sharp salute. 'Good evening *sah'b*,' he said in a brisk but quiet voice. I returned the salute and the sergeant moved closer, lowering his voice. 'Also *sah'b*,' he said, 'I am happy to report that the riflemen have perfect hearing. Please do not strain your voice further.' He flashed me a dazzling smile, I was gently but effectively chastened.

They fell in behind me and I led the way across the plaza. We stopped in front of the general store where I wanted to give the sergeant the usual speech about the PLA, their weapons, their unfailing discipline and their downright toughness. I was about to start when I noticed the Chinese sentry seemed nervous. His lips were pale. His eyes flickered between the Ghurkhas and me. He fingered the trigger guard of his Kalashnikov then removed his hands from the assault rifle altogether. I looked at the Ghurkhas and the hairs on my neck prickled. Each man had a hand resting on the hilt of his *kukri*. Each had a smile on his lips but their eyes were like polished bullets. They radiated the wicked confidence of wolves with a cornered fawn. They were relaxed, assured, in charge. Without taking his eyes from the sentry, the sergeant spoke to me. 'I think, *sah'b*, we have made our point. May we now continue the patrol?'

Baz invited me for dinner with his soldiers in their billet. That evening we stuffed ourselves with rice and fiery dal washed down with ice-cold Tiger beer from Singapore. Later, a rifleman did the rounds with a one-gallon container of treacle-thick rum. I was never fond of hard liquor but the Ghurkha rum was soft and warming. As the evening passed, Ghurkha faces turned from nut brown to fire engine red and their voices rose as they laughed and talked of past campaigns and old campaigners. Baz reminisced about the Nepal trek when, as the Brigade's youngest lieutenant, he led an expedition along Nepal's mountain paths with rucksacks full of cash to pay the pensions of retired soldiers. The old soldiers had worn their medals and many had tears in their eyes. They had touched Baz with their kindness and he returned to his regiment with an abiding affection for his troops, a rooted understanding of their culture and a fluent command of their language. That night, Baz taught me survival Ghurkhali, which comprised just three phrases.

'*Malai doorbin, dino hos,*' meant 'lend me your binoculars.'

'*Malai chiso bir, dino hos,*' always got me a cold beer.

'*Pisser?*' translated roughly as: 'I say old chap, could you please direct me to the gentlemen's convenience.'

Those three little phrases never let me down. My fluency in Ghurkhali impressed the hell out of my bosses and to my lasting shame, I never found the need to set them right.

Our stretch of the border ran from Shataukok village to Linmahang, a drab collection of houses a few miles inland. The border took no account of ancient, ancestral land boundaries. As a result, the Sumchun People's Collective worked land on our side of the border while some Hong Kong farmers worked land on the Chinese side. The arrangement worked fine but rather than walk to the official crossing points, most farmers cut holes in the chain-link fence that marked the border. Each month we had to survey the fence for damage. A dirt road ran along the Chinese side and the People's Liberation Army manned little guard posts every quarter mile. When they saw us, the PLA always made a great show of cocking their assault rifles and shouting defiance at the forces of imperialism.

As a rule, the duty inspector always led the primary fence patrol. We took transport out to Linmahang then walked back. However, Ghurkha soldiers distrust anything mechanical and on our first patrol, they grumbled throughout the outward trip.

The mood changed when we reached Linmahang. The Ghurkhas piled out of the truck and as it rumbled off back to Shataukok, there was laughter and banter. With Baz back at the village, the Ghurkhas decided to treat the patrol as a day out. I have heard that if a Ghurkha draws his *kukri* then he must draw blood, even if it his own. Sorry, but that is just a myth. As soon as the truck disappeared, the Ghurkhas scampered up the nearest hill, drew their *kukris* and cut armfuls of wildflowers which they used to decorate their combat uniforms. I told the sergeant to get a grip of the patrol and was amazed that the soldiers even heard his almost whispered command. They joined us on the road, but one, a rifleman called Gurung was slow coming back down the slope. His face was pale and he was nursing his forearm. Pain creased his brow and his eyes stared. He slumped down by the roadside and spoke to his sergeant in hushed, urgent tones.

The sergeant turned to me, his face troubled. '*Sah'b*, Rifleman Gurung reports he has been bitten by a snake.'

There were two puncture marks on rifleman Gurung's forearm. I helped remove his pack whilst the sergeant applied a pressure bandage and the radio operator arranged a casualty evacuation. I asked the sergeant to get a description of the snake.

'No need, *sah'b*. Rifleman Gurung has caught the snake and has it tucked in his pocket.' I took a step back but the sergeant waved a dismissive hand. 'Do not be alarmed, *sah'b*, before pocketing the snake, rifleman Gurung took the precaution of biting off its head.'

Through his pain, Rifleman Gurung grinned and clicked his teeth at me.

I first met Father Mario Pugilletti, alias Poppa Mario, at the Frontier officer's mess. He had wispy silver hair that hung to his shoulders and a florid hook of a nose perched above a straggling grey beard. Depending on his mood, his eyes could either freeze water or melt the coldest heart. 'You are Godless heathens,' he would shout across the bar in heavily accented English. 'But you are passable company and I will bring you all into my flock.' Poppa Mario was a missionary from the Old China school of spreading the Lord's word. He could quote scriptures in any of the Chinese dialects spoken in the New Territories. He often held court in the village squares where he enthralled children and adults alike with simple conjuring tricks and bible stories. He had a battered Vespa scooter that he drove at furious speeds along the back roads of the New Territories. Astride his Vespa, his white hair and beard streaming behind him, his cassock billowing around his bony knees, Poppa Mario was a formidable sight. Inspector Jimmy Tong came from a remote New Territories village and recalling his boyhood days, he would tell of Poppa Mario's visits. 'He scare the kids like hell,' Jimmy said, smiling at the memory. 'We didn't think he was God's messenger; we thought he was God.'

There was more to Shataukok than the border village. The sub-division had a hinterland of rolling hills and rugged coast. There were no roads, only worn footpaths connecting settlements scattered among the hills. Little *kaito* ferries served fishing villages dotted along the shoreline. There was nothing you could call a police problem: no crime, no domestic disorder or at least nothing we ever learned about. The villagers preferred to look after themselves and we sometimes heard second-hand stories of rough justice handed out to anyone breaking the rules. Shataukok's rural patrol team was there to fill a communication role, a role doubly important because they were the only organ of government making regular visits into the remote villages.

The week before payday always saw me at a loose end and I spent my leave days hanging around the main station. Seeing me thoroughly bored, Stanley suggested I spend a day with the rural patrol. It was a good way to learn about the sub-division and I did not mind giving up a leave day for a walk in the hills.

We would start at the main station, skirt Starling Inlet then make our way into the hills before dropping back to the coast to catch a police launch back to Shataukok.

The next day, we started at oh-eight hundred. The team sergeant was a grizzled, twenty-year veteran who spoke the Hakka dialect common in the New Territories. The constables were an easygoing group; they were tanned and wiry. Stanley took me aside. The sergeant had a touch of arthritis, he told me, I was not to set too fast a pace. We set off with the team striding ahead, within minutes I was gasping.

The sergeant grinned at me. There was a glint of mischief in his eyes. 'You all right, *Ah Sir?*' he asked.

'Never better,' I answered, massaging a stitch in my side.

For the first hour, we climbed rocky paths through lush hills with wonderful views out over Mirs bay and beyond to the South China Sea. Closer inshore were little bays with water of clearest emerald. At Wu Kau Tang, the village headman greeted us. He took us into his home, sat me under a ceiling fan and presented me with a dewed tumbler of Chinese Snowflake beer. An old woman smiled and nodded as she handed out freshly steamed pork dumplings. She beamed and clucked away at me in Hakka until our host gently shepherded her from the room. The sergeant and the headman fell into animated discussion, but it was all in Hakka and I could not understand a word. From time to time, the headman turned to me and in a throwback to the 1930s, addressed me as *sah-jin* -- sergeant. The snacks consumed, the pleasantries over, we resumed our patrol. The pattern repeated, village after village: a hearty welcome, delicious snacks and cold drinks. Everywhere, I was the *sah-jin*. I had stepped back in time to a quieter and more gentle place. At each village, we ate, drank and chatted then left in a haze of goodwill.

By mid-afternoon, we reached a fishing jetty where a police launch waited to take us back to Shataukok. Exhausted, I slumped down on the foredeck and enjoyed the breeze coming off the South China Sea. The launch pulled away from the shore and as we rounded the point at Wong Chuk Kok, the sergeant gave me a rundown on the day's discussions. The villagers, he told me, had a most pragmatic view of the law. To their mind, it was something best adapted to suit the occasion. So, it was fine for police to chase away townie picnickers who disturbed local tranquillity, but interfering with village tradition was something else entirely. This was particularly true if the headman was making a fortune dealing in duty-free Chinese wine or running the local gambling house.

It was in the light of this quaint view of law and order that the case of Mister Chan Ming's broken thumb needed a touch of outside, some say divine, intervention.

I was drunk with power. Stanley took a fortnight's leave and the boss appointed me sub-divisional inspector (temporary -- unpaid). Before he left, Stanley told me the cardinal rules of being SDI Shataukok. 'Rule one: don't change anything. Rules two and three: don't even think about changing anything.' All I had to do was telephone the boss at eight every morning, tell him about any crime and assure him the *bing* had not started a war.

'It's simple,' he said.

Foolishly, I believed him.

Mister Chan Ming lived in the hamlet of Hung Chuen, and I lay the blame for his broken thumb on his fondness for gambling and Snowflake beer. He worked all day on his vegetable plot and in the evening, liked nothing more than to relax with his neighbours over a cold bottle of Snowflake in the village square. Sometimes, a pack of domino-like tiles would appear and there would follow a sociable game of *pai-gow*.

One summer's day, a gentleman by the name of Mister Wong Mun, a distant relative of Chan Ming's wife, visited from the nearby village of Wu Chuen. The people of Hung Chuen and

Wu Chuen had never been on good terms although no one could remember why. Mister Chan took an instant dislike to Mister Wong but for the sake of village harmony, he tried to be polite. All went well until the evening gathering.

Snowflake, Mister Wong the visitor from Wu Chuen declared, was a drink fit only for peasants. Hung Chuen's storekeeper should stock Danish Carlsberg. This proved an interesting point and the merits of the two beers dominated the conversation for nearly an hour. As the discussion petered out, someone produced a box of tiles and suggested a neighbourly game of *pai-gow*. The visiting Mister Wong sniffed his disdain. *Pai-gow*, he said, needed as much skill as a schoolyard game of stone, paper, scissors. Sophisticated gentlemen, he said, played the western game of bridge.

This stung Mister Chan to the heart. Was not *pai-gow* a proper Chinese game of skill played by proper Chinese gentlemen? He forced a smile and with icy good manners, suggested that if the most worthy Mister Wong had the price of the game's pot, he should park his honourable backside on the unworthy chair, put his money in the place currently occupied by his noble mouth and prepare to part with a sizeable portion of his wad. Which is precisely what Mister Wong did, except for the part concerning his wad. In fact, the only wads to part company with their owners were those belonging to Mister Chan and the other players. As hand after hand fell to the visitor, the crowd of spectators grew. People jostled for the best spots and called advice to Mister Chan but to no avail. As the evening drew on, the pile of bank notes before the visiting Mister Wong grew larger whilst that in front of Mister Chan shrank to almost nothing. The more he lost, the more agitated Mister Chan became. The more agitated he became, the more recklessly he played and so the vicious cycle went. The game dragged on to the early hours. There would be sore heads the next day but nobody dared miss a second of what had become an epic duel between the villages of Hung Chuen and Wu Chuen.

It may have been Mister Wong's comment that his uncle's water buffalo played better *pai-gow* than did Mister Chan. It may have been Mister Chan's suggestion that Mister Wong's winning streak had much to do with Wu Chuen's famed skulduggery. One moment they were glaring at each other across the table and the next, the table was on its side and the two men were rolling around on the floor, kicking, punching and biting each other amongst scattered *pai-gow* tiles, ten dollar bills and the shattered remnants of empty Snowflake bottles. The crowd shouted encouragement to Mister Chan but it was not his lucky night. There was a dry *snap*. He howled in pain then rolled away from the fight, nursing his left hand. Mister Wong, the visitor from Wu Chuen staggered to his feet, his face flushed and his hair in disarray. He tugged his shirt straight and slapped the dust from his trousers. Then he squared his shoulders and with his head held high, walked into the night.

The village headman called the Hung Chuen village council together and after much discussion, the council decreed that medical treatment was in order. A group of Mister Chan's friends half-carried him to the nearest road where they flagged down a passing van and took him to the clinic in Sheungshui. The doctor diagnosed a fractured thumb, strapped up the injured digit and gave Mister Chan some painkillers.

Shataukok's detective sergeant had an ear for local gossip and the next morning, he told me all about the fight. I decided not to brief the DS, after all, it was only a village scrap. By tomorrow, I thought, everyone will have forgotten it.

Back at Hung Chuen, Mister Chan's injury was not serious but the attack on his pride and therefore on the pride of the village, was unforgivable. Nobody could remember the reason for the old feud between Hung Chuen and Wu Chuen but that did not matter because now there was a new one. Three days later, a water buffalo belonging to Mister Wong's uncle suffered a severe case of diarrhoea as he drove it through Wu Chuen's main square. The poor beast bellowed, lifted its tail and sprayed the contents of its lower gut across the whitewashed fronts of several houses. A group of village elders enjoying a quiet game of Chinese chess dived for cover. Some say the old men had not moved so fast since the last visit from land tax office staff.

The next day, a grain of concern nagged at me as I read the morning reports. The detective sergeant did not seem worried. 'It's nothing, sir,' he said and moved on to the day's crime list, which was zero.

I mentioned the case to the DS during my morning phone call. 'Don't let this get out of hand, Chris,' the boss warned.

I wish I had listened to him.

For two days, nothing happened. Then in the small hours of the morning, five bitches in season appeared in Hung Chuen. They scampered around in the narrow alleys, generating a lot of interest from the village dogs, which for village security, roamed free at night. The village dogs pursued the visitors, yelping and barking while those trapped indoors howled in frustration. Dressed in pyjamas and underwear, the villagers came bare-foot and cursing from their houses. With brooms, sticks and anything else that came to hand, they chased the interlopers into the hills. The next evening, eager for some company, the outsiders came back and did so every night until the village council called in the government dogcatchers.

It was the knockabout stuff of rural life. When I entered the officers' mess, the other SDI's chuckled and asked, 'So, young 'un, how goes the war?'

The rural patrol sergeant visited both headmen in their ancestral halls and warned them to keep the peace. Both headmen raised their hands to the heavens, rolled back their eyes and swore on the graves of their most sacred ancestors that they had nothing to do with the strange events.

Mister Ching Ma was the second nephew, third-removed of

the Wu Chuen headman and he had quite a crush on a young temptress called Mei-wu. She worked at Fanling's Better 'Ole Bar and Grill and sadly, she did not return Mister Ching's affections. However, Mei-wu's manager told her to be nice to customers so, whenever Ching Ma showed up she would smile as she served his drinks. After an evening trying in vain to work his magic on Mei-wu, a disconsolate Ching Ma paid his bill and staggered into the night. He did not see the figure that slipped from the shadows and darted after him. As he weaved down the lane leading to the main road, Ching Ma heard a noise behind him. His heart leapt, perhaps Mei-wu had followed him. He half turned as an iron bar caught him across the temple. Pain seared through his skull and lights danced before his eyes. He tried to raise his arms but all strength drained from him. As the pavement smacked against his body, he retched and tasted blood.

At four a.m., the *tailau* knocked on my bedroom door. I was to come immediately. I staggered down to the report room and found the duty officer throwing a major tantrum. The case belonged to Sheungshui, he protested, they had no right passing it to Shataukok. I rubbed the sleep from my eyes and told him to run through the facts. By the time he finished I had a sinking feeling in my stomach.

Morning prayers were grim. I had lost my grip, the DS told me. I had better get off my backside and get it sorted, he said. The job was not a game, he reminded me as I sat in miserable silence.

I sent a detective back to the clinic with instructions to sit by Ching Ma's bedside. That afternoon, he returned to the station and dropped a statement onto my desk. I skimmed through the translation.

Question: How did you come by your injuries?

Answer: Whilst planting rice, I tripped and fell.

Question: Why were you planting rice at two a.m.?

Answer: I couldn't sleep.

Question: Rice paddies are nothing but mud and water, how do you explain your serious injuries?

Answer: I fell several times.

With a tight smile, Ching Ma had told the detective that after his discharge from hospital, he would find the cause of his regrettable accident and most assuredly fix it.

In best imperial fashion, I summonsed the headmen of Hung Chuen and Wu Chuen to an audience in the Shataukok police station. I treated them like honoured guests and plied them with hot tea and tasty snacks. Then, in my sternest voice, I warned them to end the fast developing feud. Their faces took on an air of affronted dignity. Each swore that despite dastardly acts carried out by certain uncivilised people, they were innocent.

For three days, nothing happened and then, during the night, a truck belonging to a prominent resident of Hung Chuen exploded in a ball of orange flame. The driver just managed to jump clear as the flames gutted the cab.

The DS called me into his office. I sat in crushed silence as he reminded me that since I had taken command at Shataukok there had been public disorder, poisoned livestock, assaults in the street and now arson. He wanted an end to the feud and he gave me just twenty-four hours to fix everything. Frontier worked on a tested management protocol: when the DS was unhappy, everyone was unhappy. Unhappiness is of course, a matter of degree and on a scale of one to ten, Shataukok's SDI (temporary -- unpaid) had an unhappiness score of one-gazillion. I wandered round to the mess where I found Poppa Mario sipping coffee. He extended his arms in a gesture of embrace, 'Hey Chris, howsa goin' the war?'

I murmured my hellos and slumped down onto a barstool.

'That bad, eh?' Poppa Mario moved to the stool next to mine. 'Those two villages, they been at this for generations.' He put his arm across my shoulder. 'Hey, don'ta worry, Chris, they always see sense.' He made a glum face. 'But sometimes it take a decade or two.' He drained his cup, thumped me on the back and left.

That evening, my spirits sank even further when I received another visit from the *tailau*. Would I come to the report room, two Chinese gentlemen and a crazy old *gwailo* would like a word. Oh, and I had best watch what I said; the old *gwailo* spoke remarkably good Chinese. I stumped down to the report room where I found a subdued Mister Chan and a muted Mister Wong sat side by side, heads bowed. Standing over them, his hair wild and eyes blazing, was Poppa Mario. Without taking his eyes from them, Poppa Mario told me both gentlemen were eager to get something off their chests.

During the next hour, the two unburdened themselves of every element of the feud. They confessed to all attacks on man, beast and property. They wanted to accept full and undiluted responsibility. Words of remorse spilled from them faster than the reserve detective could write them down. I missed a trick that night; had I dug out the crime files for the last ten years, I am sure they would have confessed to every unsolved case.

With the feud over for at least one more generation, the villagers of Hung Chuen and Wu Chuen were happy. That made the DS happy and that in turn made the SDI Shataukok (temporary -- unpaid) happy. In fact, we were so happy that we overlooked a few loose ends. For instance, I never learned why Poppa Mario felt the need to stand so close to Mister Chan and Mister Wong whilst they gave their statements. It remains a mystery why, whenever they paused or faltered, he cracked his knuckles in such a distracting manner.

Also, I never discovered at whose hands Mister Chan and Mister Wong had suffered such livid black eyes.

The Frontier attachment for probationary inspectors was six months and I had been there a year. I had never been so content. I liked the people, I liked the work, I loved the pristine countryside. I was at home; I fitted in. Then, one morning in February,

I checked my in-tray and found a circular from the mess. It announced a curry lunch to say goodbye to several mess members who were leaving on either retirement or transfer. That was great news, I loved a good curry. I read the names of the departing members, excellent men each one. But I would say that wouldn't I?

The last name on the list was mine.

CHAPTER 7
SHIELDS AND HELMETS

BEFORE THE PRO-TAIWAN riots of 1956, Hong Kong Police anti-riot strategy was pretty basic. Each division had three anti-riot platoons which, under the command of the divisional superintendent, formed the divisional anti-riot company. A platoon had four sections, each representing an increasing level of force. Number one section carried three-foot long batons and rattan shields. Number two section was the tear gas and baton shell section. Number three section carried shotguns and semi-automatic carbines. Number four section was the arrest section with orders to pick up what was left after the other three sections had done their job. Platoon members were not anti-riot specialists, they were ordinary beat constables drafted in when needed. Other than basic weapon handling, there was no formal training and it was the divisional superintendent's job to make sure it all worked.

As far as operational policy went, this was a bad one and the 1956 riots revealed gaping holes in police ability to deal with a major disturbance. The force needed standardised tactics and, more importantly, it needed officers who were properly trained to put the new tactics into action. Then, in 1958, the army vacated their barracks at Volunteer Slopes, near Fanling railway station. The police jumped at the chance to take over a facility tailor made for military style training. There was a drill-square, a firing range, a gymnasium, a canteen and sleeping accommodation. In 1958, Volunteer Slopes reopened as the Police Training Contingent. Police headquarters issued orders requiring every officer between the ranks of constable and inspector to undergo PTC training.

Having taken over the barracks, the force discovered why the army had vacated it. The place was on its last legs. The camp buildings were just a scattering of semi-cylindrical structures made of corrugated iron. Called Nissen huts, they were painted silver and from the air, looked like a scattering of drinks cans half buried on their sides. On the basis that it was better than nothing, the force gritted its teeth and classified Volunteer Slopes as temporary accommodation, a status it kept for twenty-eight years.

With specialist training, the force's ability to counter public disorder improved beyond measure. When faced with pro-communist riots in 1967, the force proved well up to the job. Later, the Police Training Contingent became the Police Tactical Unit and its officers started to wear the headgear that earned them their more popular name -- the Blue Berets.

On a crisp February morning, my battered old Ford banged across the level crossing at Fanling railway station. Beyond the station was a tree-lined lane and within a few minutes I came to a sign that read:

'POLICE TACTICAL UNIT
HOME OF THE BLUE BERETS'

A constable waved me to a stop. He wore black trousers and a khaki jumper over his bush shirt. On his head was a navy-blue beret. Behind the cap badge a diagonal stripe bore the force colours of gold and maroon. He checked my name on his clipboard. 'Emmett ... Emmett ... Ah, Mister Emmett, Charlie company cadre course. Drive to officers' mess.' He pointed with his pen to a road that climbed a wooded slope then arced round to the right. 'Meet company commander there.' He stood aside and waved me through.

From the main gate, the road looped around a central knoll then back to the main gate. The buildings were still the Nissen huts inherited from the army, back in 1958. The administration block was the only concrete structure.

The place was green and open. It had a country feel and for a while, I felt at home. I passed a parking lot filled with Saracen armoured cars with the words 'POLICE' written in English and Chinese on their steel flanks. I pulled to the side of the road as a forty-one man platoon, dressed in PT kit jogged past in step. The inspectors were both Westerners; the corporals and constables Chinese. They looked fit and purposeful. As one, they shouted out the timing: '*One-two-three-four.*' A muscular physical training instructor trotted along behind them. The men all wore gleaming white T-shirts with green piping at the neck and sleeves. Each shirt bore the logo:

'PTU DELTA COMPANY
WARNING
THIS T-SHIRT CONTAINS APPROXIMATELY
ONE STEELY EYED ORIENTAL CRIME BUSTER'

A Landrover, leading two Bedford J3 trucks rounded the bend towards me. The Landrover's public address system blared out the theme to 'The Good, The Bad and The Ugly.' They moved onto the drill-square, their tailgates crashed open and a platoon of helmeted men vaulted to the tarmac. The platoon sprinted to the front of the convoy and formed a tight square. There was a shouted command and the men at the flanks and rear faced out, presenting a protective array of shields, batons and riot guns.

I found a parking bay near the officers' mess and climbed a short flight of steps to a patio overlooking the drill-square. The mess was an iron Nissen hut with air conditioners rattling at the windows. Inside, it was like an oak-panelled tunnel. A well-trodden carpet covered the floor, armchairs and low coffee tables filled the corners and other crannies. Plaques and witty little mementos covered the walls. Grainy black and white photographs showed PTU men in action: a bereted sergeant plucked a child from floodwaters, a dozen helmeted constables stood firm before hundreds of chanting Red Guards, a handful of PTU constables shepherded dozens of cowed triads into prisoner vans. Two men sipped coffee at the bar; one European, one Chinese. Their uniforms were that same as the gate guard's: dark trousers and khaki bush shirts.

'Mister Emmett?' The European spoke with a Scottish burr. 'You're the last one,' he said. 'The chief instructor's briefing the others in there.' He jerked his thumb towards a door marked 'Dining Room'.

I let myself in. A dining table ran the full length of the room, almost filling it. Sitting at its head was the CI, a grey-haired avuncular man with an eye-crinkling smile. He waved me in, 'A very good morning to you. Come in, come in, just going over a few mess rules.'

The others were in plain clothes, but it was easy to see who was who. The earnest looking one had to be the company commander, a newly promoted superintendent. The company's second-in-command was a chief inspector: three years in his rank and knocking on the promotion door. The others were like me, one-pip *bongban-jais*, coming up for confirmation in the coming year. They seemed nervous and eager to please. One was older than the rest and he made a big show of writing down the CI's every word. His name was Jasper Codd and he had an oily quality to which I took instant dislike. I had heard of Codd: he was a two-pip inspector from the Hong Kong Island district where rumour had it, he had not covered himself with glory. There were stories of a rainy night, a badly sited roadblock and a whacking great bill from the bus company. No injuries, thank goodness but Codd's attempt to blame it on his sergeant had failed and Codd found himself outbound for PTU.

The CI ran through the mess rules. 'No shorts after five p.m., shirts to be worn in the bar and dining room at all times. No flip-flops, no puking on the bar top. All quite clear?'

Clear enough, I thought, it sounded like an Australian finishing school.

With the mess niceties sorted out, the CI handed us to the barrack sergeant who issued our training kit: three pairs of black trousers, three bush shirts and a navy blue beret. One word describes a beret: *cool*. It is comfortable, practical and has that, 'what's your problem, pal?' quality that silences bar room heroes and turns women into play-dough. Make sure the badge is above the left eyebrow and angle the beret forward. *Voila*, you are now a tough guy. And that's official.

There would be a three-week cadre course for the inspectors, sergeants and corporals. After that, the constables would arrive and the real training would start. Ten weeks later, there would be a big parade and the company would move to a land district where it would stay for twenty weeks before it disbanded and everyone went back to normal duties. Charlie company was a Hong Kong Island unit and my New Territories platoon had been tagged on the end. This brought the number of platoons to four instead of the normal three. After the graduation parade, the company commander would take three platoons to the Island and my single platoon would move to the New Territories PTU base in Tsuenwan.

'This company upgrade has never been tried before,' the company commander told me. 'And the New Territories has never had its own PTU.' He was silent for a moment then he lowered his voice. 'Watch your back,' he said. 'There are some who want to see this experiment fail.' He flashed me a smile that seemed a little forced. 'Remember, your confirmation to full inspector will depend on you doing a good job.' Reassuring type, the company commander.

The Scottish staff inspector introduced himself as Sandy Magee and he oversaw the issue of our gas masks, or as he preferred to call them, respirators. They were the world's finest: proof against nuclear, biological and chemical attack. At least, that is what Sandy Magee said but the lettering inside my respirator read: WARNING -- FOR TEAR GAS ONLY.

Sandy led us to a windowless hut at the top of the camp's central knoll. Inside it was stuffy and carried a vague smell of marzipan. Sandy closed the door and showed us how to fit the respirators snug against our faces. I put my palm against the intake valve, inhaled and felt the rubber seal tighten against my cheeks. Good, it was a perfect fit. I exhaled and the eyepieces fogged up.

'Just breathe normally and report any discomfort,' Sandy said and produced what looked like a stubby candle. 'On the order, "remove respirators," you will take off your respirator, approach me and give me your name, rank and identity number. You may then leave through the door behind me.' Sandy pulled on his respirator and tested the seal. He put the candle on the floor and lit it. The candle fizzed like a roman candle and I felt a knot of alarm as it gave off thick clouds of white smoke. Within seconds, I could not see across the room. The temperature rose. The gas burned my neck then crept down the back of my shirt. It seeped through the cotton of my uniform; my whole body began to burn. Sweat trickled down my spine and where the CS touched damp skin the burning became fiercer. My armpits and groin were on fire. The smoke thickened and I felt the first heart-snatching stir of panic.

'*Remove respirators.*'

I pulled off the respirator and my eyes filled with scalding CS. It scorched my face, tongue and throat. It reached into my nose and scoured my lungs. The door opened and daylight cut through the fog. Our disciplined circle turned into a tangle of milling bodies and jostling elbows. I stumbled towards the light and there was another moment of panic as three of us became jammed in the door. We clawed at each other trying to get free. A push from inside the chamber carried me through the door and we all spilled coughing and retching onto the grass. I felt a flash of shame as the company commander and his number two emerged from the chamber, staggering and spluttering but at a dignified pace. Sandy followed and closed the door, his respirator still strapped to his face.

In minutes, the burning effect passed. We laughed and chatted, glad to be out of the chamber. Sandy rummaged around in his pockets and, like a conjurer with a trick bouquet, produced another candle. 'Will you look at this, gentlemen,' he cried. 'Aren't we the lucky ones? This time round, we'll have a little decorum.'

After our second turn in the gas chamber, we collapsed on the grass gasping and cursing. 'Congratulations,' Sandy said as he removed his respirator. 'Today you have seen the physical and psychological effects of tear gas. In a few moments, I will give you another tip.'

The effects of the gas eased and we staggered to our feet. An inspector lit a cigarette and took a deep pull. He frowned then spluttered; his eyes bulged and his face turned crimson. He sank to his knees and clawed at his throat. His breath came in sobs. He doubled over with his forehead pressed against the ground.

'Tip of the day,' Sandy chortled. 'Leave your cigarettes outside, bloody gas gets everywhere.'

In week two, I found I would share command of number four platoon with Andrew Chang. No surprise there, Andrew was the only other New Territories inspector. He came from an old merchant family and before PTU, had served in the market town of Yuenlong. He was tall, had cropped hair and was built like a welterweight. His capacity for French brandy was bottomless. 'You British are a barbarous race,' he would declare as he prepared to down a tumbler full of brandy. 'But the French. Ah, the French have Chinese hearts.'

As training progressed, I came to renew my profound dislike of physical training instructors. PTIs speak a language that is all their own. For example, 'Good morning, gentlemen,' means: 'For me it is good; for you, the nightmare begins.' The phrase, 'Gentle warm-up,' means 'Agony beyond belief.' And so it goes, there is not an ounce of truth in any of them. On our first day, a Chinese PTI stood waiting for us in the gymnasium. He wore dark tracksuit trousers and his pectorals bulged under a spotless white singlet. He arranged us around a canvas mat.

'Good morning, gentlemen,' he barked.

Oh dear, I thought.

'Today, we learn some simple restraints,' he said

Bring on the stretcher, I thought.

The PTI called on one of our sergeants who stepped forward with all the enthusiasm of a human sacrifice. The PTI made it seem easy. He took hold of the sergeant's wrist and applied the grip in a practised movement. 'Just a little pressure ... *here.*'

'*Arrrgh!*'

'Remember, police general orders say you must use minimum force. Never apply too much pressure, like so ...'

'*Arrrrrggghh!*'

'Maintain hold with one hand, leaving other hand free to use your radio. Do not loosen grip.'

'*Arrrrruuugggghhh!*'

He released the sergeant who dropped to the mat like a floppy doll.

'Mister Chang, Mister Emmett,' The PTI waved us forward. 'Mister Emmett, you will punch Mister Chang.'

I winked at Andrew, just to let him know I would not be hard on him. I stepped forward and swung a punch at his head. At that moment, something slammed into my back. There was a collective 'Waaaah,' from the cadre course. I stared up at the gym ceiling and realised the thing that had slammed into my back was the mat. Andrew's face swam into focus and he helped me to my feet. 'No offence, Chris,' he said. 'But you fight like a white guy.'

In the third week, we got our platoon transport: a Landrover and two Bedford J3 trucks. Let me take a minute to savour that moment again, we were two *bongban-jais* with our very own transport. Andrew jumped into the Landrover and switched on the public address system. His voice blasted across the square, heavy and metallic. 'Testing, testing. I am probationary inspector Andrew Chang and I have *transport*. Duty officers and transport sergeants, eat out your bloody hearts.'

For the next few days, whenever I saw my driver I could not resist asking if the Landrover was available. Every time he said, 'Yes,' it was as if the man with the gruel pot had said, 'Certainly, young Oliver, of course you can have more.' I did not care that the driver saw right through me and would accompany each answer with a heavy sigh.

Later that week, a team from the road safety section arrived in their little van, which was a happy, but to my mind rather garish shade of sky blue. The road safety officers gave our drivers a slide show and a lecture. The drivers sat through the presentation in morose silence and the RS team left without having to field a single question.

On the fourth week, our constables arrived. Assisted by gleeful corporals, Andrew and I bullied them into four sections. We marched them from barracks to lecture room and from canteen to assault course. We expressed outrage at the length of their hair, fury at the condition of their equipment and despair at their physical state. By the end of that first day, the corporals were hoarse and the constables were confused, dazed and worn out.

In short, they were ready for the tactical training.

Mornings started with light physical training followed by a run along one of three cross-country courses. One course led through the Wo Hop Shek cemetery where the grave plots were only temporary. In early spring, during the Ching Ming festival, families opened time-expired graves and took the remains of their loved ones to permanent resting places. Then, that particular cross-country run took us past rows of open graves and we saw the course record broken several times.

The Police Tactical Unit had many roles. Blue bereted police were a common sight at festivals, firework displays and the Chinese New Year exodus to China. In high crime areas, PTU officers bolstered normal beat duties. If commanders needed backup for a special operation, they called on PTU. We called these duties, 'soft order.' In soft order, PTU officers wore standard, day-to-day uniform, topped off with a beret instead of the normal police cap. But our tactical training was not about soft order, it was about 'hard order.' The main role of PTU was to provide every division with a core of officers trained in riot suppression. Everyone was supposed to attend PTU training and with few exceptions, everyone did. From the first day's tactical training, the working uniform was hard order: helmets, respirators and riot weapons. There had been improvements in weaponry since 1956 but platoon formation had not changed. There were still four, eight man sections, each commanded by a corporal. The first section carried batons and shields. The second section carried Federal riot guns, which looked like stubby rifles with a pistol grip behind the trigger and a short length of drainpipe as a barrel. They could fire either tear gas canisters or wooden baton shells. The third section comprised a mix of Remington shotguns and Armalite rifles. The fourth section was still the arrest section. The platoon commander, the platoon sergeant and the orderly took position between the first and second sections.

There was a fearsome grace in the way a platoon moved

through its drills. As the level of force increased, the platoon rolled forward. First the baton section advanced on an imaginary crowd. At the same time came the order, *'number two section, up,'* and the tear gas section moved to the front. A whistle blast ordered the baton section to disengage and withdraw to the rear of the platoon. Next, the orderly raised a banner with English and Chinese lettering that read, 'Warning -- Tear Smoke.' Tear gas canisters slid into the Federals' breeches and the order came, *fire!* Finally came the order, *'number three section, up,'* and the shotguns and Armalites moved to the front.

Day after day, we went through the drills: *'Number one section, advance.' 'Number two section, up.' 'Number two section, load, present. Fire!' 'Number three section, up.'* Sequence complete, we did it again. We went from the cross-country run to the drill-square, from the drill-square to the firing ranges, and from the firing ranges back to the drill-square. We lived and breathed the drills, they became part of us. We drilled until we no longer had to think them through. Finally, we were ready for the platoon test. Test done, we could relax but not for long. Soon, it would be time to move to the next stage.

The company commander held a T-shirt design contest. We were 'C' for 'Charlie' company and the winning logo was a picture of a glum looking Charlie Chaplin wearing a PTU beret, baggy shorts and scorched running shoes. Under the picture was the caption:

'PTU CHARLIE COMPANY-
HAVIN' FUN IN THE SUN'

A local TV station was airing old episodes of The Lone Ranger and for our company tune, we chose Rossini's William Tell Overture.

Throughout the training, our sergeants and constables got

credit for any success while we inspectors caught the blame for any failings. It seemed to work. Within weeks, each platoon was an extended family. The constables came to trust the inspectors and the inspectors learned a lot about command. That is except for Jasper Codd. Codd's platoon was always slowest to pick up the drills, last home during the cross-country runs and was never on time for company briefings. Codd found more and more imaginative ways to blame his men for his failings.

'You are a bunch of loafers,' he would snarl at his platoon.

His platoon sergeant, a twelve-year veteran, would mumble a half-translation.

'What's that, sergeant?' Codd would ask, making the sergeant's misery even worse. 'You'll translate what I said, you cloth-eared bugger.'

The constables would cringe, embarrassed for their sergeant. The louder and more potent his bollockings, the worse Codd's platoon performed. After each drill session, the constables sat grumbling in the canteen whilst the platoon sergeant shook his head and held his own counsel.

Even the mess did nothing for Jasper Codd's mood. For Jasper Codd, the mess was a place in which to grace us with the benefit of his experience.

I felt good after the first round of platoon tests, the boys had done us proud. I sluiced off the day's grime under a hot shower, slipped into a light cotton shirt and slacks, then adjourned to the bar for a cold one. A familiar voice soured the mood. 'Call your platoon disciplined?' Codd crowed. 'A trip round the cross-country course in full hard order would do them the world of good. It worked for mine.'

The lights behind the bar buzzed and flickered and Codd stiffened. He scuttled from the room and returned a few minutes later brandishing a screwdriver as though it were Excalibur fresh drawn from the stone.

'Should have been fixed ages ago,' he said ducking down behind the bar. 'Just needs someone with a bit of get up and ...'

There was a flash, a crack like a pistol shot and the bar plummeted into darkness. Air conditioners whirred to a stop and the hum of the refrigerator fell silent. Codd's voice emerged, muffled from behind the bar.

'It's okay, I think I've found the problem.'

A Scottish burr mused in the dark. 'Funny, that's just what I was saying about your platoon.'

The Bedford J3 was a wonderful truck. It could battle into the teeth of a typhoon or spend hours in gridlocked traffic during a tropical summer. No matter how we abused it, it refused to break down. However, if we needed to put men onto a secluded hilltop or the roof of a barricaded building, then the Bedford was useless. To set this right, we trained on Royal Air Force Wessex helicopters. The Wessex is a rugged piece of kit but it is not unbreakable. The same is true for the average PTU man, so before the staff let us near a real helicopter, we had to learn the basics. We spent half a day on the simulator, a small caravan fitted out like the cabin of a Wessex. We learned where to sit and how to disembark, first while the helicopter was on the ground, then from a height of three feet, then finally we learned to rappel down a twenty-foot rope. With the basics mastered, the real thing would surely be easy. After all, what could go wrong?

The RAF paid a visit and a Wessex pilot told us about the next day's drill. First, we would disembark with the Wessex on the ground. Next, the Wessex would hover at two or three feet as we jumped to the ground. Finally, we would rappel down from twenty feet. After the talk, Sandy walked them to their transport. I could not help notice that their farewells were remarkably cheerful and took rather a long time.

The Wessex looks like a cross between a bullfrog and a dragonfly but for all its lumpy ugliness, it is surprisingly nimble. My platoon, along with Jasper Codd's, drew the morning session and at oh-nine hundred sharp, our transport rolled past the guardhouse at the Shek Kong joint services depot. We stopped at the RAF hangars and a young airman directed us to a shabby briefing room. Sandy introduced our aircrew. The briefing seemed to drag on forever but at last, we made our way to the apron where our sergeants had divided the platoons into groups of ten, each called a stick.

A Wessex engine coughed a wad of white smoke and the rotors started to turn. A second Wessex started and the whine of turbines mingled with the thump of rotors. A RAF corporal appeared in the open door of the first Wessex. Attached to his helmet was a visor of dark perspex that hid his eyes. A safety strap held him to an anchor point inside the cabin. He spoke into a slim microphone attached to his helmet, pointed at me and gave me a thumbs up sign. I crouched, ran forward and scrambled aboard, taking the seat opposite the door. The noise was deafening and the cabin shook like an overloaded spin dryer. The first stick followed and I counted them aboard, making sure each man took the right seat. I gave the corporal the thumbs up and he made an exaggerated, vertical clapping motion, which meant we were to disembark with the helicopter firmly on the ground.

I signalled to the men and they piled out of the doorway, jumped onto the tarmac and fanned out in a defensive arc. One by one, each of my four sticks took their turn to board the Wessex and one by one, they exited with no problem.

After the ground level exercise, it was time for the proximity disembark, which meant we would exit the helicopter while it hovered a few feet above the ground. By now, the cabin was hot; it smelled of aviation fuel and exhaust fumes. I checked the men and gave the corporal the thumbs up. The Wessex rocked on its gear and rose a few feet before crabbing off to the side. The tarmac gave way to grass and the Wessex went into the hover. The corporal gave me the clapping sign again but this time his hands did not meet. This was trickier and the constables stumbled and rolled as they hit the ground. I crouched in the doorway and realised that with nine men gone, the Wessex had drifted upwards to a height of half a mile. All right, it was only about six feet, but that was high enough. With everyone watching, I could not hesitate. I landed with a knee-jarring crunch and glared up at the corporal who flashed me an innocent smile. He spoke into his microphone and the Wessex descended. It wobbled on its landing gear then settled.

I checked off the drills. Ground disembark -- done. Proximity disembark -- done. It was time for the main drill. The plan was for the Wessex to take us into the hills to show us how a low-level approach works. After that, we would return to Shek Kong and make the short rappel to the ground. An absolute doddle, Sandy promised. He was all smiles and encouragement.

I had an uneasy feeling as I strapped myself into the tiny canvas seat. A rope lay in a heap inside the cabin, the steel eyelet of one end bolted to a ring in the cabin floor. I looked around the cabin but the men were all staring straight ahead. There was no banter, no laughter. The whine of the engine increased, the rotors made a percussive 'Whumpwhumpwhump.' The Wessex swayed on its undercarriage then I felt myself pressed hard against the seat as the ground dropped away at an appalling rate. The pilot banked and we hung against our lap straps with the cabin floor almost vertical. Shek Kong's hangars, runways and tracks filled the open door. I looked around the cabin, the men had their eyes screwed shut as if in prayer. The corporal, hanging on his safety strap by the door seemed bored. The Wessex righted itself and dived, picking up speed as it headed east towards the Lamchuen Valley. I could not take my eyes from the door. The valley wall drew closer and closer. Rocky outcrops flashed by within yards. The downwash from the rotors flattened grass in the valley's meadows. The roar of the engine and the smack of the rotors filled my ears. The valley gave way to shallow gullies nestled between craggy hills. The Wessex bucked and twisted like a rodeo mustang as the pilot charged ahead, following the ground contours. I suddenly remembered that according to the laws of aeronautics, bumblebees and helicopters could not fly. Memory is a funny old thing — this was where the tone began to parody itself. The Wessex climbed. My limbs grew heavy; multi-G stresses tugged at my face. The helicopter stood on its rotor tips and my stomach hit my gullet. The Wessex dropped sideways and accelerated back towards the hillside. It levelled out then sprinted back towards Shek Kong, following every dip and rise of the terrain. Shek Kong's perimeter fence zipped past a few feet below. My head, arms and legs became leaden as the nose of the Wessex lifted and it clawed itself to a juddering standstill, using the main rotor as a brake. The corporal flung out the rope and signalled that I should stay put. One by one, the constables slid on their backsides across the cabin floor. By turn, each grabbed the rope and disappeared through the door. With the cabin empty, the corporal waved me forward. I grabbed the rope and as I swung myself clear of the door, I saw scraps of foliage lodged in the helicopter's undercarriage. On all sides, buildings, drill-squares, sports fields and runways lay stretched out. I started to descend hand under hand. The engine note changed but I did not care, I was nearly back on the good earth. It felt like I was climbing down the rope forever. I looked down but I was no nearer the ground. I looked up and realised there was about twenty feet of rope above me. The corporal waved and gave me a cherubic smile. I climbed down a few feet and the Wessex moved up a few feet. I looked down and saw the ground, now thirty feet below. I thought nothing could scare me more than that dreadful flight down the valley but as the end of the rope left the ground, I learned the meaning of true horror.

I do not know if it was the, 'just shoot me now,' look in my eyes or the signal that Sandy waved to the pilot, but the Wessex inched downwards and a few seconds later, my feet touched the ground. I massaged the palms of my hands. My fingers were stiff and painful. Everyone thought it hilarious and not wanting them to think me wimpish, I grinned through gritted teeth.

With a massive clatter, another Wessex skimmed the perimeter fence and reared to a halt a few yards from where we huddled against its downdraft. A rope snaked from the door and Codd's platoon sergeant swung away from the helicopter's door. One by one, more men followed until there was a defensive circle kneeling at the foot of the rope. Last man out was Codd and as he started his descent, the Wessex climbed a few feet. Codd froze. He looked at the ground, then at the crewman then back at the ground. He scrambled a few feet down the rope then stopped as the Wessex climbed a little more. Now it was not me dangling from the rope, I could see the funny side. The Wessex edged higher. I flexed my fingers and could almost see Codd tighten his grip. The circle of constables on the ground shielded their eyes and looked up, smiling. The rope-end drifted clear of the ground but the Wessex continued to climb. It edged forwards and the rope swung like a pendulum. The Wessex banked and climbed higher. I was not smiling now. I pictured poor Jasper: white knuckled, eyes screwed shut, heart pounding, stomach knotted. My heart went out to him. Even a shameless little bully like Jasper Codd did not deserve to go through that undistilled terror.

But then, on second thoughts ...

Sandy stood with his hands on his hips and his mouth set in grim satisfaction. I am not sure, but as the Wessex disappeared beyond the fence, I swear I heard a plaintive howl above the clatter of the rotors.

We returned to Fanling and found the camp alive with the story. Back in the mess, I listened to an account by an inspector who was barely coherent. He forced himself to speak slowly and told me how a Wessex helicopter had flown in unannounced from the South. It had hovered over the drill-square, rattling the mess windows and blasting the patio with dust. It took a while for anyone to realise that hanging from a rope below the Wessex, was a PTU inspector. The Wessex deposited Jasper Codd gently onto the square.

'It was hovering for ages,' the inspector gabbled, his eyes gleaming. 'It took two PTIs to prise Jasper's fingers off the rope.'

Behind the scenes, an argument raged between PTU staff veterans and younger staff members. The veterans believed disciplined drill worked well in street operations; the youngsters thought flexibility and speed was key.

Compromise came in the shape of flexibility training. We had practiced the drills until we could do them without thinking. Now, we got a free hand to develop new tactics. There was no way to do that on the drill-square but high-rise housing projects were springing up all over the New Territories. Some were still empty. Their deserted road networks were ideal for trying new tactics. The empty corridors of the tower blocks were perfect for practising high-rise cordon and search techniques.

The tower blocks may have been empty but they were far from safe. Sandy Magee and his staff sergeants would lay in wait and punish us with flour bombs and high pressure hoses if we left ourselves exposed. The bombings and soakings went on for weeks then stopped just as abruptly as they had started.

'I guess they think we've got it right,' I said to Andrew after a day's training.

'Maybe,' he said. There was a twinkle in his eye.

'What do you mean, maybe?' I demanded.

Andrew flashed a wicked grin. '*Ohhhh* nothing,' he said.

'What do you mean, *maybe?*'

'I had a night out with some of the staff sergeants,' he said. 'And I may have suggested something.'

'Like what?' I asked, knowing I would not like the answer.

'Like, if there were any more flour bombs, there might be a

real baton charge.'

The words hit me like a mallet. 'Are you mad?' I said. 'They'll get you for that. They'll find some way to punish you for sure.'

Andrew did not seem worried. He shrugged. 'It's OK,' he said. 'I didn't really say I would order a baton charge. ' He chuckled and leaned closer to me. 'I said my crazy *gwailo* partner would.'

During drill sessions, our vehicles moved at a sedate pace and decanted orderly columns of men onto the drill-square. But flexibility training was about speed. It meant racing to the exercise area and sliding the vehicles to a halt with a squeal of brakes and a smell of hot rubber. Before the vehicles came to a full stop, men in riot gear spilled over the tailgates and through the side-panels. Within seconds, a milling body of men would crystallise into a solid square, its perimeter bristling with weapons. Sometimes, it seemed there was telepathy at work. We were fast, we were a team, everything we touched turned to gold. Then, the day before the dress rehearsal for our graduation parade, we had the accident.

The driver of the number one Bedford slid into a strategic road junction and stopped on a dime. Unfortunately, he forgot to leave enough room for the number two Bedford. There was an expensive *crunch* and by the time I got there, the platoon sergeant was umpiring a lively chat between the drivers concerning who had caused the large dent in the number two Bedford's wing. I was not worried, after all, it was just a training accident. The transport inspector would get it fixed and lend us a replacement truck for the parade rehearsal. At that suggestion, the aggrieved driver, who carried the nickname Wah Jai, blanched. The platoon sergeant motioned me aside. 'It is ... *cough* ... not so simple, *Ah Sir*.' He was clearly unhappy. 'The PTU major does not like Wah Jai.' Wah Jai nodded, his eyes flicked between the two of us. The platoon sergeant lowered his voice. 'PTU major wants to send Wah Jai back to ...' his face took on a pained expression '... normal police duties.'

At the words, 'normal police duties,' the colour drained from Wah Jai's cheeks.

The platoon sergeant spoke in a conspiratorial whisper. 'Wah Jai's cousin is in car body repairing business. He will fix damage and have Bedford back before off-duty time.' He slapped his hands together as though he had disposed of a dusty chore.

Wah Jai was nodding like an over-sprung trip hammer.

The platoon sergeant looked around to make sure there were no eavesdroppers. 'Trust me, *Ah Sir*. I *gau dim* everything.'

Those very words should have been a loud enough warning shot. *Gau dim* -- the back door fix. I should have talked it over with Andrew but it was Friday afternoon, it was hot and I was tired. What's more, the platoon sergeant was the most persuasive man I have ever met. For that, I will never forgive him.

We crammed the platoon into the undamaged Bedford and scurried back to base. Charlie company's transport formed a navy-blue line along the square's rear perimeter. If no one noticed there were seven Bedfords instead of eight, we had it cracked. I briefed Andrew and he stamped away in a major sulk.

Of course, nothing goes according to plan. In my heart of hearts, I knew the damaged Bedford would not appear at the end of the working day. I tried to relax but doubts gnawed at me. There was a chance some sharp-eyed staff inspector would notice the missing truck. Other 'what ifs' started to nag me. What if the repair was noticeable? What if Wah Jai's cousin could not match the police navy-blue? What if the respray did not match the other company vehicles? I went through a pointless 'if only' checklist. If only I had done things by the book, if only the drivers had paid attention during the road safety lecture, if only I had told them to take extra care during flexible deployment exercises.

If only it wasn't the dress rehearsal tomorrow.

'All ready for tomorrow, Chris?' I nearly fainted, it was the company commander.

'What? Of course we are. Sorry, I mean of course we are, *sir*.

Transport's tiptop. Weapons gleaming. Transport's great. The men are ready. Did I mention the transport?'

By eight p.m., I could not contain myself so I wandered round to the platoon barracks. 'Don't worry, *Ah Sir*,' the platoon sergeant said. 'I've phoned to Wah Jai's cousin. Repair is all finished.' He grinned and gave me a thumbs up. 'Very good job. Better than government workshop. Now, only damaged wing to paint and all is *gau-dim*.' He lowered his voice. 'Paint is from police stores.' He held up his hand in a gesture that said, 'Don't ask.'

At ten, I demanded another progress report and did not like the way Wah Jai and the platoon sergeant swapped glances. 'Paint *nearly* matching rest of cab,' Wah Jai stammered. He gave me a pained smile. 'But not *exactly* matching.'

I was about to explode but the platoon sergeant chipped in, a bit too smooth for my liking. 'No problem,' he said. 'Old paintwork must have faded. Wah Jai's cousin will repaint whole cab. Relax, *Ah Sir*, nothing can go wrong.'

By midnight, there was still no sign of the Bedford.

'Whole cab done; very good job,' the platoon sergeant assured me. 'Better than government workshop. Do you want to inspect platoon's weapons now?'

'The cab's perfect?' I asked, not convinced.

'*Verrry* good job,' the sergeant said, his face earnest. He held up his hand with the thumb and forefinger all but touching, as though describing something very small. 'But looks *tiny, tiny* bit newer than rest of truck.'

'So it doesn't match?'

'Don't be angry, *Ah Sir*. Wah Jai's cousin is top notch car repainter. You want good match, don't you?'

I beat down my fears. Wah Jai's cousin was using paint from police stores, I told myself. He would keep going until he got it right. Everything would be great, at least that's what Wah Jai said.

Next morning, I stepped bleary eyed onto the mess patio. In

their barrack rooms, the constables were putting the last touches to their uniforms. They smoothed an extra layer of polish on their boots and picked the last scrap of lint from their berets. They ran stiff brushes over canvas ammunition pouches and rubbed a smear of oil on their weapons.

I had no appetite for breakfast. Andrew's mouth was a thin line. 'You're on your own with this one,' he said, his voice icy.

I half glanced at the transport and tried to pluck up courage to count the Bedfords. The drivers were polishing inside the engine compartments. I held my breath and counted Charlie company's trucks.

Seven.

I looked away, gave the Bedford fairy a chance to work her magic then counted again.

Still seven.

Pure, one hundred and twenty proof panic burned my neck. My ears stung. Sweat trickled down my spine.

The roar of engines and the crunch of gearboxes broke the morning's peace. Wisps of oily blue smoke drifted across the square as the drivers manoeuvred the company transport into parade formation. Five Saracen armoured cars grumbled onto the square and moved onto the places usually taken by the Landrovers. The company commander's Saracen was front and centre. Behind it, the platoon Saracens formed a perfect line abreast. A surge of pride nearly popped my shirt buttons, then I sagged like a day old balloon. Behind three of the Saracens stood two gleaming Bedfords but behind my Saracen, there stood only one. Soon I would change into uniform, go down to the armoury, sign the register and take my revolver from its rack. Sadly, no ammunition for a parade. I wanted to make one final request of the armoury sergeant. 'Two rounds only please; one for the platoon bloody sergeant and one for Wah Jai.'

Andrew's voice interrupted my plans for revenge. 'Looks like *your* platoon sergeant has his knickers in a twist.'

The platoon sergeant was at the foot of the patio steps. He was hopping from foot to foot and giving me the thumbs up sign with both hands. I bounded down the steps, not daring to hope. He was bouncing with glee. 'All finished, *Ah Sir*,' he chuckled. 'Full respray. Official police paint. Perfect job. Better than government workshop. Wah Jai's cousin is driving back now. It will be here by the time you are in uniform.' He read my mind and took a step back. Smart move, I could have kissed him.

I changed into uniform, the starched cotton was stiff and scratchy. I tightened my belt an extra notch and made sure the cross-strap lay flat across my chest. I adjusted my beret so the badge was one inch above my left eye. I saluted myself in the mirror then headed back to the patio. By the time I got back there, Charlie company's four platoons had formed up on the road and the band was playing, 'Will ye ne'er come back again?' The mood was bright. Soon the lectures, the square-bashing, the practical exercises and the physical training would end. The company commander and his second-in-command fidgeted in the shadows of the mess lobby.

The empty space behind my Saracen gaped at me and I began to implode with despair. Then I heard a sound sweeter than all the choirs of paradise. It was the low-geared snarl of a Bedford J3 truck labouring up the road on the other side of the camp's central knoll. My Bedford, my beautiful Bedford swung into view and a hush radiated through the lines of men waiting on the road. The band groaned and squeaked into silence. Andrew clamped both hands to his head. Someone cheered. Then the whole company was cheering and clapping as my number two Bedford took its place on the square. The company commander and the second-in-command stared at the truck, open-mouthed. Then their eyes swivelled towards me like a brace of twelve-inch naval guns.

The Bedford was beautiful. Not a ripple broke the sweep of its previously damaged wing. The cab and bodywork gleamed under its coat of police issue paint. Indeed, nothing could possibly go wrong. After all, Hong Kong police vehicles are, without exception, a standard navy-blue, right? Well, nearly all. There is only one tiny exception. Nobody notices the road safety teams. They do an excellent job and get themselves around in little vans that are a happy, but to my mind, garish shade of sky blue.

Just like my number two Bedford.

Then it was over. No more hours on the drill-square, in the gym or on the firing range. No more armoured car training, helicopter training, hill walks, cross-country runs, map-reading exercises, mass arrest management exercises and no more tactical training. There was just one item on the programme and that was baton shell practice. Tear gas is great for dispersing rioters but it has drawbacks. After the rowdies have fled, the gas hangs around for ages and people must put up with the vile stuff seeping into their homes. To get round this, the American company, Federal Inc. developed a handy piece of kit called the baton shell. It is a bright red, wooden projectile. It is eight and a half inches long and one and a half inches in diameter. It is tapered at one end and weighted at the other. The shell fits the Federal riot gun and the idea is to fire it at the ground in front of a rioting mob. With that first bounce, it loses most of its power but it still raises a few yelps as it tumbles into the mob and whacks a lot of disorderly shins.

I delayed the practice for half an hour. On this day of all days, timing was critical. We set up a line of wicker targets on the square beside the gymnasium. Each target was the size of man and looked like an *Ali Baba* laundry basket. At the last moment, I grabbed a Federal from one of the constables and joined the firing line. The section corporal called out the standard orders.

'*One round, load.*'

I opened the breech and the baton shell slid in with a satisfying *tonk*.

'Low angle, present.'
I snapped the breech shut and settled the Federal against my shoulder.
'Fire!'
Eight Federals banged as one. The butt slammed into my shoulder and white smoke drifted across the square. The shells streaked across the square, clattered against the tarmac and *whacked* into the wicker targets, rocking them on their bases. One baton shell however, did not rattle against the tarmac. Instead, it flashed high above the targets in an arcing red blur. It slammed against the gym's corrugated iron wall. The building quivered like an over-stiff jelly and emitted a low rumble that rolled across the square and grew into an iron-jacketed boom that would have brought a lump to a bell ringer's throat. A figure wearing shorts and a staff T-shirt stumbled from the gym. He threw a badminton racquet onto the ground and sank to his knees, palms pressed against his ears. Three more followed, the last man out was Sandy Magee. His eyes bulged, he worked his bottom jaw in wide circles. My constables bit their lips and concentrated on plucking empty shell casings from their Federals. I pulled a hot casing from the breech and snapped the Federal shut. Sandy walked towards me holding his racquet before him like a nightstick. His lips were white, a small muscle throbbed in his cheek. He stopped with his face just inches from mine.
'You bugger, Emmett, you did that on purpose.'
It was a wounding remark, particularly after everything Sandy Magee had done for me. He had teargassed me, chased me around the square wearing full hard order and had me dangled from a helicopter. He had pelted me with flour bombs and soaked me with high-pressure hoses. I put on my best puppy-dog expression. Yes, some ruffian had half deafened him with a baton shell, but why pick on me?
Heaven forbid I should do such a thing.

CHAPTER 8
A POACHER'S TALE

LIKE MOST OF MY bold initiatives, everyone thought it was crazy.

Let me recap. Ours was the first Tactical Unit platoon based in New Territories. We did not slot into the command structure and found ourselves tagged onto NT headquarters like an extra thumb. Each Friday, a dispatch constable appeared in our office and dumped tasking sheets for the following week on the desk. Pinned to the sheets were crime reports listing blackspots for robberies, burglaries, vehicle thefts and any other crime that captured the assistant commissioner's interest. I soon realised that each crime sheet was identical to the one from the week before, the only thing that changed was the date. We were supposed to attend divisional conferences but we were not on the notification lists. We were supposed to meet with the SDIs but they were too busy. We talked to subunit commanders but most were fresh from police training school and had no idea what was going on. After months of training with helicopters, armoured cars and almost every weapon in the police inventory, the New Territories seemed quiet. We bounced from one crime blackspot to another but the sight of forty para-military cops piling over the Bedfords' tailgates did the trick every time. As soon as they spotted us, the local hooligans melted into the shadows. A quick look through the crime reports showed that when we were on duty there was no crime. Good, yes? Well, no, not always. We brought down the crime rate but caught flak for making too few arrests. The phone would ring and a chief inspector from NT headquarters would harp on about our poor productivity. 'It's no good strutting around in those fancy, sodding berets,' he would snarl. 'Stop trying to impress the ladies and start arresting some crooks.'

It was just a numbers game. The more arrests, the higher the score. High score, good cop; low score, bad cop. Andrew and I both hated the numbers game, it got in the way of good police work. The constables started to pull in all kinds of rubbish just to make up the figures. I often found myself called back to a report room to explain why our men were wasting everyone's time by bringing in street hawkers and other petty obstruction cases.

'I thought you *gwailos* were clever,' Andrew grumbled after a gruesome meeting with the chief inspector from NTHQ. A few days later, he wished he had kept his mouth shut.

I found the answer in a magazine article about the English countryside. I became convinced that the answer to our problems lay in the semi-criminal practice of 'lamping.' It sounded easy. A poacher shone a bright light onto a pheasant or a rabbit. The animal's first instinct was to freeze and whilst it thought about what to do next, the poacher whacked it on the head and scooped it into a bag. I figured if lamping worked for poachers, then it would work for policeman. I talked it over Andrew and he roared with laughter.

'You aren't serious,' he scoffed.

Like all my favourite plans, it was simple. After dark, one of our Bedfords would move at walking pace into a target area. The driver would keep his headlights on full beam. Walking behind the Bedford would be a column comprising one corporal and seven constables. If we found anyone up to no good, the Bedford would head straight at them with its headlights burning into their eyes. If everything went to plan, we would be all over them before they knew what was happening.

Andrew rubbed his chin. I could see he did not like the idea but we had nothing to lose. If it did not work, so what?

We called in the platoon for a briefing. The corporals swapped, 'Shall we throw the net over him now?' looks but said nothing. The next evening's tasking sheet called for an anti-crime patrol of Taiwohau public housing project in Tsuenwan. Taiwohau was an old estate. It was grubby, ill-lit and in a bad state of repair. People went in fear of young toughs who had taken over the staircases and corridors. Andrew and I walked into the Tsuen-wan briefing room and did our best to exude confidence. The platoon sergeant called the men to attention and the clamour in the briefing room turned to instant silence. They were so different from the nervous young men we had chased around the camp on their first day. Now, they were tough and self-assured. There was 'Giant' Chan, he was short, slim and a good bet for the forthcoming sergeant's board. Beside him stood 'Big Dragon' Ming and his lifelong friend, 'Little Dragon' Cho. Both were tall and muscular. Danny Soong was a lady's man who tried to balance his hair stylist's advice against the demands of the platoon sergeant. So many characters, each one special. I told them to relax and went through the plan.

'Hey, *Ah Sir*,' the Big Dragon called. 'Give me an hour with no corporals. I get many cases. All plead guilty, guaranteed.'

'Give him a chance,' someone called. 'It's not often we see *bongban-jais* act stupid.'

'Yes it is,' shouted another and they all burst into laughter. I laughed too because there was no malice in them. No matter how tough it got, they always found a reason to laugh.

Andrew smiled, 'Don't ever let me forget how good they are, Chris,' he said. 'They're not convinced but they'll give it their best.'

At twenty-one hundred hours, we parked a quarter mile from Taiwohau and I sent in two plainclothes constables to look around. They were gone for thirty minutes, leaving me to dwell on everything that could go wrong. Every scenario ended with me the laughing stock of the New Territories. By contrast, the platoon was relaxed, everyone was looking forward to a bit of action. The platoon fell silent when the plainclothes men returned. Their faces shone with excitement.

'There's ten *laan jais, Ah Sir*. Ten ratbags.' The plainclothes men were tripping over each other in their hurry to tell what they had seen. 'Anyone who goes into Block Five must pay door fee.'

That was only part of it. The gang had been drinking. They were taunting elderly residents, shouting lewd comments at young women and using triad slang to challenge other passers-by.

'They act like big bosses,' one of the plainclothes men said. He pumped himself up and strutted a few paces, a caricature of a local hard case.

In the darkness, a constable gave a wicked chuckle.

At last, we had some real targets and the plan did not seem so bad. We went through it again. Andrew would go in first with three columns. Two of his columns would work around the gang's flanks whilst the third would slip in through the building's utility door. 'It might work,' Andrew muttered, 'but only if they're blind, deaf and stupid.' He rounded on a knot of men who were chattering like school kids. '*Mo cho.*'-- Shut up. 'Like I said, they'll have to be deaf.'

Andrew and his three columns faded into the night. I gave them ten minutes then squeezed into the Bedford's cab, alongside the platoon sergeant. The driver was Wah Jai. He started up the engine and switched the headlights onto full beam. PTU officers always had a dig at the drivers because they were famously work-shy but bless him, Wah Jai was the only one who truly believed in the plan. He clunked the Bedford into gear and we set off at walking pace. Number four column followed on foot. We trundled through the estate until we rounded a corner and there, caught in the glare of the headlights, were ten young men. They were in their twenties, unshaven and with lank hair.

They wore grubby jeans and rubber sandals. In the warm evening, they had unbuttoned their shirts to the waist. Cigarettes dangled from their lips and some held open cans of beer. As our headlights caught them, they craned their necks like stagehands surprised by a spotlight. Wah Jai edged the Bedford forward and the circle of light around the group narrowed. One young man dashed his beer can into the street and pointed at the truck. His voice was harsh and slurred. *'Jo m'ye, leng jai?'* -- What's your game, pretty boy?

The Bedford inched forward. The other young men gathered behind their leader. They pointed at us and thrust out their chests. One of them shouted, *'Wei. Hai bin do lei?'* I allowed myself a smile, *'Hai bin do lei?'* -- street slang for, 'What triad group are you?'

One of the gang picked up a length of wood and strutted to the front. He brandished it at the Bedford and made 'come on,' signs with his other hand. They all began to shout. One drew his finger across his throat. Another stood with his feet planted wide and his hands on his hips.

Behind them, eight bereted PTU officers stepped from the shadows. All were grinning like guests at a surprise party.

The gang's leader took a step towards the Bedford and raised a fist. *'Fai di gong, saai lo.'* -- Hurry up with that answer, youngster.

From the left, eight more PTU men stepped into the light, then eight more from the right. Andrew appeared, smiling and shaking his head. It was like an English Christmas pantomime show where the bad guy sneaks up on the hero and the audience shouts, *'He's behind you.'* I stepped from the cab and slammed the door. Somewhere, a dull mental alarm must have rung because one by one, the young men fell silent. They squinted into the headlights. What they saw was the silhouettes of the fourth column as it moved forward into the light.

And still they did not move. From their left flank came a fair imitation of a popular children's television presenter, 'Hi, *gok wai siu pang yau.*'-- Hi, my little friends. The young toughs turned towards the voice and their jaws dropped. They turned in the other direction only to find themselves facing a wall of smiling constables. One young man threw a punch. He let out a cry as Giant Cho swatted the blow aside, grabbed the young man's wrist and twisted hard. The young thug cried out as he found himself face down on the concrete with Giant Cho's knee in his back. The Bedford's headlights caught a flash of steel. There was the *crack* of a truncheon on bone. A gang member sat down hard, cursing and cradling his wrist. He shouted to me in English. 'Inspector, he hit me; he *hit* me.'

Andrew bent down and picked up something from the ground. It was a triangular file, about nine inches long. The file's three abrasive faces had been hollow ground. They were machine shop smooth and the edges were as sharp as straight-razors. It was the trademark blade of a street triad; an ugly weapon, made for slashing and stabbing. The gang fell silent, shoulders slumped, heads bowed. We lined them up facing the wall; feet spread, arms stretched above their heads. One called out to passers-by. '*Pang yau, tai jue,*' -- Friends, witness this. '*Chai lo jun m jun ha yan?*'-- Can the cops oppress people like this?

From nowhere, a crowd formed and rewarded us with nods of approval. Someone even clapped. I chose a constable to handle the case exhibits and he soon had a collection of hunting knives and sharpened files. Andrew clapped his hands together, glee flashed in his eyes. 'Did you see looks on their faces? Did you *see* them?' He punched the air. '*Yes*, that did me good.' He put his left hand on my head and raised his right hand. He threw back his head and shouted, 'I hereby adopt Chris Emmett into the Chinese race.' Then he laughed and gripped me in a headlock. 'But only if he sticks to his own language and stops crucifying mine.'

One uneventful day blended into another. New Territories

HQ bounced us from one crime blackspot to another but it was always the same, as soon as they saw the berets, the local hoodlums simply disappeared. Andrew and I visited the New Territories SDIs and we took our meals in the officers' messes and station canteens. We were a familiar sight but somehow separate; not part of any divisional family. The sad fact was that so long as we did not stir up any trouble, the divisional people were not interested in us. They were friendly enough and we always had an ear for any local gossip. Inspector so-and-so was up for promotion, superintendent such-and-such had been caught in a vice raid, the new anti-corruption laws had come into effect. I remembered Tsuenwan's chief of detectives mentioning the new corruption laws but it all seemed ages ago. I did not give it another thought, after all, it is the nature of youth not to realise the impact of important events. Then, in early June, we dropped in on the SDI of a busy station and found him engaged in an animated telephone call.

'What?' he said. '*What?* Jesus.'

He leaned back and showed us the palm of his hand, silencing any questions.

'Are you sure? *Jesus.*' He put down the phone. 'Godber's in the shit,' he said and shook his head. 'Anti-Corruption Branch has searched his office and car. He's been suspended from duty.'

The name was familiar. Yes, chief superintendent Peter Godber. The same witty and highly intelligent Peter Godber who had delivered the after dinner speech at the training school. It seemed impossible. *Peter Godber?* Never.

The SDI was already back on the phone, spreading the news. 'Have you heard? Yes, Godber. They searched his office and car. Home? Don't know but it seems logical they'd search there as well.'

Andrew nodded to the door and we left the SDI to his phone calls. 'Have you any idea what this means?' he asked when we were alone in the corridor. 'My God, it changes everything. Godber's the Kowloon number two. If they hit Godber, they will hit anyone. A lot of bosses will be sweating.'

I shrugged, ever the cynic.

'Wait and see,' Andrew said. 'Just wait and see.'

A week later, Peter Fitzroy Godber used his airport security pass to bypass immigration checks and escape to the United Kingdom. Hong Kong's governor immediately appointed a senior judge to inquire into the whole mess. Eight months after Godber's escape, the Royal Hong Kong Police handed all corruption investigations to the new Independent Commission Against Corruption, known as the ICAC. Cruel pundits claimed the initials stood for: 'Investigating Chinese Ancient Customs' or 'I Can Accept Cash.' The jokes did not last long. As the list of senior government officers awaiting trial grew, the jokes became hollow. As Andrew predicted, everything had indeed changed. Within twelve months, the corruption bus was still running, but there were far fewer passengers on board.

But that was not the end of it. For years, every Hong Kong policeman suffered Godber's legacy. Whether from a knowing look or a harsh comment, there was always someone who assumed a Hong Kong copper was a bent copper. Stand up comedians the world over quipped that Hong Kong had the best police force money could buy. The stain on our reputation went deep and no matter how hard we scrubbed it, there was always a trace ingrained in the force fabric.

The coin of Hong Kong's wealth had two faces. Elegant villas overlooked squatter villages built of wood and corrugated iron. Villagers ran power lines from street lights and water from fire hydrants. The toilets were simple pits. Chikung village was like any hillside squatter village but on the day our platoon went there, all was utter chaos.

One moment we had been patrolling a public housing project, the next, I had orders to return to base. I was to load the platoon's riot gear into transit boxes, get to Chikung village and report to a detective inspector called John Yen. That was it; there was no other information and we had no idea what to expect. We loaded our riot weapons into their boxes and bullied our way along the busy road between Taipo and Fanling. As we neared the village, we found the main road jammed with police cars. Red and white plates identified them as coming from Shatin division, NT head-quarters and the district emergency unit. Their radios chattered, some still had their blue lights flashing. Constables attended each vehicle, busying themselves with radio messages and writ-ten logs. Nearby stood an ambulance, its crew lounging in the shade. Meanwhile, other road users fumed as a flustered traffic constable tried his best to unsnarl the road.

I told the platoon sergeant to keep the men on the trucks then Andrew and I walked up a steep path leading into the village. Our platoon orderly tagged along behind. As we stepped away from the main road, the metallic chirp of insects surrounded us. The shade given by scrubby trees did not ease the heat. We splashed across a shallow stream that smelled of sewage. The path wound upwards until we came to a cluster of huts. By now, my bush shirt was soaked with sweat. I swatted at mosquitoes that buzzed around my head. My beret seemed tighter.

The command post was easy to find. Police officers ranging from constable to inspector milled around one of the huts. There was the crackling of radios and from inside the hut I could hear the babble of raised voices. Inspectors shouted commands at sergeants who bellowed at constables who scrambled back and forth along the village paths. A constable carrying a Remington shotgun barged past me. The atmosphere was heavy with urgen-cy. A group of men and women perked up when they saw our berets. Pinned to their shirtfronts were rectangular badges that read 'PRESS.' A camera flash dazzled me. The press crowded round and for a few seconds, we could not move forward.

'*Bongban*. What weapons will you use?'

'Over here, here.'

'Anything? Any comment at all?'

Their voices were a jumbled racket and we shouldered our way through. I bowed my head to enter the hut's doorway and found myself in a small living room with a lumpy sofa and a battered sideboard. A stone-faced woman sat on a straight-backed chair against a wall, her arms folded across her bosom and fury burning in her eyes. I guessed the police had taken over her home with no regard to social niceties.

Sitting at a table with a telephone lodged between his ear and his shoulder was a young Chinese man. The hem of his jacket had ridden up, exposing the butt of a Colt Detective Special. Hovering over him was a uniformed superintendent. The superintendent was slim, he had fleshy lips and a receding chin. In a reedy voice, he fired off a string of questions. 'What news on the victims? What are the negotiators doing? Have you got the cordon in place? Where the hell's PTU?'

Detective senior inspector John Yen looked like he needed to catch up on some sleep. He was a glum-looking man in his late twenties. He put down the telephone and raised both hands as if to ward off an attack.

'Please, *please*, sir. Let me brief PTU.'

The superintendent pursed his lips and John Yen waved Andrew and me forward. He pinched the bridge of his nose. 'Glad to see you,' he said, massaging his neck with both hands. 'Here's the story.'

I glanced at the door to make sure the press were not eavesdropping.

John Yen spoke in a clipped voice. 'Subject: Chinese Male Wai Dak, Dak Jai to his friends.' I nodded and he continued. 'Oh-three hundred hours, Dak Jai woke to find wife missing. For whatever reason, he went straight to his neighbour's house, breaks open the door and found wife and neighbour ... how do you say? Intimate.'

I swapped looks with Andrew. We had a hillside full of police-men, a superintendent teetering on the edge of panic and a size-able portion of the press corps clamouring round the command post. This was more than a dispute over Mrs Wai's indiscretions.

John Yen continued. 'So, what next? Dak Jai rushes home where he keeps an illegal collection of martial arts weapons.'

Oh shit, I thought.

John had read my thoughts. 'You got it,' he said, 'Dak Jai grabs a samurai sword, goes back to neighbour's hut and slices up wife and boyfriend like roast geese.'

I hardly dared ask. 'Where's Dak Jai now?'

John pulled a sour face, he was a one-man bad news factory. 'Barricaded inside his home ...'

I finished the sentence for him, '... and now some poor sod's got to dig him out?'

John Yen nodded. There was a short silence then Andrew chipped in.

'*Katana.*'

'What?'

'Samurai sword. It's called a *katana*. Beaten from a single steel bar. Heavy, very heavy, but balanced like a goldsmith's scale. Sharp, very sharp.'

I gave him a tight stare.

'Why look at me? I just want to get it right.' He fell into a sul-len silence.

The superintendent spoke. 'So, PTU will just have to earn their pay for a change.'

His face was pale and there was a quaver in his voice. He was trying to project an air of jaunty confidence but he was on the verge of cracking.

'Of course, it's up to you how you handle things,' he said. 'But if you want my advice ...' His voice trailed off. I let him stew for a few seconds then turned back to John Yen and asked him to show me Dak Jai's hut.

John relaxed as we left the command post. We pushed our way through the reporters and together, climbed a narrow path.

It was a mess, John explained. Mrs Wai and her lover were in critical condition in Queen Elizabeth Hospital. Police negotiators were trying to coax Dak Jai out of his hut but they were having no luck. It did not help that the superintendent who was supposed to be running things was hiding behind a barrage of useless orders. We paused at a fork in the path. The narrower of the two paths led up the slope to a small house that hugged the hillside. Broad-leafed plants almost hid it from view. The hut had a sagging roof and walls of splintered plywood. The only things holding the shabby little building together were baling wire and desperation. The door was closed and there were shutters at the windows. Two men crouched by the door; I recognised them as police negotiators.

From somewhere near the command post, a sergeant shouted. A constable shouted back then ran back to the main road. A half dozen more pushed past us and formed a line in front of the hut. A one-pip inspector joined them, his revolver drawn.

'Jesus,' Andrew groaned. 'Let's get rid of this lot before they hurt themselves.' He turned to our orderly. 'Tell the platoon sergeant to get two columns up here on the double.' The orderly turned to obey but Andrew grabbed his arm. 'Tell him: helmets, respirators, shields, batons, mace spray, teargas grenades.'

The orderly scurried off.

'And,' I called after him, 'bring breaking equipment and the Bedfords' CO2 extinguishers.' Teargas grenades used a burning compound; I had seen one glow cherry red. If we used them up here, we could end up with the whole hillside ablaze.

Further down the hillside, someone was on the receiving end of a fierce bollocking. Sergeants and constables ran up and down the path on meaningless errands. The whole operation was a shambles. The superintendent should have been pulling things together but he was hiding in the command post. It was more than a mess, it had the makings of a major cock-up.

I spoke softly trying to ease the tension. I told the young inspector to put away his revolver and suggested he calm his men. Our first column arrived. They carried rattan shields and three-foot long riot batons. Each man had his riot helmet slung across his shoulder by its chinstrap. In addition to his own helmet, the orderly had brought Andrew's and mine. The young inspector seemed not to have heard me so I spoke directly to his constables and told them to regroup back at the command post. They trotted back down the path, leaving their inspector high and dry. He re-holstered his revolver, threw me a glare and followed them. Our second column arrived a minute later. I told the corporals to cover the rear and both sides of the hut. They moved into place in silence. The corporals went from man to man, giving whispered orders. The men removed their berets, jammed on their helmets and snapped down the perspex visors.

The negotiators shrugged and moved away from the door. 'It's no good,' one said. 'He won't say anything. No requests, no demands, nothing.'

We were running out of choices. I had a gut-gnawing feeling this day would end badly. The hubbub faded; a flat stillness spread like spilled ink on fresh tissue. A cockatoo screeched and for a moment I thought it an idyllic scene. Then I looked at the shuttered house and remembered that inside, an angry man with a keen-edged sword waited for us to go in and get him.

I called up the remaining two columns and told the platoon sergeant to keep them in reserve nearby. With the area secure, Andrew and I went back to the command post and talked over our options with John Yen. The superintendent hovered nearby. It was essential to keep everything calm, I told them. 'All the shouting and running about makes the constables nervous and it'll get Dak Jai jumpy.' I looked around the room and to my surprise, everyone agreed. 'Okay,' I invited, 'suggestions?'

The superintendent jumped in. 'Gas the bugger,' he huffed.

'Lob in some grenades. When he comes out, jump him. If he's still got the carving knife, shoot the sod. Simple. But it's your decision, of course.'

Our decision? Our responsibility if it went wrong, more like.

'We could wait him out,' I said. 'Less chance of anyone getting hurt that way.'

'Good God, no,' said the superintendent. 'We'll be here for days. Get in there; winkle him out; that's the job.' He turned to John Yen. 'You tell him, John. After all, it's your investigation.'

John Yen gave me a sorrowful look and shrugged. 'You heard. I'm in charge but we do it his way.' He frowned and lowered his voice. 'Let us hope he's right.'

I looked at Andrew; Andrew looked at me. There was nothing more to say. We ducked through the door and headed back to Dak Jai's hut. I ordered one of the reserve columns to come with us and in silence, we headed back up the path.

A hush shrouded the village. Helmeted PTU men surrounded the hut. Their breath misted the inside of their visors. Rattan shields hid the lower half of their faces. I dropped to one knee and raised my binoculars. Through the lenses, the hut's walls leapt at me. They were water-stained and rotten, at the corners the joints were cracked and warped. There was a way in, dangerous but not suicidal. I lowered the binoculars.

'Forget the door,' I said. 'We should take down a wall.'

I handed the binoculars to Andrew and he examined the hut in silence. The wall on the left flank looked the flimsiest. We called the corporals together and had a hurried strategy meeting. The plan was simple. One column would attack the weakest wall with axes and crowbars. With the wall down, the second column would rush in and pin Dak Jai down with their shields and batons. The third column would cover the front door in case Dak Jai decided to dash out and attack us in the open. If that happened, there would be life or death decisions to make. Doubt chewed at me. Speed was vital; surprise everything. I willed Andrew to come up with a better idea but he just turned down the corners of his mouth and nodded.

'Might work,' he said. He nodded to the platoon orderly who had the Bedford's fire extinguishers with him. 'We'll give him a blast of CO_2 as we go in.'

We tossed a coin and I called heads. Andrew would lead the assault through the wall, I would command the column guarding the door. That was the plan; simple and uncluttered. We looked at each other in silence. The silence dragged. Andrew shrugged, his voice was casual. 'Let's go.'

My column bunched at the door. Andrew's men gathered at the side wall. This is not a drill, I told myself but could not believe it. I focussed my thoughts on a wrathful man ready to strike at the first policeman he saw. I imagined the curved blade slicing through cotton, flesh, bone. How much protection would a rattan shield give?

Andrew flipped down his visor and gave me the 'okay' sign by circling his thumb and index finger. I returned the signal. Men with axes and crowbars moved up to the wall. The entry party raised their shields. Their eyes were hard, their bodies taut. Andrew mouthed the words, 'let's go.' Time telescoped. Everything moved in slow motion. I snapped down the visor of my helmet. I nodded.

And clamorous bloody mayhem came to Chikung village.

'DA. DA. DA.' -- STRIKE. STRIKE. STRIKE. The men were shouting in unison. Their voices pummelled my ears. They beat their batons against their shields, *chukachuckachuck*. Axes and crowbars smashed into the wall.

'DA. DA. DA.'

There was a tearing crash. A section of plywood wall fell away and tumbled down the slope, then another, then one more. It was too slow. Seconds seemed like minutes. We were losing surprise. I pictured Dak Jai waiting in the dark, sword raised.

'DA. DA. DA.'

The hissing roar of the fire extinguisher mingled with the chanted shouts and the crash of hammered shields. Inside my head a voice pounded, 'Don't hurt my men. Please don't hurt ...'

'Man down.'

'Bastard.' I kicked at the front door. The doorframe split but did not give.

'Man down. Man down.'

I unsnapped the flap of my holster and snatched out my revolver. I kicked at the door again. The doorframe shattered and the door banged open.

Kill him.

I barrelled into the hut holding my revolver stiff-armed before me. I pivoted left and right. *Where was he?* My breath came in hard gasps. I had a fleeting impression of visored faces beyond the remnants of a shattered wall. The shouting and hammering stopped. On the floor was something crumpled and broken. I took a breath and stepped closer. There was a man kneeling in the middle of the room. His head was bowed. He was still and silent. His eyes were screwed shut. At first, I thought he was praying. Sticking from the middle of his naked back was twenty-four inches of blood-smeared steel. I took another step forward and Dak Jai toppled onto his side. Both his hands grasped the sword's grip; the hilt guard was flat against his stomach. Blood puddled on the floor. My mouth was like old sand, my pulse thumped in my skull, a white mist filled my eyes, I felt dizzy. I stood over Dak Jai, my legs straddling his body. A great cruelty uncoiled inside me. I raised the revolver and sighted on his temple. Then it hit me.

It was safe.

Dak Jai was the man down, the sword buried in his guts. Not Andrew's guts, not a constable's and not mine. *His* guts. I stepped back, slid the revolver back into my holster and clipped the fastener. Andrew's hand was on my shoulder. He shook me like a sleepwalker. *'Jesus,* I thought ...'

I knelt beside Dak Jai and saw how ordinary he looked. I had expected a crazed giant, instead he was small and thin. Emotions rolled around in me like blankets in a tumble-dryer: rage, pity, exultation, sadness.

Dak Jai gave a small gasp. His eyelids fluttered.

'He's alive.' I said, not believing it.

Andrew dropped to one knee beside me. 'He's *what?'*

'He's alive.' A great rush of relief flooded through me. No, it was not relief, it was joy. Was it minutes or just seconds earlier I had wanted him dead? Now I was joyful. He was *alive.*

Helmeted men threw aside their shields, clambered into the house and ripped field dressings from their pockets. Andrew had a radio to his lips, 'Scene secure. Roger so far?'

The radio crackled back. *'Roger so far.'*

'No police injuries.'

'Roger so far.'

'Suspect has a severe stab wound. So far?'

'Roger so far.'

'Confirm when ambulance crew on the way, over.'

'Roger.'

A flash bulb popped. A man wearing a press badge stood at the broken wall, he leaned into the room and snapped off another photograph. Rage boiled inside me. Other reporters crowded and jostled behind him.

'Get those bastard vultures out of here,' I shouted.

The reporters parted as the superintendent pushed his way through. 'They're with me,' he said, his voice imperious and uncaring. He stepped into the room and looked at Dak Jai as though he were a stain on his office carpet. 'Is he dead?'

'No,' I said. 'Ambulance crew's on the way.'

The superintendent frowned. 'You should have shot him. Would've saved everyone a lot of trouble.'

My mouth felt full of wax. I wanted to speak but no sound

came. I stood. I knew what I had to do. I would grab this super-cilious prick by his throat and demand to know where he had been hiding. The press would love it. Andrew moved between us and put his arm around my shoulder. His grip was hard and insistent. He steered me from the hut. His voice was loud with artificial jauntiness.

'Right, let's get down to the command post.' To me, he spoke in an urgent hiss. 'Punching a senior officer. Oh yes, smart move.'

Behind us, the superintendent was addressing the press. 'Of course, *my* plan had three aims: safeguard the public, safeguard my men and finally, use minimum force against the perpetrator ...'

I tried to pull away but Andrew would not let me go. I looked at my hands, they were trembling. The strength drained from my legs and I sat heavily on a low stone wall. The ambulance crew scurried up the path carrying a stretcher and an oxygen bottle. The platoon filed past, heads bowed, shields and batons trailing on the ground.

There was something wet on my cheek. I dashed it away with the back of my hand.

Andrew stood in front of me so no one would see. 'It's okay, Chris,' he said. 'The boys are okay. Everything's okay.'

And it was. It really was all right.

So why could I not catch my breath? It was ridiculous, I could not speak, I tried to stand but my legs would not carry my weight. Why were my shoulders shaking? I bowed my head as shameful tears burned my cheek.

November, as always, was perfect. The skies were clear; the weather was dry and cool. In November, we were near the end of our district attachment. Soon PTU Charlie company would disband and we would go back to normal duties. Behind us were months of rapid shift changes, forced overtime, cancelled leave, and months of being treated like Little Orphan Annie. The platoon's mood was sombre, we were glad to be going back to our divisions but we had grown close and would miss each other.

The company commander summoned me to his headquarters on Hong Kong Island and I made the journey wondering what was wrong. I recalled undetected sins and conjured up non-existent problems. I went into his office a nervous, one-pip probationer and emerged a dazed but happy two-pip inspector. But where was the glow of inner confidence, the weight of extra dignity? I was no longer a *bongban-jai*, -- a boy inspector; I was a proper *bongban* -- a grown-up inspector. But I was not two feet taller and my IQ had not expanded into the cosmos. Nothing had changed, dammit. Then I passed the company major's desk.

'Congratulations, sir.'

That stopped me dead.

'Pardon, major?'

The major gave me a warm smile.

'I said, congratulations, sir.'

I felt the first stirrings of true authority.

'Thank you, major. Are you well?'

'Very well, sir.'

There it was again, the major was calling me 'sir' and not struggling to keep his face straight. I was on a roll.

'Looking forward to getting back to your old division, major?'

'I shall miss Charlie company, sir.' His eyes narrowed. He had seen through me, so I headed back to the safety of my Landrover.

We spent the last few days on platoon administration. There were final staff reports to write and men to interview. There was a backlog of travel allowance and overtime claims to process. The PTU transport officer inspected our vehicles and the force armourer spent a day checking our weapons. The incoming commander visited with his platoon sergeant and orderly in tow. My platoon sergeant went up to Fanling and engaged in serious haggling with the PTU barrack sergeant. Between them, they sorted out all the missing equipment, which were two water bottles, one webbing belt and forty-one berets.

The final Friday was an auspicious day to pay homage to Kwandai, our patron deity. There was a small shrine on the wall of the rank and file canteen and in a simple ceremony, we each presented three pungent joss sticks to the god's scowling icon. We ate suckling pork, greasy goose and drank too much beer. After the last red-faced constable bid a boozy and comradely farewell, Andrew and I checked the barracks, armoury, washrooms and platoon office. Everything was clean and in good order. We realised there was nothing left to do. Our PTU attachment was over. An uncomfortable silence hung between us. I felt a sudden fondness for Andrew but the words I wanted to say would not come. Andrew scuffed his feet and for the first time since we had met, he seemed lost for words. We exchanged muttered promises to stay in touch, shook hands and went home. A few months later, Andrew left the police to join his family business.

I never saw him again.

CHAPTER 9
HARRY'S LAW

To ENTER COURT IS to enter hell, at least that is what the Chinese say. And who can blame them? For centuries, imperial Chinese magistrates would order court attendants to grab shifty or just plain forgetful witnesses and beat their backsides with wooden poles until they became more talkative. When they passed into history, the emperor's magistrates left a yawning gulf between the forces of justice and the common people. Collective memory is a powerful force. Just ask a Hong Kong detective who has spent days canvassing a public housing estate for witnesses.

Queen Victoria gave British justice to her empire, but in a uniquely imperial form. Hong Kong's magistrates, sitting all alone, could hand down sentences of three years imprisonment. District court judges, also sitting alone, could dish out a seven-year stretch. Only murderers, rapists, drug barons and the like got anywhere near a jury. Luckily, our judges and magistrates were not the gin-soaked fuddy-duddies of popular myth. They were generally learnéd and honourable people. Any police officers who tried to get away with sloppy casework would find themselves on the receiving end of a judicial bollocking that would make their head spin. Many of my colleagues complained that magistrates acted like part of the defence team.

The courthouse at Fanling was a two-storey edifice with a featureless exterior. Inside, the building was a grander affair. The entrance opened onto a lofty atrium with a broad staircase leading to a spacious gallery. The gallery led to two courtrooms, each with high ceilings and wood panelled walls. Each courtroom had a terraced section for the public and an elevated bench where the magistrate could settle into a chair of crimson leather and look down into the well of the court. The Royal crest adorned the wall behind his seat.

The Royal crest may have adorned the walls, but Fanling court belonged to just one person and that was His Worship, Harry Lyonns Esquire. Harry Lyonns was an owlish man with jam-jar bottom spectacles and a mop of unruly hair. He always seemed distracted, as though he had just mislaid something. Harry's court interpreter was Ricco Pong. Ricco understood Harry perfectly and translated not only Harry's words, but also his every nuance. That is not as easy as it sounds, I know because I have tried it. Harry and Ricco were two parts of a three-man act. The third was the police prosecutor and that was me.

There were two courtrooms in Fanling magistracy but Harry resisted all attempts to appoint a second sitting magistrate. Harry liked being the only New Territories magistrate; no, Harry *loved* being the only New Territories magistrate, even if it meant a caseload that would floor anyone else.

On my first day, I sat at the counsel's desk and shuffled my papers. I had been up all night going over the prosecution files and I tried to convince myself there was no need to worry. There were five cases for trial and they were straightforward. All I had to do was to call the witnesses in the right order, get them started and prompt them if they lost the thread of their evidence. But first, we had to deal with all the thugs, triads and drug addicts arrested over the last twenty-four hours.

The clerk drew himself to his feet and called, '*Court.*' The door to Harry's chambers banged open and Harry strode up the steps to his bench. Everyone rose and bowed. Harry returned the bow, sat down and searched for something among his papers. He blinked from behind his spectacles and beamed at the clerk.

'First case?'

The clerk called the name of a defendant caught trying to snatch an old lady's handbag. Harry smiled as the thief's lawyer rose to his feet.

'My client pleads not guilty, your worship.'

Harry called for the court diary and peered at me over his spectacles. 'How many witnesses, inspector?'

'Two, your worship. My witness examination should last about twenty minutes.'

'Mister Worthington?'

'Defence needs at least a day to cross-examine and maybe two days to present our case. I will apply for an adjournment if necessary.'

Harry licked his fingertips and turned the pages of the diary. 'Is it true, Mister Worthington, that you calculate your fees by the hour?' he asked.

'I ... er ... believe, that is, I ... um ... normal practice, your worship.'

'Yes, yes; indeed yes,' Harry said, jabbing his finger onto a page. 'Ah good. I can fit you in a month from now. I have a nice afternoon slot between two careless driving cases ...'

'I can't possibly ... that's nowhere near enough ...' the defence counsel huffed, but Harry seemed not to have heard.

In the coming months, I saw Harry Lyonns get through motoring cases in half an hour. Blackmail and street robbery took a little longer. Harry could hear a half dozen cases a day and still get home for high tea. His trials were legendary, as was his reputation for fairness. In all his years on the bench, Harry never had a judgement overturned on appeal. When Harry scheduled an hour for trial, that is how long it took.

As the day's list of fresh cases filed past, Ricco Pong read the charges and the case summaries then handed down Harry's pronouncements with the alacrity of a Virginia tobacco auctioneer. I struggled to keep Harry supplied with case papers and criminal record folders. With just one case left, the clerk called upon a Mister Wing Cho. I checked the papers, it was an opium case. I had the case facts and a chemist's certificate that showed the case exhibits were, indeed, opium. Mister Wing was a frail looking man with a wispy white beard and thinning hair. He had bony cheeks and rheumy eyes. He wore baggy trousers and a high-necked tunic made of blue silk. A snow-white scarf hung around his neck. As he reached the well of the court, there was the briefest flash of mischief in his eyes. He bowed to the bench.

Ricco Pong read out the charge and invited a plea.

Mister Wing bowed again. '*Sing ying, fat gwoon dai yan,*' he said in a clear, strong voice.

Ricco translated, 'Guilty, honourable magistrate.' He even copied Mr Wong's bow.

I handed Harry the case report and passed a copy to Ricco who translated it aloud. A constable, patrolling a rear lane in Yuenlong had detected the liquorice-aniseed smell of opium drifting from a lean-to shed. There was no door, just a blanket hanging from the lintel so the constable stuck his head inside to investigate. A small paraffin lamp lit the lean-to and there, lying on a wooden bed was Mister Wing. In both hands, he cradled a slim bamboo pipe, its clay head inverted over the lamp. A porcelain pot filled with sticky black resin stood at the side of the bed. Clear as day, Mister Wing was smoking opium.

'Any previous, inspector?'

I picked up the criminal record folder and totted up Mister Wing's previous convictions.

'Well, inspector?'

Mister Wing's criminal record sheet had a dozen or more pages. All his convictions were for possessing and smoking opium.

'A moment, your worship,' I said and started counting as fast as I could.

'How many in the last six months, inspector?'

'Two, your worship; both similar.'

Harry turned to Mister Wing.

'How old are you?'

Ricco translated Harry's question, taking care to echo his solicitude.

Mister Wing bowed yet again. Ricco translated perfectly, 'Ninety, honourable magistrate.'

'How long have you been smoking opium?'

'Over sixty years, sir.' Ricco's translation mirrored Mr Wing's respectful but friendly tone.

'How do you feel? How's your health?' Harry asked.

'I'm ninety years old, your honour, how do you think I feel?'

Harry chuckled and awarded Mister Wing ten dollars from the court's poor box. 'Just be sure not to spend it on opium,' he cautioned.

Mister Wing bowed. 'Thank you, honourable magistrate. I promise.' As Mister Wing turned and walked from the court, his eyes twinkled.

I was outraged. How were the police supposed to keep public order when the courts were not even slapping the wrists of hard-core drug addicts? I decided to pen a fierce report to New Territories HQ and demand a sentence review.

After the day's last case, Harry called me into his chambers. He pulled two beers from a refrigerator then enlightened me about his views on opium. 'Opium is the drug of the elderly,' Harry said, pouring the beers into two frosted glasses. 'Fellows like the delightful Mister Wing Cho have been smoking the stuff since it was legal.' He loosened his tie and leaned back. 'Opium's cheap, you see, but it's a bugger to smoke. Your average Mister Wing needs a bed-board, a headrest, an assortment of small pots, little metal scrapers, a paraffin lamp and a bamboo pipe.'

Yes, yes, I knew all that. Harry would have to do better if he wanted me to forget about the sentence review.

'Now, take your average heroin smoker,' Harry continued, ignoring my impatience. 'Compared to opium smokers, he's got it easy. A small packet of heroin, a tin foil, a paper tube and a cigarette lighter; that's all he needs. Heroin addicts sort themselves out in back lanes or public toilets, which is where your mates often find their corpses.'

True, I thought.

Harry fixed me with eyes that were no longer smiling. 'Most robbers and petty thieves appearing before me are heroin addicts. Opium addicts, on the other hand, can afford to eat and look after themselves. If I bring the full weight of the law down on the likes of Mister Wing Cho, he'll switch to heroin and be dead in months.'

I nodded, it was hard to fault Harry's reasoning.

'I hate drugs,' Harry said and his voice took on an edge. 'Before me, possession of heroin is worth six months in detox or eight months in jail. Traffickers won't get much change out of two years. When was the last time you saw an opium addict beat up a street hawker for a few dollars?'

I could only shrug.

'I'll give opium smokers a fifty-dollar fine, *plus* another fifty dollars for every prior conviction in the last six months,' Harry's brows furrowed. 'If they can't pay or if they're proud old gentlemen like Mister Wing, I give 'em ten dollars from the poor box and hope I don't see 'em again for a few months.'

Then he was his old self again. He sipped his beer and put his feet up on the desk. 'Anything you'd like to ask?'

I had no questions; it was the law according to Harry Lyonns. And it made perfect sense to me.

Harry was so transparent that after a few weeks, I could anticipate just what he expected from a case. Everything went fine until the day I tried my hand at the court interpreter's job.

From time to time, inspectors prosecuted their own cases. At first, I thought this a slight on my skills but most detective inspectors had spent time as prosecutors and Harry was always glad to see them make the effort. One afternoon, I returned from lunch and noticed a nervous European sitting at the front of the public gallery. He wore razor-creased, grey flannel trousers and a blazer with an embossed badge on the breast pocket. His shoes had a military gleam. Around his neck was the regimental tie of the 3rd Fusilier Highlanders, better known as 'The Poison Picts.' Tattooed on the knuckles of one hand were the letters L-O-V-E and on the other H-A-T-E.

There was also a new face at the counsel's table. He was young and had a 'can do' smile. He pumped my hand. 'Jaimeson, Army Legal Service.' He nodded to the young European. 'That's my boy.' He lowered his voice. 'Indecent assault. High spirits of course. Any chance of reducing it to breach of the peace?'

I shook my head but panic snatched at me. Indecent assault, what indecent assault? Here was an army barrister, briefed and ready to go and I had not even seen the file. I shuffled through the files on the desk. Nothing. It must still be in my office, neglected and unread.

A case file thumped onto the desk and I turned to see a heavy-set Chinese scowling at me. His voice was harsh. 'Joe Chow, CID Yuenlong. This is my case. The boss told me to prosecute. Stay if you want.'

I was not a happy man. Joe Chow should have told me days ago he would prosecute. I had almost wet myself looking for a file that I had never received. Without asking, Joe Chow sat in my seat and shuffled his papers. I sent my clerk back to the office and took his spot at the end of the table.

'*Court.*'

We stood and bowed as Harry clumped to the bench, leaving a trail of court papers behind him. The clerk called the first case. 'Cormack, Ian Stewart,' he said, as officious as any mandarin. The young soldier stood and looked around. The clerk was at his pompous best. 'Step forward and listen to the charge.'

Ian Stewart Cormack was nineteen years old. One balmy evening in August he had visited the Roseland Bar in Kamtin, a small village about a mile from the Shek Kong army base. There he struck up a conversation with a young waitress called Flossie Woo. After some convivial chat and two pints of San Miguel tops, Mister Cormack had placed his unwelcome hand upon Miss Woo's left breast.

Jaimeson stood. 'Your worship, my client pleads not guilty to indecent assault but will accept a binding over order.' He nodded to me. 'The police prosecutor has no objection to reducing the charge to breach of the peace.'

I spluttered my denials and caught a flinty look from Joe Chow.

Joe Chow stood and his voice grated through the court. 'Your worship. I am detective senior inspector Joe Chow of CID Yuenlong. *I* am officer in charge of this case and *I* represent the Crown.' He gave me a withering look. 'We proceed with the charge as presented.'

Joe Chow was a good prosecutor. He called Flossie to the stand and led her through her evidence. Flossie described the incident with commendable clarity and when asked to identify her assailant, she pointed unerringly to Fusilier Cormack. She dabbed a tear from her eye and smiled bravely as she finished her evidence.

Jaimeson cross-examined on the basis that women who worked in bars should expect the occasional fondle. Flossie would not be intimidated and at the end of the cross-examination, she was unruffled; her evidence unshaken.

Joe called the bar owner, a fierce middle-aged Chinese lady who told of comforting Flossie and single-handedly detaining Fusilier Cormack until the arrival of the military police. She glared thunderbolts at Jaimeson as he cross-examined her. When Joe closed his case, young Cormack's future did not seem bright.

Jaimeson tried to have the case thrown out on a technicality but Harry was having none of it. Jaimeson sighed and called his only witness. 'Your worship, I call my client, Fusilier Cormack.'

Ricco Pong administered the oath and returned to his seat, his role in the trial over. As Jaimeson rose to ask his first question, Joe Chow opened a notepad and prepared to write down Cormack's evidence word for word. He meant to eat the young soldier alive, literally by the look of him.

Jaimeson tried to sound reassuring. 'Don't be nervous, Fusilier Cormack, just use your own words to tell the court what happened on the evening in question.'

Cormack took a deep breath and screwed up his face in concentration. 'Like ... *ahwentdoontaKamtinferaweebevvy.*'

Joe gaped at Cormack, then at his notepad as if he expected the words to transcribe themselves. He looked like a student who finds his examination board speaks only Esperanto. I leaned closer to him and whispered. 'He says he went to Kamtin for a little drink.'

Joe scribbled in his notepad then blinked at the words as though he did not believe them. Sweat trickled down his temple.

Jaimeson's voice was silky. 'Then what happened, Fusilier Cormack?'

'Well ... *ahhadtwapintso'tops.*'

Joe blinked and shook his head.

'He had two pints of lager with a dash of lemonade.' I placed a reassuring hand on Joe's sleeve. He gave me a half smile and made a note on his pad.

Jaimeson continued to coax Cormack's evidence from him. 'Did you meet anyone in the bar, Fusilier Cormack?'

I caught Ricco from the corner of my eye. He raised an eyebrow. He was enjoying himself and I realised I had learned nothing during the last few weeks. I asked myself how would Ricco translate young Cormack's evidence? Answer: not only would he translate Cormack's words correctly, he would deliver every inflection and nuance of Cormack's speech. He would infuse his translation with every morsel of the young soldier's desperation.

A smile touched Ricco's lips, he did not think I could do it.

Jaimeson continued to nudge Cormack's evidence along, 'Well, Fusilier Cormack, did you meet anyone there?'

Cormack hunched his shoulders and licked his lips, '*Aye, ahdeed,*' he said. '*TherewuzaweetottycalledFlossie.*'

Joe turned to me, pen poised, his expression pleading. I imagined being in Cormack's shoes. I closed my eyes and reached out to feel his desperation. *Yes,* I was ready to give the perfect translation, a translation with every inflection and each linguistic hue in place. I cleared my throat then spoke. 'He said: "*Aye, ahdeed ... therewuzaweetottycalledFlossie.*"'

Ricco gave a snorting laugh and shook his head.

Joe did a three-sixty-degree scan of the court, convinced it was full of lunatics.

My self-confidence withered and I went back to plan A. 'Sorry ... that is ... he said: yes, he did meet someone. There was a young lady by the name of Flossie.'

'*Shesezahgrabbedhertittiesbutahdidna.* Honest.'

'She said that Mister Cormack touched her breasts but he most strenuously denies it.'

Ricco pretended to lose interest in the rest of the proceedings. He examined a piece of lint on his jacket, he tidied the papers on his desk and he checked the points of all his pencils but all the time a thin smile played on his lips. He was still the master.

'No further questions, Your Worship,' Jaimeson said. He sat down and Harry nodded to Joe.

'Your witness, Mister Chow.'

Joe looked from his notepad, to Cormack, to Harry, to me then back to his notepad. '*Er ...*'

'Any cross-examination, Mister Chow?' Harry looked at his watch.

'Ah ... no. No questions, your worship.' Joe dropped back onto his seat.

'What, Mister Chow, no questions at all?'

'No ... sorry. No, Your Worship.'

Harry retired to his chambers and ten minutes later he was back with his verdict. Flossie Woo and her manageress he declared, were truthful and dependable witnesses. He found Fusilier Cormack guilty and despite an impassioned plea for leniency, the young soldier celebrated Hogmanay as a guest of the Hong Kong prisons service.

Although he always punished sloppy casework, there was no malice in Harry and he was a regular at the Frontier officers' mess. Harry had just one complaint: he believed the police used the courts as detective training grounds. He moaned constantly that as soon as he broke in one prosecutor, the force gave him another. There was no arguing with that, the average posting to court was only six months. Many ex-prosecutors ended up as detectives, narcotics officers or in the traffic branch, where their court experience was invaluable. True to form, six months after I took my place at the counsel's table, my replacement arrived and I went back to England.

Colonial governments once thought that if British civil servants did not return home every few years, they would don grass skirts, weave flowers into their hair and go native. This made for an amazing perk to the job, the long home leave. It seemed impossible, but my first tour of duty was up. I had my leave papers tucked in my pocket and I was going home for four months.

I arrived in England at six in the morning on a glorious Sunday in June. It is hard to believe now but then, England was closed on Sundays. Heathrow's taxi rank was empty and there were shutters at the car hire booths. An old newspaper blew across the deserted bus station. There were no smiling faces at the tourist information desk, and the tourist board's twenty-four hour telephone number went unanswered. In desperation, I called a limousine service and half an hour later, a uniformed but sceptical chauffeur stowed my rucksack in the trunk of his Austin Princess. He sniffed as he opened the door for me so I picked some lint from the seat covers and made a show of dropping it into the gutter. Didn't want to mess up my jeans, did I? I boarded a northbound train at Euston and stunned the crowd in the club car by asking the barman for a cold Perrier. Behind me, a customer sniggered and the barman's voice quivered with outrage. 'There ... there's nuffin' cold in 'ere, mate.'

I got off the train in my hometown and took the bus back to my parents' house. While I had been away, the bus fare had tripled. It was great to see my parents, they were older and my room seemed smaller. I took my dad to the local pub and he told me outrageous stories about his army days in Hong Kong. My old friends were harder to find. The gang had either married or moved away. I dropped into an old watering hole and a group of regulars greeted me from their usual table. 'It's young what's-his-name,' one said. 'Where've you been, lad? Not seen you for weeks.'

I explained I had served for three years in the Royal Hong Kong Police. I told them of the unbending para-military discipline. I regaled them with yarns from the furthest outpost of empire. I told them how I had stood shoulder to shoulder with stout-hearted men whom I was proud to call friend.

The regulars swapped dour looks. 'Hong Kong, eh? So, can you get English telly in Japan?'

It was like four months adrift in an open boat. I bought a car and saw more of England than ever before. England was as green and pleasant as ever but even during that splendid summer, it was a lonely place and I felt a surge of relief when the envelope arrived. Along the top left hand border were the words 'On Her Majesty's Service' printed in English and Chinese. It told me that my first working day was in early October. I would not return to the New Territories but instead, should report to Hong Kong

185

Island district headquarters where the superintendent (administration) would give me my new assignment.

My rural coppering days were over. I was going to walk the hard streets of the city.

CHAPTER 10
THE KWANDAI'S APPRENTICE

As far as gods go, Kwandai is pretty cool. He likes good food and has been known to enjoy a drink or two. His shrine comprises an ornate frame with a small shelf on which there is a brass, sand-filled pot for receiving incense sticks. The centrepiece is an image of Kwandai himself, a dark visaged warrior. Every Hong Kong police station has at least one of these shrines and most have several. Not to be outdone, the criminal classes also pay homage to Kwandai and his shrine adorns the walls of vice establishments, opium dens and gambling divans. He gets around a bit, does our Kwandai.

Usually, Kwandai is pretty relaxed but he gets annoyed if people ignore him and the last thing a police station needs is a grumpy Kwandai. So, every now and then, we pay homage to Kwandai in a ceremony called *Baai Kwandai*. The ceremony is simple. Guests line up in order of rank, each grabs three incense sticks and takes a turn to stand before the shrine. Bow three times and it's done. Well, almost. The next part of the ceremony involves drinking beer and eating lots of suckling pig. As I said, for a god, Kwandai is pretty cool. It is amazing what a good *Baai Kwandai* will achieve. Crime rate up? Hold a *Baai Kwandai*. Productivity low? Same thing. Kwandai did it all: he made the streets safe, he brought crooks to book, he could even boost a flagging career.

But given half a chance, he could also ruin a promising one.

Hong Island's North division found itself with a divisional detective inspector called Jonathan Sowerby. The DDI was the detective chief inspector commanding the division's criminal investigation department and he carried real clout. Sowerby was an ambitious sort who demanded nothing short of perfection. After a two-week management course, he was chock-a-block with bright ideas. He was quick to try his new skills but somewhere along the line he hit a solid wall of resistance. Some blamed a few old-style detective sergeants, others said that Sowerby's ideas were just not workable. Whatever the reason, everyone's paperwork doubled and time spent investigating crime halved.

Detectives are an easygoing bunch and could have forgiven Sowerby just about anything. But things changed the day Jonathan Sowerby stepped across an invisible line drawn many years earlier on the floor of the detective squadroom. On that day, Sowerby decreed that in a climate of streamlined management, the detective staff sergeant, the legendary D/major, was surplus to requirements. Bit by bit, Sowerby cut his D/major from the command loop. He did not ask the D/major's advice on serious crime, he did not discuss team performance or even speak to him about staff welfare. The D/major was out in the cold and he did not like it one bit. Morale suffered, detection rates plummeted and Sowerby got a discreet phone call from the divisional superintendent.

'These setbacks are systemic but transitional obstacles,' Sowerby explained. 'They are a product of an ingrained culture of resistance to change. Things will be fine when people get used to the new integrated working systems.'

Hmm ... when he put it that way, the DS had to agree.

The problem lay in the communications gap; no one could understand a word Sowerby said. The final cut came when he told the D/major to prepare a written job charter for himself. The station held its breath. D/majors did not have job charters; their job was to be the D/major, everyone knew that. The D/major took it very well, too well as it turned out. The next day he laid a comprehensive list of his duties on Sowerby's desk. He turned to go, then as an afterthought, reminded Sowerby that the men expected to welcome their new DDI in the traditional manner. They wanted a *Baai Kwandai*.

Sowerby pooh-poohed the idea. Superstition, he declared, had no part in the modern police force.

Of course, that was not the end of it. As the detection rate fell further, the D/major appealed to the modern manager in Sowerby. Staff performance, he explained, went hand in hand with morale. Sowerby nodded, the management course had taught him that much. Morale, the D/major continued, had to do with perception. Even false perceptions played a part in poor productivity. Sowerby was amazed, the D/major's insight into human resource management equalled that of the force management gurus.

The date was set and as *Baai Kwandais* go, it was a big one. The CID Kwandai glowered down from the squadroom wall. There were four suckling pigs laid out before the shrine. Trestles sagged under the weight of goose, chicken and piles of steamed *dim sum*. The San Miguel brewery sent some leggy public relations girls to work the beer pumps. All of the division's detectives were there, so was the divisional superintendent and his deputy. A detective chief inspector escorted by a coterie of inspectors came all the way from Hong Kong Island headquarters. The beer disappeared quicker than the San Miguel girls could pour it. Faces turned brick red and the hum of conversation rose to a deafening babble. The D/major stepped forward with an armful of paper offerings. There were good luck characters painted on crimson paper. There was paper shaped to look like gold bullion and one in the shape of a Mercedes limousine. The roomboy put a match to the offerings. The D/major made three hasty bows to the shrine then handed the blazing offerings to the roomboy who dashed out to the compound before the sprinklers went off. The assembly lined up in strict order of rank but as Sowerby was the new DDI, he was to go first. The roomboy prepared incense sticks for the divisional superintendent and the other senior officers. Blue-grey smoke filled the room; it roughened throats and stung the eyes. Sowerby took the proffered incense sticks and stepped forward. He held the joss sticks between the palms of both hands. He bowed once.

And then Kwandai's shrine fell off the wall.

There was a heart wrenching crash. The brass pot clanged against the floor, spilling sand everywhere. There was a collective gasp followed by a crushing silence. Sowerby blanched and looked around, searching for guidance. The divisional superintendent and his deputies swapped looks of horror. Nobody had heard of such a thing, it was as if Kwandai had excommunicated the whole division. The circle around Sowerby widened as though he had become a plague carrier. Those nearest the door slipped outside.

Within twenty-four hours, the whole force was talking about it. Half North division's detectives called in sick. CID Island headquarters received a delegation of D/majors. One day later, a transfer memo wafted into Sowerby's in-tray.

It cost the D/major a fortune. He dug deep to pay for a new shrine and he hosted a huge *Baai Kwandai* to consecrate it. On top of that was the small matter of the renovation work. With the old Kwandai in ruins on the floor, the D/major told a station labourer to clear up the mess. As he dropped the last splinter into his waste trolley, the labourer saw what looked like a mark on the wall where the shrine had once hung. When he looked closer, he found it was not a mark at all, it was a hole. The hole went all the way through to the next office and was just large enough to accommodate a steel skewer. When he told the D/major what he had found, the D/major put his forefinger to his lips and gave the labourer a wad of ten-dollar bills. For years, the labourer did not tell another soul.

The tiger really bothered me. In the spring of 1915, a police-man shot the beast not far from where Fanling court now stands. By rights, the pelt should have graced the wall of Frontier mess, not the lobby of Central police station.

Central police station was home to Hong Kong Island head-quarters and it was one of a few colonial buildings spared the wrecker's hammer. It had deep verandas, high ceilings and a spacious courtyard. It had stood on its site in Hollywood Road since the 1860s and was part of a complex that included the old magistrate's court and Victoria prison. My interview with the superintendent (administration) had been brief.

'Congratulations. You're the new boss of the Island special duty squad. Hope you're up to speed on drugs and gambling. See the superintendent ops. Good luck.'

He bent back over his papers and made one-handed shooing signs.

The superintendent (operations) was a tired looking man with a cluttered desk and a brimming 'in' tray. He thumped a file into his 'out' tray and waved me to a chair.

'Ah, the new SDS inspector,' he said. 'I hope you have better luck than the last one.'

That did not sound good.

'Of course, you're just back from leave, you haven't heard,' he said and rummaged around in his 'in' tray. He pulled out a report and ran a finger down the page, musing aloud as he went.

'At sixteen hundred hours ... no parking zone ... traffic warden ... *ah*, here it is.'

He held the report at arm's length and read from it aloud. 'After the traffic warden issued the parking ticket, OC SDS leapt from his car, roared like a wild animal and chased said traffic warden along Queens' Road whilst making ...' he screwed up his eyes, '... whilst making giant monster arms.' He slid the report back into its tray. 'Bloody fool took the job too seriously, if you ask me.'

I was desperate to get to grips with city policing and the special duty squad seemed perfect. I wanted to be out on the streets, but first the superintendent (operations) was keen to give me the benefit of his experience. The job, he explained, was a challenge made all the harder by constant scrutiny from the assistant commissioner Hong Kong Island. AC Island was an old fashioned copper who would judge me by my arrest statistics. He would push the squad for cases then use our case figures as a cudgel to beat any underperforming divisional superintendents.

There was more. Special duty squads were prime targets for the new anti-corruption body called the Independent Commission Against Corruption. Any whiff of suspicion and the ICAC would visit the prisons and interview people we had arrested. There was even a chance they would hook their surveillance teams onto us. If that were not enough, some of my targets were also targets of the narcotics and triad society bureaux. If we cropped up in their surveillance operations, I would have to explain what we were doing. The key words were, 'Watch your back -- always.' He paused for a few seconds. 'Apart from that, the job's great fun.' He shook my hand and wished me luck.

The special duty squad office was in the bowels of Central police station and if there is anything more depressing than a Victorian basement, I would like to see it. Low wattage light bulbs cast a grubby light, the walls were mildewed, the floor was cracked and scuffed. There was a hum of conversation from behind a door at the end of the passageway. The conversation stopped the moment I opened the door and fourteen pairs of eyes swung towards me. Strip lighting made everyone look hollow-eyed and sallow.

The Chinese love puns. Country stores often bore the Chinese characters *si* meaning 'business' and *dor* meaning 'much.' *Si dor*, sounds like 'store.' Clever, right? On Hong Kong Island, police slang for a Frontier policeman was *fan day har*. It sounds like

'Frontier,' but translates as, 'one who sleeps on the floor.' Also clever, they must have thought I had straw in my hair.

A thirty-something year old man gave me a lukewarm smile. 'I am squad sergeant,' he said. 'Call me Choi Jai.' *Choi Jai*, it was Cantonese for 'Lucky Guy.' Good, we could use some of that. Choi Jai rattled off a list of nicknames, each time pointing at a member of the squad. Dee Jai: designer jeans, styled hair. The Bull: black T-shirt, body-builder's physique. Ah Fan: a fragile, pretty girl. Two-Zero: studious type. He seemed out of place. Auntie: middle aged and homely. The introductions were quick and I gave up trying to remember them all. With each name, an officer would nod in my direction, their expressions a mix of curiosity and amusement. To me he said, 'And you are our *Dai-lo*. OK?' There was a hint of challenge in his voice. 'This is small squad. We must be ...' he hunted for the right word. '... Tight, yes? Yes, tight and solid.'

Dai-lo -- elder brother; a mix of respect and familiarity. I looked around the faces in the room. '*Dai-lo* is fine,' I said and they grinned back at me.

Choi Jai relaxed. 'Right, *Dai-lo*,' he said. 'Any instructions?'

I thought for a moment and suggested a visit to some of the island's blackspots. We boarded Choi Jai's car, a modest Japanese compact, and set off for Western divisional police station.

'Divisions do not like us,' Choi Jai said as he battled through the late morning traffic. 'They think we are an enemy. They think we try to make them look bad.'

As we drove into Western station compound, the gate guard scowled at us and spoke into his phone link with the duty officer. Choi Jai eased into an empty parking space. A sign on the tarmac demanded, 'POLICE VEHICLES ONLY.'

'They know my car,' Choi Jai said. 'They know we are working. When we come back, maybe the car will be padlocked to security barrier. Always, the man with padlock key is bloody *sau gung* -- off duty.'

We left the station and walked to Des Voeux Road West. The pavements were narrow and jammed with people. There was the blare of car horns, ancient trams creaked and grumbled on iron tracks. From upstairs windows came the *clackclackclack* of mahjong tiles. Bicycles carrying impossible loads darted in and out of the traffic. The shops were open-fronted. There were dried fish merchants, herbalists, tea emporiums and ships' chandlers. There were furniture stores and lighting shops. Cut-price fashion shops pumped out Canto-pop music. Lanes and alleys connected Des Voeux Road West with the island's western waterfront. We turned into a side street and I saw the derricks of cargo lighters moored by the cargo basin. Beyond them lay the waters of the harbour. Within seconds, we were on the waterfront. This was Connaught Road West and in Connaught Road West, heroin was the tyrant king.

Connaught Road was just two lanes of potholed and oil-flecked tarmac. Crumbling tenements and dowdy waterfront warehouses known as godowns, lined one side of the road. On the other side, ranks of trucks stood with their backs to the harbour. Stubby cargo lighters bobbed on the harbour swell. Swarms of sun-darkened workers called *gu-leis* bounced along perilous gangplanks, carrying sacks and cartons ashore on their backs. Derricks swung pendulous cargo nets over men's heads and dumped them onto the road. Diesel smoke curled from the lighters' winches. The air was thick with shouts, curses and the smell of burnt fuel. As we stepped into the road, the shouted chatter fell away to silence. A bare-chested *gu-lei* stepped in front of me. Sinewy muscle covered his shoulders and arms. He held a baling hook, the point shiny from use. His eyes were dull, his smile had the idle arrogance of a recently satisfied heroin craving. He looked at me, eyes unblinking. He raised the hook then scratched his chin with the point. His work-mates laughed.

'Show fear and you never walk this street again,' Choi Jai hissed. He glared at a group of *gu-leis* who had stopped work to watch us, their eyes narrow. 'Bloody *do yau*, bloody drug addicts,' he growled. 'Paid part cash, part drugs. No work, no drugs,' He scowled. 'Here is very bad place on quiet working day.'

I stared into the *gu-lei's* face with feigned confidence. I put my hand on his shoulder and eased him aside. His shoulder felt like polished stone but he was unsteady on his feet and he staggered away.

We walked on and behind us, silent resentment turned to curses.

'*Ham gar chan.*' -- Death to your whole family.

'*Sau gung, jau faan lai,*' -- Come back when you're off duty.

Off to our left, a man squatted in the space between two trucks. White smoke billowed from something in front of him. There was a warning shout and he half-turned towards us. He was playing the flame of a cigarette lighter against the underside of a tinfoil strip. Clasped between his lips was a matchbox cover. He saw us, dropped everything and scampered away. A line of *gu-leis* moved in to block our path. Choi Jai shouldered his way through. Where the man had been squatting there was a blackened strip of tinfoil and a small square of paper. On the paper were a few grains of what looked like cat litter.

'You have this in New Territories?' he asked.

Indeed we did. It was number three heroin. It was bad stuff: up to fifty percent pure, cut with caffeine, brick dust and just a trace of strychnine. It had a rotting vinegar smell. Number three heroin was strictly for smoking. Anyone who pumped number three into a vein was lucky to make it to hospital.

Choi Jai picked up the tin foil and the square of paper. 'General orders say we must get court destruction order,' he grumbled. 'Waste of time.' He rolled tinfoil and paper into a ball and tossed it into the harbour.

We carried on along Connaught Road West and I felt a rush of relief when we left the cargo-handling basin behind. Adrenaline still pumped through me but Choi Jai seemed relaxed. 'Drug dealers complain like crazy when we search them. If we're not quick, many *gu-leis* block our way to the transport. That's if we can get any transport.' The set of his jaw told me transport was a luxury. 'The addicts fight like wild animals. Get them after they smoke and they feel no pain; catch them before they smoke and they do not care if they get hurt. Some uniform boys will not walk down this stretch of road.' He scowled and shook his head. 'I do not blame them.'

Back at Western police station, we found The Bull in a bare office next to the report room. He was doing the paperwork for a drug case. He sat, hunched over a chemical analysis form, chewing his lip as he wrote it out in longhand. He made a gesture with the pen. 'Report room clerk's using the typewriter.'

A man watched in silence. His clothes were grimed and threadbare. His hands were hard; his nails were cracked and blackened. He had parchment-like skin and hollow eyes. The Bull held up an exhibit envelope and made a show of dropping a small paper packet into it. He sealed the envelope and pushed it towards the prisoner. He pointed to a printed section on the envelope and offered his pen. The prisoner folded his arms and looked at the ceiling.

'Ask him where he got it,' I demanded.

The Bull flashed Choi Jai a look that said, 'This new boy's truly *fan day har.*' Choi Jai scowled at him and The Bull translated my question.

The prisoner kept his eyes on the ceiling. '*Hong Lok Do Sai,*' he said -- Connaught Road West.

The Bull started to translate but I waved him into silence.

'Ask him who sold him the stuff.'

The Bull rolled his eyes then spoke again to the prisoner.

The prisoner gave harsh laugh and snapped back, '*Ah Bin Goh.*'

A half smile played on the Bull's lips as he translated. 'He says he got stuff from "what's-his-name."'

Choi Jai spoke. '*Dai-lo*, tomorrow, court will give him bail. Arrest his dealer today, no drugs tomorrow. Dangle him from the station roof; still, he will say nothing.'

The Bull and Dee Jai had arrested the addict in a side street off Connaught Road West. They had telephoned the report room from a corner shop then waited ten long minutes for the promised transport. Meanwhile, a growing crowd of *gu-leis* had taunted them. Eventually, they had walked the addict back to the station, followed part of the way by a jeering crowd.

So that's they way of it, I thought: no transport, no admin support, no radios, no nothing. I went to the assistant sub-divisional Inspector's office, intending to kick up a fuss.

'What do you expect?' he snorted 'There's never any transport, there's only one clerk and just the one typewriter. As for back-up, we don't know your boys are in the area until you front up with a prisoner.'

We went back to our office and I pulled out the visits and inspections register. The last time a senior officer had set foot in our office had been two years earlier. I opened a file cabinet and found it jammed with loose memos and intelligence reports. I pulled a memo at random from the drawer, it was over a year old. I climbed the stairs to the superintendent (operations)'s office. As always, his door was open. He smiled when I asked for an administration clerk. He chuckled at my request for radios and when I suggested we have our own transport, he laughed so hard I thought he would burst an artery. The best he could manage was some obsolete 'Storno' radios. Each was the size of a house brick and weighed the same. They worked in direct line of sight but only if the weather was good. When switched on, they hissed like a campfire in a blizzard and the batteries went flat if anyone looked at them too hard. They were better than nothing, but only just.

I called Two-Zero back to the office and set him the task of sorting out the admin. He opened the filing cabinet and summed it up in a word. *'Waaaah.'*

I telephoned around the divisional special duty squads and pumped them for ideas. One squad commander had bought an old banger of a car then sold it to his successor when he moved on. I did a mental check of my finances and hoped someone in my squad had a friend in the trade.

Choi Jai came up trumps. Two days later, we stood in the compound of Central police station and looked over the squad transport. It was an old Nissan taxi. Its boxy bodywork was a faded fire engine red. It had a list to starboard and the tyres held only the memory of a tread. The Bull shook his head. Ah Fan folded her arms and made a show of looking away. Dee Jai just stared at it in silence.

I hardly dared ask. 'How much?'

Choi Jai was delighted with himself. 'No cost,' he chortled. 'But we give it back when tax expires.'

I asked what kind of car dealer his friend was.

Choi Jai grinned. 'Not car dealer; scrap merchant.'

He showed me a clunky lever snuggled between the driver's seat and the driver's door. The lever was standard in Hong Kong taxis. Choi Jai jerked it upwards and with a groan, the rear door swung open. He pushed the handle down and the door slammed shut. Instantly, the window disappeared inside the door and there was a tinkle of breaking glass. Choi Jai invited The Bull to sit behind the steering wheel. He settled onto the bench seat and a seat spring popped. The Bull turned the ignition key and to everyone's surprise, the engine started first time. Black smoke shot from the exhaust and drifted across the compound. He eased off the accelerator and apart from the diesel's characteristic clatter, it sounded fine. The floor was bare metal, the bench seats were torn and lumpy. It was big, ugly and it was falling apart. It was perfect.

I headed back to the office. Two-Zero met me with a satisfied smile. I opened the filing cabinet and found it stuffed with neatly jacketed files. I flicked through them: 'Correspondence In,' 'Correspondence Out,' 'Narcotics,' 'Gambling,' and 'Monthly Report.' He had prepared case registers, witness lists, exhibit folios and the all-important court dates. The office was clean and he had even placed fresh fruit on the Kwandai shrine's offerings shelf. I opened the file marked 'Monthly Report.' There were rows of neat figures showing the number of arrests for narcotics and gambling. Every month, the same kind of cases and virtually in the same number. There was no shortage of arrests but they were mostly for petty offences: street gambling or possessing a small packet of heroin. This was lazy policing: easy cases and in just the right quantity to keep the bosses happy. I refused to blame the squad, this was down to a leadership culture. Something had to change.

I ordered a plastic display board to show our arrest figures. It carried two main headings. The first was, 'Narcotics,' and under it were two sub-heads: 'Possession' and 'Trafficking.' The other heading was, 'Gambling,' and under that were the sub-heads, 'Players' and 'Organisers.' At the top of the board in English and Chinese was our new mission statement:

'IT'S NOT IMPOSSIBLE -- IT'S ONLY VERY DIFFICULT.'

I had done all I could. We had transport of a sort, we had radios that might work in line of sight on a clear day, and we had a make-do administration system. All that was missing was Kwandai's blessing.

Our *Baai Kwandai* started just before noon. We laid a small suckling pig on a table before the shrine. We burnt paper offerings and filled our little office with eye-stinging incense. We ate the pork and drank the beer. The shrine stayed fixed to the wall and we did not set fire to the building. Kwandai seemed to approve of his new apprentice, which was good because as things turned out, we would need all the help we could get.

CHAPTER 11
DEALERS AND PLAYERS

THEY SAY SHIT rolls downhill, and so it does. The assistant commissioner in charge of Hong Kong Island wanted more cases so he leaned on the superintendent (operations) who looked for the nearest person downslope. That was me.

The easy course would have been to follow the same old pattern: pull in more drug addicts and nab a few more workers relaxing over a game of *pai-gow* in the street. But I wanted something better. Street-level trafficking is easier to prove than most people think. Mister Chan gives Mister Wong a packet of drugs and that's it, another honest-to-goodness drug trafficker is in the cells. No need to prove sale, just handing the stuff over is good enough for the case to stick. It takes time, though. Good operations need planning, reconnaissance and lots of luck. I wheedled some binoculars and a camera from the Island CID intelligence unit then found a useful spot on the roof of a Connaught Road West godown.

The next day, Dee Jai and I sweated in our rooftop post. We watched *gu-leis* toiling under the weight of sacks and cartons. Trucks came and went. There was the constant din of truck engines and derrick motors. A uniformed constable stepped from a side street. A man lounging by the roadside put two fingers to his mouth and gave a long whistle. *Gu-leis* squatting behind piles of cargo stood, then ran in different directions leaving behind a detritus of matchbox covers and scorched tinfoil. With a *THWACK*, a *gu-lei* dropped a carton on the sidewalk behind the constable. The constable flinched then his neck reddened as the cargo basin filled with jeers. As he continued along Connaught Road, a *gu-lei* followed, making lewd gestures with his fingers.

'Got him, *Dai-lo.*' Dee Jai handed me the binoculars and pointed to a man near the harbour wall. He was middle-aged and looked tense, like a deer at a waterhole. He wore the grubby shorts and singlet of a waterfront labourer but his skin was pale, his muscles soft, his hair styled. Nearby stood a younger man, also dressed in work clothes. In a loose circle around them, others watched the street. They were having a busy day; it took just half an hour to figure out how it all worked. Addicts approached the younger man and gave him the money. The younger man passed a single packet to the older man who gave it to the addict. The older man was running the show but did not trust his assistant to complete the deal. Drug traffickers often took the money then refused to hand over the drugs. This led to fights and the older man wanted no problems on that score. Fights attracted the police.

I gave them nicknames. Nicknames made log-keeping easier and showed we had not concocted the log afterwards. We called the younger man 'Banker' and the older man 'Dealer.' Dealer was smart; he never held more than one packet and it was clear he dealt only with known customers. Banker took all the risks. I figured he was holding lots of little packets of heroin. If there was a raid, he had to choose between hanging onto the drugs or dumping them in the harbour. He risked hefty jail time if he hung onto them but if he dumped them too soon he would have to cover the loss. On top of that, he would no doubt take a punishment beating.

Dealer thought he was safe but there was a hole in his plan. If we grabbed a customer after he made the deal, we would have the case nailed; one dealer, one addict, one packet of heroin, the courts loved it. But it was tricky; if we lost sight of the addict, even for a second, the evidence chain would break and the case would be a dud.

I left Dee Jai at the observation post with orders to get photographs and to write everything into the log. I went back to the office to brief the rest of the squad. The plan was simple, Dee Jai would man the observation post whilst Choi Jai and I would wait nearby with a raiding party. When Dee Jai saw a deal go down, he would alert us by radio. Choi Jai would move in, arrest the addict and seize his drugs. This should distract the lookouts while the rest of us slipped in to scoop up Dealer. He would be clean and unworried. I doubted he would put up resistance, but for the plan to work, we had to stay calm. No headlong charge down Connaught Road, no noisy confrontations with the lookouts. Success lay with an unhurried infiltration. Key words were: *calm, slow, quiet.*

I briefed the squad but they kept throwing little spanners into my finely oiled works.

'What if the radios don't work?'

'What if someone sees us in the side streets?'

'What if the first arrest doesn't distract them?'

The plan that had at first seemed great was now full of holes. I could see dozens of things that might go wrong. But it was too late; it was time to get started.

Choi Jai switched on the Storno and it made a noise like a summer rainstorm. 'Dee Jai, this is Choi Jai. Testing, over.' A blare of static answered him. He banged the radio against the dashboard then held it to his ear and shook it like a mysterious parcel. 'Bloody *lap-sap*. Bloody rubbish,' he grumbled.

I told him to relax, we were still in the station compound and it would take a miracle to contact Dee Jai from here with a Storno.

Choi Jai was not convinced. '*Lap-sap* radios; *lap-sap* car.' He nodded towards the station report room. '*Lap-sap* bloody cooperation.'

'*Mo cho jue* -- shut up,' I snapped and instantly regretted it. We were all stressed.

Choi Jai hunkered down in the seat. 'No overtime pay, no plain clothes allowance ...' He caught my warning glare and fell silent.

The Bull slipped into the back seat next to Ah Fan. By now the rest of the squad would be taking up position in the alleys and lanes. If anyone spotted them, the operation was blown. The Nissan's engine coughed then clattered to life. I crunched it into gear and we rolled out of the station yard. The traffic was heavy and we were behind schedule. As we inched along Des Voeux Road West, I pictured Dee Jai on the godown roof, checking his watch, wondering where we were. I turned off the main road and pulled into the kerb. A few yards ahead was the Connaught Road West cargo basin. I pulled on a baseball cap and tugged at the peak, concealing my Western eyes. I nodded to Choi Jai and he pressed the Storno's transmit button.

'Dee Jai, this is Choi Jai. Over.' The radio hissed. I felt the operation start to unravel.

'Dee Jai, this is Choi Jai. Over.'

A voice crackled back. 'Choi Jai. This is Dee ... *hiss* ... Jai. Over.'

'Dee Jai, this is Choi Jai. *Yue bei* -- get ready, over.'

Dee Jai acknowledged and the radio went silent.

Choi Jai unfastened his door and tensed like a sprinter on the blocks. I pulled the baseball cap lower and hunched down in the seat. I could hear The Bull breathing, fast and heavy. Ah Fan was still. The radio was silent. What was happening? The sun streamed through the windscreen and the temperature climbed. An addict wandered into our side street from Connaught Road. He peered at us and stopped. If he turned back, it was all over. For a moment, the addict paused then he walked on past us. Next time we might not be so lucky. *What was happening?* The radio poured out a stream of static. I checked my watch, only three minutes since our arrival.

The radio chattered into life. 'Choi Jai, this is Dee Jai ... *Go. Go. Go.*'

Choi Jai was half out of the car but I held him back. I snatched the Storno from him. 'Dee Jai, description of buyer.'

More static hissed from the Storno. '*Shit* ... Dee Jai, description. Descri ...'

Dee Jai's transmission cut across mine. 'Male, blue T-shirt, red shorts. Heading ... *hiss* ... right for you. *Go. Go.*'

I swore as Choi Jai shot from the car and sprinted for the waterfront. *Slow down.* I put the car into gear. It juddered and nearly stalled. *Calm, slow, quiet*; easy to say during the briefing. I wanted to floor the accelerator but instead, I hunched my shoulders and chugged along in first gear. We reached the junction as Choi Jai grabbed a man wearing a blue T-shirt and red shorts. I scanned the junction, the *gu-leis* had stopped to watch the show. Two of them wore blue T-shirts and red shorts. *Shit*, had we got the wrong man? Choi Jai pushed his prisoner into the middle of the road; a floorshow for the crowd. I eased into Connaught Road and drove past lookouts too busy abusing Choi Jai to pay attention to a battered illegal taxi. We were yards from Dealer and Banker. They must see us. In seconds, they could be gone, swallowed by the crowd of hook-wielding *gu-leis*. Dealer was calm; Banker was twitchy. I eased off the accelerator and the car slowed to a crawl. Dealer saw us. I lowered my head. He shot me a scowl and signalled me to keep moving.

I braked to a halt, the rear door level with Dealer. He banged on the roof and jerked his thumb, signalling me to move on. The Bull reached for the door catch and for the first time, I saw a flaw in my plan. How could I have missed it? I grabbed the lever by the driver's seat and forced it down. The Bull could not open his door. He threw me an angry look and the lever bucked as he put his shoulder to the door. I eased the car forward as though obeying Dealer's instruction. Banker squinted at me and horror darkened his face. I stamped on the brake. Ah Fan yelped as she shot

CHRIS EMMETT

forward and smacked into the back of my seat. The Bull flashed me a grin. Call it coppers' telepathy, call it what you like but he knew what I wanted. I let go the door lever and banged my fist on the steering wheel. *'Go. Bloody go.'*

The Bull bolted from the car like a greyhound from the traps. Banker snatched a bag from his pocket and took a step towards the sea wall. The Bull charged across the short stretch of pavement and grabbed him in a giant hug, pinning his arms. I climbed from the driver's seat. Ah Fan raced ahead of me. She pointed at Dealer. Her voice was shrill. *'Chai Yan. Mo yuk!'--* Police. Freeze.

Dealer smiled like the victim of a good-natured joke. He raised his arms in a gesture that said, 'Go ahead, search me.'

As Ah Fan wrenched his arms behind his back, he flashed her a lewd grin and whispered something to her. He winced as she snapped handcuffs onto his wrists and ratcheted them into place. 'Tight enough?' she asked, with a wicked smile.

The rest of the squad emerged from the side streets and formed a circle around us. Nearby, *gu-leis* muttered threats but stayed back.

'Dai-lo, look.' The Bull was grinning like a schoolboy. He shoved a paper bag at me and peeled back the opening to reveal dozens of small packets. He reached into Banker's pocket and fished out a ball of crumpled banknotes. Choi Jai joined us with his prisoner and showed me a packet of number three heroin. Dee Jai appeared, he was fizzing with excitement. He had photographed the deal and the addict's arrest. The evidence chain was intact. I almost dared not believe it, it was a clean sweep.

We'd got the lot.

In 1850, Hong Kong saw an outbreak of common sense, but it did not last long.

The governor, Sir John Bowring realised that if he legalised gambling, he could tax it. His masters in Whitehall muttered into their beards about the profane sins of gambling and scotched the whole notion. Satisfied they had saved the vice-ridden Chinese from themselves, the good men of the colonial office repaired to their clubs for snifter of brandy, a hand of cards and maybe a turn or two at the wheel. A decade later, a new governor, Sir Richard MacDonnell had the same idea. He was a tough old nut and he resisted Whitehall's attempts to interfere. For five years, Hong Kong used gambling taxes to fund its police force. Then the secretary of state stepped in and over MacDonnell's fiery objections, brought an end to legalised gambling. The casinos closed their doors, Hong Kong's triad societies thanked the gods of fortune and a century later it was part of my job was to suppress illegal gambling.

My first-ever gambling raid had been two years earlier in a small border village and it had turned into a farce when a goose attacked the raiding party. Like they say: you live and learn. Lesson number one: expect the unexpected. Lesson number two: don't forget lesson number one.

Good lessons. If only I had remembered them.

The senior superintendent (general duties) called me in for a routine interview. He was an agreeable Irishman but had a fearsome reputation for stamping on dissent. However, on that day he could not have been more affable. In fact he was so affable I let my guard slip. Big mistake. We talked about the island's narcotics and gambling problems then I let slip it had been two years since a senior officer had spent time with the squad.

'Really?' he said. 'Can't have that. No, no, no. We can't have that at all. No, we can't. Can we? No.' He reached for his desk diary. 'Give me a date and time.'

I had not expected him to take me up on it and I babbled on about shift patterns and operational commitments. But it was too late, he had called my bluff and he sat with his pen poised over the open diary. Then I saw it: the perfect chance to show what the squad could do. I had some reliable gambling information and this was the perfect chance to act on it. It was time for a little self-promotion.

Choi Jai had received information about a gambling divan on a hillside overlooking Bay View. We had checked it out and it looked good. It stood half hidden in foliage next to a hillside construction site. It was the size of a large house. It had a flat roof and an iron frame. The walls were of unpainted plywood. It had one door and no windows. It was a policeman's dream: a gambling divan with only one way in and, more importantly, only one way out. We had spent days watching and picking up on the divan's working pattern. We had seen a constant stream of hard-hatted construction workers enter and leave. There were no watchmen and that bothered me; there were always watchmen. Either the divan keeper was sloppy or the information was wrong. We could not see inside but the noise was unmistakable. Gambling divans have a noise all of their own, a supercharged babble of triumph and despair. Our hillside structure was a gambling divan all right, and a big one.

But still, it niggled me; something was wrong. We checked it out again. The unpainted plywood walls were unmarked and the iron frame did not carry even a hint of rust. It was just weeks old and no doubt served workers from the nearby building site. Hong Kong building sites had a fast turnover of workers so slipping the squad inside the place would be easy. I should have been a happy inspector. I had a juicy divan ready for plucking and I had a senior superintendent willing to watch me pluck it. What more could I want?

The boss arrived at the squad office just before dusk. He chatted with the team then signed the visits and inspections register. He leaned back in the chair and folded his hands across his stomach.

'Well now,' he said. 'You said something about a gambling raid, so you did. Didn't you? Yes you did.'

I felt a twinge of uncertainty but persuaded myself there was nothing to worry about. I had borrowed some builders' hard hats and that afternoon two of my men had walked unchallenged into the divan. Inside they found six tables and dozens of construction workers laying bets worth thousands of dollars. All was going to plan. On top of the assortment of helpers and bouncers, there were six table captains reporting to one divan keeper who oversaw everything from a perch on top of a high stool. There would be no mistaking him, he was a one-eyed dwarf with a wicked scar running from forehead to jaw.

It was a fifteen-minute drive to Bay View police station. The senior superintendent declined my offer of a seat in our scrapyard Nissan and took his staff car. The Bay View gate guard babbled a warning down the phone as the staff car swept past him. We settled ourselves into the station briefing room and I went through the plan again. Dressed in helmets and work-clothes, the squad looked like a gang of construction workers. In groups of twos and threes, they would infiltrate the divan, identify the operators, cover the tables and guard the only exit. When the boss and I made our entrance, that would be the signal for the squad to grab the exhibits and declare the arrest of everyone in sight. We had done it all before and the mood in the briefing room was relaxed, some might say we were even a little cocky.

We rendezvoused at a track leading to the construction site. The staff car would attract too much attention so the boss rode in the Nissan. Choi Jai and Ah Fan were in the back where they sat in intimidated silence. I put The Bull in charge and sent the squad up ahead. I gave them ten minutes then set off after them. Where the track petered out, I pulled into the shadows. A man in a hardhat emerged from the dark. I held my breath but he was one of my constables. He bent his head close to my window and tried to ignore the boss.

'Squad all inside now, *Dai-lo*,' he said. He looked around, making sure we were alone. 'Many construction workers playing *pai-gow, fan-tan, dai-saai, yue ha hai*. Many games. Thousands of dollars.'

From where I sat, I could hear the telltale din of a gambling divan working at full steam. It was all going fine, I could not figure why I was so nervous and put it down to having the senior superintendent along for the ride. I turned to Choi Jai. 'I'll give you a couple of minutes,' I said. 'When we walk in, go for it.'

Choi Jai and Ah Fan moved off. There was a blast of noise as they opened the door. For a moment, the divan's lights threw hard shadows then the door closed behind them and they were gone. I waited two long minutes then nodded to the boss and we followed. We paused at the door. Doubt nagged at me but I shrugged it off. I opened the door and the noise hit me like a shock wave. It was a noise unlike any other; it was joy and despair all mashed together. I stepped across the threshold and blinked in the glare of unshaded ceiling lights. Gaming tables lined the walls. Slick table captains threw dice, dealt cards and counted off *fan-tan* beads. The air was thick with tobacco smoke. The rank tobacco smell mingled with the stench of stale sweat. Punters clamoured around the games, jostling, shouting and throwing banknotes onto the tables. There were brown five-dollar bills, green ten-dollar bills, red one hundreds and some blue five hundreds. In an instant, the captains scooped them up and jammed them into their cashboxes. Two muscular bouncers moved in behind an animated player who was disputing a game call.

A ripple of silence started at the door and spread through the divan as the gamblers caught sight of two Europeans. Into this silence came Choi Jai's voice. '*Chai yan. Kei jue.*' -- Police. Don't move. '*Kei jue, kei jue.*' He was holding up his warrant card and turning full circle. At the tables, the captains could only gape as my squad members produced warrant cards and shouted, '*Chai yan. Kei jue.*'

At the far end of the room, perched on a tall stool, was the dwarf. A livid scar cut across his forehead, disappeared behind a black eye-patch then scoured his cheek from eye-patch to jaw.

In the hard lights, it was the face from a nightmare. Triumph surged through me. I looked at the dwarf expecting to see panic but instead, a crooked smile formed on his lips. Hanging from the ceiling above his head was what looked like a large stirrup. I thought it was to help him climb on and off the stool but I was wrong. He reached up, grabbed the stirrup with both hands and pulled down. Instantly, the lights snapped out and there were a series of loud *thunks*, as though someone had shot the bolts to a dozen doors. There came a creak, like a rusty hinge on an ironbound door. The noise came from every direction, it filled the room. I had no idea what it was but knew it had to be really, really bad.

And then there was light. It seeped in from where the walls joined the roof. It was an eerie silver light, like moonlight. Indeed, it was moonlight. I had not noticed before but there was a gap between the walls and the roof. The creaking grew louder, the gap grew wider. Now I could see shapes of people, surprised and motionless like a school play tableau. It took a second for me to realise that all four walls were collapsing outwards. With a splintering *whack*, they hit the ground, covering everyone with stinging grit. Around me, players, table captains, bouncers and policemen stood frozen as if in a tableau. Then, in an instant, the tableau sprung to life. Moments earlier, I had a room full of prisoners; now they were all clumping over the fallen plywood and fanning out in every direction. The squad danced around, arms outstretched like a one-sided game of catch-me-if-you-can. My prisoners disappeared into the undergrowth and along the road. We were alone: a perplexed inspector and a dozen bemused special duty squad officers.

And the most bad-tempered, foul-mouthed senior superintendent I have ever known.

That spring, my six-month tour with the special duty squad ended. Just one last piece of gambling information to deal with and I would be ready for a new posting. As usual, our informant was a disgruntled punter who had bet a month's pay on a horse that came in fourth. He had placed the bet with an illegal bookie working out of a staircase landing in a Chai Wan public housing project. Come the day, I sent in two of my new constables to confirm the location, place a bet and bring back the evidence of a betting slip. Within half an hour, they were back. No problems, the bookie was on the landing between the fifth and sixth floors. He had taken our ten dollar bet and issued a hand-written betting slip. All we had to do was step in and scoop him up. I put half the squad on the fifth floor, half on the sixth and within ten minutes, we had ourselves a tasty little bookmaking case. We had the bookie cold and he came along like a little lamb. For me, this final case was doubly rewarding. The bookie was a dwarf. A livid scar cut across his forehead, disappeared behind a black eye-patch then scoured his cheek from eye-patch to jaw.

'Got you,' I crowed.

With his one good eye, the dwarf shot me a quizzical look. He spoke English with an accent straight from the streets of South L.A.

'*Huh?* What the hell you talkin' about?'

'I got you,' I said again. 'Causeway Bay, three weeks ago.'

He looked puzzled.

'Your trick gambling divan, the one with the collapsing walls. You were head keeper. I saw you; you can't deny it.'

The dwarf fixed me with a glittering eye then shook his head. '*Nah*, not me bud,' he said. 'I think you got me mixed up with someone else.'

We held a small party in the squad room. Choi Jai brought cakes and I splashed out on a bottle of champagne. In my final month, we had notched up fourteen drug trafficking cases, a squad record. I filled plastic cups with champagne and toasted the squad. The Bull sipped the champagne then pulled a face and topped it up with lemonade. I wrote a glowing staff report for each member of the squad, thanked them for their support and that was it. I prepared a handover report for my successor and reported to the superintendent (operations). He read over my transfer report and told me I could look forward to a cushy, nine-to-five job. The administration wing needed someone to carry out a review of overtime claims and, joy-oh-joy, the job was all mine. It sounded perfect: an air-conditioned office, regular hours, weekends and public holidays off. My brain would rot but so what? I would be a staff inspector. Staff inspectors wrote curt memos, set impossible deadlines and, under the protection of their boss, assumed authority far beyond their rank. Staff inspectors were special; they were the anointed ones. Of course, everyone hated them.

Superintendent (operations) must have guessed I was not keen on the idea. I suppose there was some hint of that in my body language: a fixed grin, pleading eyes and white knuckles gripping the edge of his desk. He leaned forward and gave me the last word in persuasive argument. 'It's either that or CID.'

No sane Hong Kong policeman volunteered for the criminal investigation department. Detective work sounds great; everyone thought detectives spent their days solving crossword puzzles and their nights checking out nightclubs. Reality was very different: the basic working week was more than sixty hours and detective inspectors were so busy wading through paperwork, they had no time to solve crime let alone crossword puzzles. CID was always last in line for decent equipment, detectives even bought their own typewriters.

CID or overtime review? Tough call.

CHAPTER 12
DAIRYMEN AND FOLLOWERS

IAN TOSHACH MADRUGER was everything a detective chief inspector should be. He stood six foot tall, weighed 200 pounds and had a face only a rock-climber could love. He was middle-aged and had thick jet-black hair brushed back in the style of a 1950s teddy boy. He spoke with an Edinburgh accent that sounded like chipped granite. He also had a prominent lisp and as he talked, he would wipe flecks of saliva from his chin. Madruger was the detective training school's course director and on our first day, he stood before the class, feet apart, hands clasped behind his back. There were a dozen inspectors in the classroom. Beside me sat a fair-haired man called Jeremy Kays and I remember thinking he did not look tough enough for CID. First impressions were never my strong point; years later, this quiet and intelligent man took command of the force's elite counter terrorist unit.

Madruger's voice filled the room. 'I take it you have read the joining instructions.' He pronounced it, 'joining inthtructhionth' and wiped his chin.

We all nodded.

'Good. Then you have all brought with you two, pathportthized photographth.'

We grabbed our joining instructions and shuffled through them. Ah, there it was, clear and simple: 'Bring two passport-sized photographs.' As one, we smiled at Madruger and shook our heads. Madruger sighed and stormed out of the classroom, slamming the door behind him. That was a turnaround; I could not believe a few missing photographs would so upset someone with Madruger's hard-man reputation.

All became clear when a slim Chinese officer entered the room and handed out single sheets of typing paper. He spoke in an imperious voice. 'You will now write a detailed description of the officer who just left the room. Include physical details, dress and peculiarities. You have five minutes.'

We huddled over our papers and scribbled descriptions of Madruger. No problem, we were professional police officers, right? Now, was that a blue shirt or was it green? I tried to sneak a look at my neighbour's work but he saw me and shielded it with his arm. Five minutes later, Madruger returned and went around the desks collecting the descriptions. He shuffled through them, pausing to read one aloud.

'Average height. Athletic build.' He jiggled his paunch, a veteran of every downtown police bar. 'What the bloody hell?' He held another sheet at arm's length and squinted at it. 'Broad Irish bloody acthent.' As he read the final sheet, his face reddened and his voice choked, whether with anger or laughter, I was never sure. 'Mithter Kayth.' The trainee closest to Madruger ducked to avoid the spray. 'Which one of you bloody lot ith Mithter, bloody Kayths.'

Jeremy raised his hand. 'That would be me, sir.'

Madruger thrust the sheet of paper at Kays. 'Read it out, boy,' he growled. 'Read it now.'

Jeremy Kays took the sheet and cleared his throat. '*Ahem* ... Peculiarities: His mouth waters when he talks about homosexuals.' He returned Madruger's glare with a saintly smile. 'First thing I noticed, sir. Do I pass?'

We spent the first five weeks going over the nuts and bolts of divisional CID work. After the classroom phase, there would be practical exercises under the critical eyes of the training staff, all of whom were experienced detectives. But first, we had to sit through lectures on the law concerning theft, assaults, public order and triads. We studied the rights of prisoners and the legal authority for police to arrest and detain suspects. We learned how to manage a crime scene and what specialist units to call upon. We had talks from fingerprint experts, scientific evidence officers, ballistics officers and the government chemist but the most memorable talk came from the pathologist. No one forgets the pathologists' lecture because the pathologists did not come to the detective training school; the detective training school went to them.

Mortuaries are cheerful places. They are clean, tidy, well lit and there is a constant stream of banter between pathologists and mortuary assistants. Despite this, our mood was grim as we took our places around an examination table where a cadaver waited under a plastic sheet. The pathologist was a jolly man who did his best to put us at ease. He pulled back the sheet and briefed us on post-mortem procedures. There were a few pale faces when he made the first incision but he was an excellent speaker and we started to take a real interest in what he was doing. We remained commendably stoic until half way through the examination.

'This is most unusual.' the pathologist said, bending nearer to the cadaver. 'Indeed, most unusual. Come closer.'

We pressed closer. Too late, I saw the mortuary attendants exchange knowing smiles. The pathologist probed with his scalpel and sprayed us with some unspeakable body fluid. Two trainees rolled back their eyes and crumpled to the mortuary floor. The rest of us gagged, swore and staggered back. The mortuary crew broke into applause and the pathologist bowed in return.

'Sorry, just a little pathology humour,' he said. 'Now, come back and I'll show you something really fascinating.' There were no takers.

We skipped lunch and returned to the training school. By the afternoon, we had recovered enough to sit through a talk by a sociology professor on the subject of community policing. The professor proposed that in modern times, Hong Kong citizens should not have to put up with the ever-looming presence of armed and booted policemen.

'When I see a policeman, I see a man with a gun,' he declared. 'In my books, that's institutional violence.'

I put on my wide-eyed choirboy look. 'But if the police stay off the streets,' I asked, 'who'll control the ratbags?'

The professor looked at me as though I were a much-loved puppy caught next to a suspicious puddle on the kitchen floor. 'My *dear* boy,' he said, in a pained voice, 'to call them "ratbags" is crass oversimplification. Modern society creates a disenfranchised underclass that can express its frustrations only through empowering acts such as vandalism or violence.'

'*Ahhh*, of course,' I said, the picture of an enlightened convert. 'And there's me thinking they were just a bunch of arseholes.'

The afternoon wore on and our exchanges became more vigorous, the professor's tone more fiery. The afternoon ended with him shouting in white-lipped fury that we were all colonial fascists and one day, the will of the great proletariat masses would sweep us into the ashcan of history. I found later that he drew a salary equal to the police commissioner and lived in one of the island's swankiest apartment blocks.

A visiting magistrate told us that evidence of confessions was almost worthless because magistrates believed detectives extracted them by force. Sadly, this view was due almost entirely to a spectacular own goal scored ten years earlier by a detective inspector called 'Hooker' White.

Hooker had been in CID for a year when uniform branch handed him the case that would make him famous. It concerned a piece of street thuggery that was nasty but not unusual. In fact, if not for the failure of a beat constable, a station duty officer and a CID inspector to search the shirt pocket of a triad bully called Ricky Chong, no one would have paid the case any attention.

It started when Ricky demanded money with menaces from a newspaper hawker. The hawker was slow to react so Ricky gave him a sharp punch on the nose. Ricky's timing could not have been worse. No sooner had his victim's backside hit the sidewalk when who should round the corner but the local beat constable. The constable grabbed Ricky and marched him off to the police station with the unhappy newspaper hawker trailing behind.

The case found its way to the CID squadroom on the station's fourth floor. Afraid of repercussions, the hawker refused to press charges and Hooker found himself without a case. That would not do at all; detection-wise, Hooker was having a lean month. If he could lay a charge against Ricky, then the statistics would credit him with a detected crime. Hooker thought about the problem, but the hawker's refusal to lay a complaint left him no choice; Hooker would charge Ricky Chong with 'motsi.'

Membership of a triad society had been a criminal offence since 1845 but MOTS, known as 'motsi,' was hard to prove. Victims were too frightened to speak and unless a police officer overheard someone admitting they were a triad, then there was never enough evidence. If Hooker wanted to nail Ricky for motsi, he would need a confession. Hooker told his sergeant to bring Ricky into his office and to shut the door.

One hour later, Ricky Chong scowled at the statement form before him but signed it anyway. It began with the familiar phrase: 'You are not obliged to say anything ...' It went on to tell of a childhood during which bigger boys had bullied Ricky without mercy. Everything changed when a young man called Ah Keung took Ricky under his wing and changed his life forever. At the mention of Ah Keung's name, bullies backed down and street vendors would slip Ricky a few dollars. Then, one day, Ah Keung asked Ricky to join him and some other boys in a secret oath that would bind them closer than family. Ricky agreed and

so became a full member of the 14K triad society. With this statement, Ricky Chong admitted he was a triad soldier. Hooker read
the English translation with satisfaction. It was a story of pathos
and drama, it was the best damned confession he had ever read.
It was perfect.

The sergeant sorted the paperwork and took Ricky to the report room. He handed him to the duty officer who logged the arrest then handed Ricky to the cell guard constable. The constable
took Ricky into his care but before locking him up, he searched
him. And that is where the keystone to Hooker's downfall
clunked into place. This was the very first time since his arrest
that anyone had searched Ricky. The constable took Ricky's belt,
his shoelaces, his wallet, his ballpoint pen, his wristwatch and
cigarettes. He frowned, did no one search prisoners any more?
He sealed everything in a property envelope, made an entry in
the register and locked up Ricky for the night. Had the script
played out properly, Ricky would have gone to court, pleaded
guilty and the magistrate would have slapped his wrist. Instead,
the divisional detective inspector got a morning call from the
court prosecutor. After the briefest of chats with the prosecutor,
it was a very upset DDI who called Hooker into his office. Without inviting Hooker to sit, he came to the point, 'Did you dangle
a prisoner from your window to make him admit to motsi?'

Hooker was outraged, how could anyone dream of such a
thing?

The DDI told Hooker that not only had Ricky Chong dreamed
up such a thing, he had convinced the magistrate he could prove
it. At that very moment, the magistrate and his entourage were
on their way to the station.

Hooker decided to stay quiet. He knew he was guilty and so
did the DDI but knowing it and proving it were two different
things. Hooker was worried but not panicked.

The DDI lowered his voice. 'Is there anything you want to tell
me before they arrive?'

'No, of course not,' said Hooker and with those words, lost any chance of salvation.

Later that morning, the magistrate presented himself before the DDI. With him was the court interpreter, the magistrate's clerk, the prosecutor and finally, handcuffed to a constable, was Ricky himself. The magistrate wiped his brow with a huge handkerchief and demanded to see Hooker's office. The DDI led the way; the magistrate and his group followed. Behind them trudged an increasingly worried Hooker White.

The magistrate opened the window, letting in a blast of summer heat. 'Bad do, chief inspector,' he said. He ran his hands over the window ledge. 'Can't see anything though.' He leaned further out of the window and squawked as his feet left the floor. If the DDI had not grabbed his belt, he would have tumbled into the compound, four floors below. The DDI decided an external examination was needed. He called for a ladder and looked around for a volunteer to climb it. His eyes zeroed in on Hooker, 'Not scared of heights are you, Mister White?'

The barrack sergeant produced a ladder and Hooker began to climb. By the time he reached the first floor, he could make out a blue mark a few feet below his office window. His knees weakened but the mark drew him on. He prayed the mark was just a touch of mildew. No such luck; the writing was shaky but legible:

Ricky Chong

Hooker looked down into the compound. Below him, the DDI stood waiting. And with him was a crime scene photographer.

Our final lecture was on criminal intelligence gathering, which for me was something mythical. For years, I had read CID arrest reports that included phrases like, 'acting on information received' and 'following covert intelligence gathering.' Intelligence gathering was what set detectives apart from the mortals in uniform. On the day of the lecture, I felt like an acolyte awaiting the mystic rites of an ancient guild.

Jack Owens would deliver the talk. Jack was a force training officer but what marked him out from the other FTOs was that he was an ex-London detective. Jack Owens was an honest-to-goodness Scotland Yard man. He was dapper and youthful. His eyes were bright and his voice carried the slightest hint of cockney twang. He stood before the lectern and took a few seconds to organise his notes before starting.

'All detectives need good informants.'

I wrote it down, eager not to miss anything.

'So, tell me,' he continued. 'Who's your best informant?'

That threw me, I did not know. I wrote down the question and sat, pen poised, waiting for Jack to enlighten me. The question met a wall of silence but Jack was not ruffled. He smiled encouragement. 'Come on, it's no great mystery.' He pointed to the nearest trainee who looked hopefully over his shoulder at the man behind. 'No, not him,' Jack chided. 'Think about it. Who's your best informant?'

'I think ...' the trainee furrowed his brow. '... I'm not sure.'

Jack pointed at another trainee.

'Drug addicts,' came back the answer.

'No.' Jack pointed at somebody else.

'Other criminals.'

Jack warmed to the challenge. 'No. Next. Come on, it's obvious. I'll give you a clue. Who knows everyone? Who sees everything?' He worked his way around the class, no one escaped. He met each answer with a chuckle. 'No, no, no. More obvious than that, much more.'

I felt I was on the verge of a great discovery but lacked eyes to see it.

'You'll kick yourselves.' Jack looked round the classroom making 'come on, come on,' gestures with both hands. He folded his arms, shook his head and leaned on the lectern. 'It's ... the milkman.'

I wrote down, 'milkman' then reread my notes. So far, I had written, 'detectives need informants,' 'best informant is?' and 'milkman.' I thought it might be a code and tried to see the hidden meaning. Jack beamed at the trainees. The trainees stared back. Then it struck me: from the English copper's viewpoint, Jack was right. Back in England, every neighbourhood had a friendly milk delivery man who knew the name of everyone on his round. He was up to date on all the local gossip but, bound by the milkman's unwritten code, he kept it all to himself. In fact, England had lots of neighbourhood service providers who were so familiar, they were almost invisible. There was Bob the postman, Eric the window cleaner, Peter who read the gas meter, and all the others. Between them, they knew everything and they were an invaluable source of information. It was a copper's dream but in Hong Kong, it would never be more than a daydream. I folded up my notes and checked the schedule for our next lecture.

It was the nature of Hong Kong policemen not to question the wisdom of their tutors and in deference to Jack, no one said a word. The British inspectors did not scoff at the idea of a cheerful milk float clinking its way around housing projects like Kwaishek Estate, delivering pints of milk, fresh eggs and yoghurt. The Chinese inspectors had never seen a milkman but sensed it was best not to ask questions. Later, a Chinese inspector told me his first reaction had been to sift through the pantheon of superheroes. He had heard of Superman, Batman and Spiderman but Milkman? That was a new one.

There was more to the detective training school than the classrooms. The complex was a maze of simulated crime scenes. There were interview rooms and incident control rooms. There was an identification parade room, a TV studio and a mock courtroom.

The training school could recreate almost every situation a junior detective would meet during his or her first year in CID. After five weeks in the classroom, we were looking forward to the practical stage. Madruger assigned each inspector a team comprising a trainee sergeant and three trainee constables. We would stay together for the rest of the course. My four officers still had the well-scrubbed uniform branch look: short hair, crisp shirts, neat slacks and shiny shoes. The sergeant was Armstrong Yee, an ex-detective constable who, some years ago, had moved back to uniform on promotion. Now he was back in CID. The constables were nervous and eager to make a good impression.

Madruger set up a simulated case for each team to investigate and we spent weeks chasing fingerprint reports, crime scene reports, building occupancy details, criminal records, intelligence reports and the million-and-one mundane but essential bits of paper that drive an investigation forward. As the simulated investigation went on, we put together an investigation file and eventually arrested a culprit. A real magistrate presided over our mock court where he found a villainous looking member of the training school staff guilty of burglary.

The final part of the practical phase was a surveillance exercise. After an hour-long lecture, we had the basics down pat; after all, how hard could it be? A staff inspector called Titch Ginty was the exercise co-ordinator and he handed out manila envelopes containing descriptions and photographs of our surveillance targets. My team's target was Titch himself. Great, Titch stood six-foot-three; the exercise would be a walkover.

Along with the description and the photograph was a list of rendezvous points. If we lost Titch, we would proceed to the next point, re-establish the tail and continue with the exercise. The stores clerk issued brand-new Motorola radios and I felt a flash of resentment when I remembered my fight to get a few battered Stornos for the special duty squad. I hefted the radio in my hand and realised they were our first problem. In its day, the Motorola was a great radio. In the concrete and steel heart of the city, it gave crystal-clear reception. A policeman could drop it, get it soaked in a tropical downpour, patrol all day under a baking sun and the Motorola would not let him down. The radio had just one drawback: like the Storno, it was the size of a house brick. If our haircuts and shiny shoes did not scream, 'plain-clothed policeman,' then the radios did the job nicely. We split a few trouser seams trying to fit the radios into our pockets. A constable tried to stuff one into the front of his waistband but after a few minutes it slipped down into his crotch where it formed an unusual and noisy bulge.

Armstrong Yee suggested we hide the radios inside envelopes but the only ones he could find bore the logo, 'On Her Majesty's Service.' In the end, we begged five, government briefcases from the stores clerk. They were black imitation leather and each had a government crest embossed on the flap. Time was running out so we boarded the transport taking us to the exercise location in Causeway Bay.

Causeway Bay was a bustling area of shops, restaurants and bars. The streets were hot and narrow, the traffic jams legendary. Day and night, crowds packed the sidewalks. Street vendors filled the alleys and lanes with their stalls. Their cries competed with storefront music for the attention of passers-by. If the police were not around, they set up their stalls on the main roads, forcing pedestrians off the sidewalks and into the already snarled traffic. Looking at the crowds, the traffic and the labyrinth of side lanes, I had a moment's doubt. Just walking along a Causeway Bay street was hard enough, let alone following someone. I calmed myself with the knowledge that the crowds would hide the team. All we had to do was keep track of a six-and-a-quarter foot tall European on a Hong Kong street full of Chinese who were more than a bit shorter.

Titch arrived and rolled his eyes. We were five young men, neatly dressed and all carrying government briefcases. We looked like a raiding party from the Census Department. A pass-er-by did a double take as a constable's briefcase crackled to life. 'Exercise control to Echo One -- radio check. Over.'

Titch told me the exercise had started. He strolled off down the street and we followed. We were masters of guile: we stuffed our hands into our pockets, we cast our eyes skyward, we scuffed our feet and whistled tunelessly. We followed Titch around a corner and it was if he had beamed into orbit. We searched the street. Nothing. I split the team into two groups and they searched the shops and alleys. Fifteen minutes later, they returned with bad news. No Titch. There was nothing for it but to move to the second rendezvous point. After an hour at the second RV, Armstrong spotted Titch ambling towards us. I chivvied the team into formation and we managed to latch onto him as he walked into a shopping mall. Titch wandered through the mall's lofty atrium and stepped onto an escalator leading to the first floor gallery. Two constables tried to follow but a group of schoolgirls cut in front of them and stood chattering and laughing on the es-calator. The girls ignored requests to move aside and made noisy complaints when the constables tried to squeeze through.

Titch began to stride up the escalator steps. From the atrium below, my heart sank as I watched his pace increase. Armstrong grabbed his remaining constable, an eager young man called Koo Jai and together they darted onto the parallel escalator. They either ignored or missed the sign that cautioned: 'Down Only.'

Armstrong tried to look casual as he bounded up the descend-ing escalator but he was not in good shape. After running flat out and not getting very far, his progress slowed and his run became a walk. He continued to climb upwards but it was clear he was moving inexorably downwards. With a jolt, the escala-tor decanted him back onto the atrium floor. He leaned, panting against a wall then looked at the escalator as though it was an unconquered mountain. He was a game so-and-so and had I not stopped him, he would have tried again, despite the 'up' escalator now being clear.

Koo Jai was younger and stronger. As Armstrong was regaining his breath, Koo Jai reached the gallery and pulled out his radio. At the bottom of the escalator, a florid woman dropped her shopping as Armstrong's brief case began to chatter. 'Sergeant Yee ... *gasp* ... Koo Jai ... over.'

Armstrong tried to open his briefcase but the catch stuck. He cursed between clenched teeth as he wrestled with it. I was dancing a circular jig in the middle of the atrium when Koo Jai's voice came across the radio. 'Target in view. First floor gallery, outside *Mundo Chinois Fashions*. Over.' I was half way up the escalator before Armstrong could answer and within seconds, the team joined me outside the fashion shop. Koo Jai pointed at the store window. 'In there, *Ah Sir*. Should be out soon.' A tall European in casual shirt and slacks stepped out of the shop. Koo Jai pulled at my shirtsleeve like a child desperate for the toilet. 'There, boss, there.' It was like a punch in the stomach; it was not Titch. I sent Armstrong into the shop to scout around. He came out a few seconds later and shrugged. No joy. He turned to Koo Jai who seemed to shrink to a third of his normal size. The other two constables closed in on him, fists clenching and unclenching. How could he have done it, how could anyone have lost a target built like an animated vaulting pole?

'*Ah Sir*, don't angry at me.' Koo Jai was close to tears. 'A *gwailo* is a *gwailo*. All look the same.'

Back at the detective training school, the debriefing room went quiet as Madruger led in a group of training staff. One by one, the staff went though their exercise notes. Most Hong Kong Police exercise debriefs focussed on what went wrong and it was good to find that DTS staff preferred to be positive. Echo Two, good use of cover. Echo Five, excellent communications and so on. I relaxed; surely, we had not done too badly. Okay, we had lost our target, twice. And okay, we had lost him within minutes but nobody is perfect, are they?

It was my turn. Titch flashed me a comforting smile. 'Ah. Mister Emmett.' The smile became wolf-like. 'Now, I don't mean to be cruel or anything.' I got a hollow feeling inside me. 'Are you ready to write this down?'

Indeed I was.

'Well, let's put it as kindly as possible,' he purred. 'You couldn't follow a five-legged donkey across fresh snow.'

That night, the inspectors, sergeants and constables all went out together. We drank lots of brandy and swore undying friendship. The next day we nursed sore heads as the DTS commandant made a speech and handed us our certificates.

Some time during the ceremony, we became detectives.

CHAPTER 13
THE KWANDAI'S LIEUTENANT

TV DETECTIVES HAVE a lot to answer for. Everyone knows how they behave: they sit in smoky rooms, surrounded by empty coffee cups, they loosen their ties and wear their hats on the back of their heads. When someone has the gall to shoot at him, the detective snatches a snub-nosed revolver from his shoulder holster and flicks open the chamber to make sure it is loaded. 'Gee, did I remember to put bullets in this gosh-darned thingamajig?' he asks himself. Then he flicks the chamber shut, thus guaranteeing that some time soon, the chamber lock will break and all his bullets will fall out. Our TV detective returns fire over amazing distances. He always hits the bad guy unless the bad guy is really an undercover detective, then he misses, but only by a smidgen.

Hong Kong detectives wore ties only to attend court and we never wore hats. Hong Kong detectives carried snub-nosed, Colt Detective Specials but our commissioner banned the use of shoulder holsters. Most detectives completed their service without firing a shot in anger. Luckily for the public, I never fired my snub-nosed revolver outside a police target range. The first time I fired my Detective Special was on the indoor range at police headquarters. At ten yards, the target was so close I thought I could touch it. I took aim and scored a nice little group between the shoulder blades. The range sergeant moved us back to the fifteen-yard mark and we fired six more shots. Again, the target seemed close but the extra five yards was too much for the Colt's stubby barrel and my tight little group hit the target's groin. As I left the range, I overheard the sergeant mutter to his assistant, 'Not bad shots, those CID boys. But they're gruesome bastards.'

My new posting was Central division on Hong Kong Island. The division covered Hong Kong's supercharged business district. In gleaming office blocks, floor directories bore the names IBM, Chase Manhattan and Sumito Corporation. Chauffeured limousines jammed the roads. Boisterous equity traders divided their times between the floor of the stock exchange and wood-panelled wine bars.

Behind the business district was Hong Kong's famous measure of social worth, Victoria Peak. The Peak was like a giant board game, the nearer you lived to the summit, the more status you had. If people drove the right car and lived at the right address, it did not matter if their forebears were counts or coolies. It was all about the money, or at least the appearance of money. Wealth meant success and success bred more money. Struggling businessmen often courted ruin by investing in a flat on the Peak and a Mercedes in the parking lot.

Central division was Hong Kong in microcosm. Anyone who has spent time in Hong Kong will tell you the place is just a big village. I suppose that is right but I always thought of it as a collection of villages. Of course, these are figurative, not actual villages but they are every bit as distinct and inward looking as the real thing. The Chinese middle class live in one village, the expatriate community live in another village, the Chinese working men and women live in yet another. The village concept was as true in the 1970s as it is now. In part, it was the basis of Hong Kong's rich diversity but at the same time, it drew invisible lines on the cultural landscape. These lines were subtle and divided us in ways not immediately clear to the newcomer. It was as if each village community lived behind walls of porous glass. We could see each other, we worked together, we socialised and we made lasting friendships. After a while, we became less aware of the cultural divides but somehow, they were always there.

The differences between us showed in small ways. At police social gatherings, Chinese and British unconsciously separated into two groups, each drawn by comfortable ties of language. This was not divisive, it was just human nature. In the street markets, there was one price for Chinese and another for foreigners. No matter how adept I became at haggling in Cantonese, I would never get as good a price as would a Chinese housewife. There was no dishonesty intended, it was just a game and the Chinese played it better than us. We expatriates did not help ourselves. There was a whole service sector built around Westerners. Need an English-speaking plumber? How about getting the parquet floor sealed and waxed? There was always someone ready to help, for a price of course. This made the busy expatriate's life easier but it perpetuated the myth that Westerners were separate from the real community. It suggested we had more money than good sense and were therefore fair game.

For the Chinese, life was very different. Many had arrived as refugees from China or were the children of refugees. Most had known great hardship and for them, life was all about pragmatic choices. Need to learn English for that vital promotion? Go to night school. Worried a colleague is outshining you? Work harder; be brighter.

So many differences between Easterner and Westerner: language, life experience, values, priorities and family background. Yet somehow, it all worked. Everyone rubbed along and did what Hong Kongers did best: worked hard and made money.

My base was Waterfront police station, which was not a police station at all but the converted first floor of a multi-storey car park. Wire mesh covered the windows and paint peeled from plywood partitions that divided the offices. My detective sergeant was Fu Jai, which meant Little Tiger. He was a quiet man with the stoic hardness of someone who has seen too much of life's uglier side. My detective constables were much the same: quiet and purposeful.

I headed one of four CID reserve teams. Every fourth day was our reserve day. Then, we worked a twenty-four hour shift that started at eight in the morning. During our reserve day, we picked up all the day's crime reports. Next day was supposed to be a rest day but if any leads needed follow-up, the shift would stretch to thirty or more hours.

I would be working for the divisional detective inspector, the DDI we called him. He was detective chief inspector Buster Kydd, a barrel of a man with the face of an ageing boxer and the booming voice of an East End street trader. His desk carried three 'in' trays, each full of blue-grey jacketed criminal investigation files. On the wall behind Buster's desk were a half-dozen commendation certificates. Buster's detective skills bordered on the legendary but he was also a hit in front of a television camera. He was not one to go in search of fame and it was by accident that he earned his reputation as the master of the perfect sound bite.

One spring morning, as Buster sat wading through his administration, the D/major put his head round the door and reported the armed robbery of a jeweller's shop in the city centre. The robbers had flashed at least one gun and escaped with a bag full of tasty merchandise. Buster dropped everything and sped to the crime scene where he found his path blocked by a phalanx of reporters. As cameras flashed and the barrage of questions merged into a clamour, a reporter from a local TV station thrust a microphone into Buster's face. 'Chief inspector, do you have any leads?'

Buster had not questioned a single witness, he had not even spoken to the investigating officer but felt he must say something. He composed himself, looked into the camera and answered with the confidence of a real pro. 'Evidence collected so far indicates that this crime was committed by armed thieves, acting with a view to financial gain.' He had a way with words, did Buster Kydd.

With a typhoon rattling around the South China Sea, I once asked him about the CID emergency standby arrangements. 'Standby?' he thundered. He leaned back in his chair and gave me his views on CID's role during typhoons. 'Crimes is for cops,' he said, nodding sagely. 'And fires is for fire services. Typhoons? Typhoons is for Royal Observatory. Cops don't do typhoons.'

Cops of course meant detectives because as far as Buster was concerned, there was no life beyond CID.

There is a start up routine to a new job: meet the DDI, meet the team, meet the other detective inspectors. I had done all that but then I received orders to see the big boss: the detective senior superintendent of police. Being the detective SSP was, and still is, a big deal. They caught flak from everyone. If the assistant commissioner asked about a case, the SSP had best know about it. When police headquarters wanted to know about crime and detection trends, the detective SSP needed an immediate answer. Detective SSPs were special; the job sorted out the real fliers from the ordinary wannabes. Hong Kong Island's detective SSP was a bit more special than most. At a time when most senior officers were Westerners, this boss was Chinese and rumour had it, he was going places.

I arrived ten minutes early for the interview. The secretary announced me then smiled. 'The SSP will see you right away,' she said.

Here we go, I thought: crushing handshake followed by, 'I hope you will be very happy here, we are one big family, my door is always open. Etcetera, etcetera.'

I went in and found myself in a well-ordered office. The man behind the desk was not what I expected. I thought he would be a corporate sort with a can-do smile and a designer suit but to be honest, he was a bit of a disappointment. If I had to describe him, it would be average: average height, average build, middle aged, normal haircut. His office was neat and his desk was tidy. He gave me a thin smile, a brief handshake and waved me to a chair. Then I noticed the commendation certificates and presentation plaques hanging in neat rows on the walls. My service record lay unopened on his desk. He steepled his fingers and leaned back in his chair.

'Tell me about yourself,' he asked.

Over the next fifteen minutes, I had the distinct impression he was truly interested in what I had to say. He spoke very little but even when silent, he projected an air of understated dignity. To this day, I remember little of what we said but as the interview ended, I knew I had met someone who was indeed special. His name was Li Kwan-ha and within a few days, he would teach me a life lesson that would guide me for many years to come.

Like most policemen, I had a sneaking regard for clever crooks, but by virtue of their cleverness, I rarely met any. Luckily for my detection rate, most of our criminals were not too bright. I have charged a shoplifter who left a supermarket with a watermelon stuffed under his T-shirt and a burglar who got his head stuck in a security grille. I once arrested a confidence trickster who bounced dishonest cheques all over Central division then watched, frustrated, as his lawyer won him an acquittal. Justice of a sort came when he paid his legal bill by cheque, which promptly bounced. A friend of mine investigated Hong Kong's most infamous serial killer. This man murdered several young women and took photographs as he dismembered their corpses. He might have been at it still, had he not taken the film to his local developer for processing. Arresting this kind of criminal was a lot easier than talking to them. Interviews had their own, special challenges.

'What's your name?'

'*Er...* Chan.'
'Chan what?'
'Chan Ming.'
'Where do you live?'
'Kowloon.'
'Kowloon, where?'
'Mongkok.'
'Mongkok, where?'
'Who? me?'
'Of course I'm talking to you.'
'Are you sure?'

The simplest question frequently got the most bewildering answer.

'What's your date of birth?'
'Can't remember. It was too long ago.'
'Have you ever been in trouble with the police?'
'No. I get into trouble on my own.'

I did not mind when criminals tried to confuse me, that was their job but I got annoyed when crime victims did the same.

When the report room constable escorted a European into the squad room, I expected just another routine crime complaint. The European had a huge girth. After the short walk from the report room, he was wheezing and wiping sweat from his jowls. The constable handed me an extract from the crime register and retreated down the corridor, muttering something about a 'jumped-up *gwailo*.' The CR extract included a summary of the European's report. The previous evening, he had visited a Wanchai massage parlour where a young lady had entertained him with some distracting sleight of hand. Whilst he was in deep discussion with this lady, someone had stolen fifty dollars from his wallet. I was about to suggest he put it down to experience but got the feeling he would not take to the idea at all well. I invited him to sit and grabbed a statement form. I started with a routine question.

'What's your name?
'Biddleforth.'
'Is that your last name?'
'Yes.'
'What's your first name?'
'Biddleforth.'

I waited for him to correct himself but he just sat staring at me, sweating and wheezing.

'So, that would be Biddleforth Biddleforth?'
'Of course not, that's silly.'

I looked into a pair of bloodshot eyes. They blinked back at me.

'What comes before Biddleforth?'

'Marquis of. *Harharharhar.*' His jowls shook and flecks of spittle gathered at the corners of his mouth. I wrote 'Marquis of Biddleforth' at the top of the statement then took his age, address and other particulars.

'Can you tell me what happened last night?'

The Marquis gave me a yellow toothed grin and rubbed his hands together. 'Oh yes indeed,' he chortled. 'The details, delighted my dear fellow.'

The Marquis remembered every bit of his contact with the pretty masseuse. He described every inch of her pert young body. He told me about each exquisite touch of her delicate hands. He could not remember the address of the massage parlour, neither could he recollect how he had got there or how he had left. An hour later, I promised I would do my best to recover his fifty dollars but to be honest, there was not much to go on. He took the news well and seemed happy enough to have shared the experience with someone. In fact, I had a hard time stopping him from telling it to me all over again.

It is hard to describe tropical rain to anyone who has not seen it. Some say it is like a curtain. I think of it more as a blanket.

234

First the sky darkens, next a few isolated drops fall like little water bombs. Then it starts. It hammers at the sidewalks, it stops
traffic, it overwhelms the storm drains. Farms become swamps,
roads become impassable. August normally marks the end of the
rainy season but in 1975, it lasted well into October. It was my
second week as a working detective and it was our reserve day.
It had been quiet, just a couple of bounced cheques when my sergeant, Fu Jai, took a message from Island Control. There was a report of a person collapsed at a small public garden in the upmar-
ket Victoria Peak area. Hardly work for the detectives, I thought.
Then Fu Jai told me the DDI was coming back to the office and
that a detective superintendent from Hong Island headquarters
was on the way to the scene. The DDI arrived as we were getting ready to leave so we jumped in his car and headed up to the
Peak. As we left the station, the rain started. It hammered at the
windscreen and within seconds, the wipers were next to useless.

   We arrived at the little park just as the rain stopped. Water
gushed through the storm drains, which had overflowed and
flooded the road to ankle depth. Blue lights mounted on an ambulance and a couple of police cars, strobed across lawns that
were now just a soggy mess. At the park entrance, the detective superintendent in charge of island (west) was speaking to
an ambulance crewman. The crewman shook his head, boarded
the ambulance and switched off his blue light. The superintendent walked to us, his face pained. He pointed to a shape lying
half-hidden in the shadows. 'It's one of your sergeants,' he said.
'Looks like he's been shot twice. His revolver's missing.'

   For a while, there was silence; maybe the superintendent had
it all wrong. He handed the DDI a blood spattered warrant card
that belonged to a newly promoted sergeant. I did not know him
well but remembered a chirpy young man who worked in the
CID action squad. We made our way to the body. He was lying
chest down in the mud, his head turned sideways so we could
see his face. There was blood on his shirt, his hair lay plastered

against his head. The eyes were half-open and dull, the face was without expression. No one spoke; no one moved. Then I must have dropped into something akin to automatic pilot. Key to a homicide investigation is action taken at the crime scene. Once released, the scene can never be recreated. At the scene, detectives have just one chance to gather up any available evidence. If they get this phase of the investigation wrong, a defence barrister will shred their case in no time. I went through a mental checklist: secure scene, establish command post, canvass area for witnesses, call for a photographer and a forensics expert, appoint exhibits officer, search scene for hard evidence. Easier said than done. The ground was sodden, footprints and bloodstains were disappearing by the second. My exhibits constable chased a broken ballpoint pen along a coursing storm drain. Fu Jai went round everyone present and collected anything they had seized. Every item needed bagging and a note made of where and when it had been collected. The owner of a nearby house ran a telephone line out to his porch and that became our command post. I phoned island control and asked for a photographer, a pathologist, the ballistics officer and a scientific evidence specialist.

Fu Jai gave me a nudge and nodded to the road where a dark saloon car had pulled up. 'SSP CID,' he whispered.

Li Kwan-ha stepped from the car and stood in silence as the DDI and the superintendent briefed him. I joined them and updated everyone on the scene of crime action. Li Kwan-ha had just one question. 'Does he have family?'

One of my detective constables knew the deceased sergeant well. He lived with his parents in Happy Valley.

'Have they been informed?' Li asked.

No, they had not.

'I must speak with the assistant commissioner,' Li said. I took him to our command post and he called the AC at home. 'The scene is well under control,' Li reported. 'I will go and break the news to the officer's family.'

That surprised me, police officers dread having to break the news of a sudden death. No one volunteered for the job, let alone a detective senior superintendent.

At first, I could hear only Li Kwan-ha's side of the conversation. 'I feel it is my duty,' he said.

Then I heard scratchy sounds coming from the telephone earpiece but I could make out no words.

'No sir,' Li said. 'It is not a job for delegation. I am his commanding officer.' He held the phone away from his ear as the noise from the earpiece became louder.

Now I could make out a few phrases. '... *Remain at scene ... get an inspector ...*'

Li was calm but insistent. 'I must disagree, sir. I will sit with them until other family members arrive.'

I could not believe what I was hearing. When an assistant commissioner gave an order, you obeyed it. Simple; no fuss. If the AC says do this or do that, you darn well do it but this quiet and dignified man was having none of it.

The voice on the other end rose until I could hear every scratchy word.

'*You will stay at the bloody scene.*'

Li Kwan-ha was silent, his face expressionless.

'*The family can take care of themselves.*'

Still nothing.

'*CAN YOU BLOODY HEAR ME?*'

And Li Kwan-ha hung up the phone on the assistant commissioner commanding Hong Kong Island.

I was stunned. Li spoke to me but his words did not register. He spoke again. 'Mr Emmett, if anyone looks for me, please tell them I am at the sergeant's home. I will remain there for as long as necessary.' His voice was as calm as ever.

I nodded. I could not speak. No one hangs up on an assistant commissioner, not even another assistant commissioner. The detective senior superintendent in charge of Hong Kong Island's

CID, a man destined for greater things, had just committed professional suicide. He swapped a few words with the DDI then boarded his car and was gone.

Next day was my rest day but I returned to the station to pick up on any fallout from the previous evening. As usual, the squadroom buzzed. There were statements to take, case diaries to fill in, court appearances to prepare. But where were the dire tales of retribution? I felt sure I would hear that Li Kwan-ha had been fired off to some remote backwater to see out the rest of his career. But no one spoke of it. There was no mention of the man who had put the welfare of a dead sergeant's family above his career.

Three weeks later, detectives from Western division arrested two men responsible for the shooting. Expecting rich pickings on Victoria Peak, and counting on a well-known police aversion to heavy rain, they had planned a burglary. They did not count on a newly promoted sergeant, keen to make a name for himself. There was a struggle, a snatched revolver and two shots. The first shot had put the sergeant down but it was the second shot, fired whilst the sergeant was unconscious, that killed him. Both burglars received life sentences.

In the coming years, I worked under Li Kwan-ha several times. Throughout his service, he never changed. He was ever the patrician gentlemen. Resolute in professional standards, faultless in kindness but unrelenting in matters of discipline. In 1989, Li Kwan-ha, CBE, QPM, CPM, became Hong Kong's first Chinese police commissioner.

Everyone thinks police work is a mix of science, teamwork and professionalism. Police forces encourage this idea, but it is not true. Behind most arrests is a healthy chunk of good luck. Hard working constables spend their shift patrolling gloomy alleys and exploring quiet rooftops. It is dangerous and thankless work. They suffer regular abuse from people who should know better. They risk a beating or worse when they question dubious characters in the secluded parts of their beat. Despite all this, by the end of shift our constable may not have arrested a single criminal. He has found no swag-laden burglars, no gold bullion thieves and no drug couriers. In need of a break, the constable slips into a rear lane for a quick smoke and trips over someone picking a lock. I do not mean to diminish the arrests made by hard-working officers, I just want to put things into perspective. Having said that, there was one arrest that earned my undying admiration and I always regretted not having played a part in it.

Cheri Tu was a teller in a sub-branch of the Tang Liu Bank in the Tai Ping Shan quarter of Central district. Tai Ping Shan was a leftover corner of old Hong Kong. Tucked away behind Central's glitzy skyscrapers, it was a bustling maze of lanes, alleyways and crumbling tenements.

To say the bank's Tai Ping Shan sub-branch was small is an understatement. It had only one teller and a modest sitting area furnished with a coffee table and some chairs. Although it was small, the sub-branch had all the modern security fittings. A perspex screen separated the teller from the public area and mounted on the wall was a closed circuit television camera. If all else failed, there was a silent alarm linked to the police control room.

Cheri joined the bank right after school and the sub-branch was her first job. Her manager had several other sub-branches to look after and he often left Cheri to run things by herself. She was a big hit with the customers and knew most of them by name. She was efficient, cheerful, pretty and she enjoyed her work. One morning, the bank was busier than usual and a queue formed in front of Cheri's counter. The manager had popped out and Cheri was alone when a stranger joined the line. He held a canvas bag and when he saw the closed circuit TV camera, he pulled the peak of his baseball cap low over his eyes. When his turn came, the stranger stepped up to the counter and looked around, making sure all other customers had left. He hefted the bag onto the counter and slipped Cheri a note. Written in child-like Chinese characters were the words, 'I HAVE A BOMB. GIVE ME THE MONEY.'

The bank had strict rules for this kind of thing: Cheri was to stay calm, sound the alarm if it was safe and, if necessary, hand over what little money there was in the till. Cheri knew the rules but as she read the note, her anger grew until she felt like a fire-cracker had gone off inside her. This was *her* little bank and no jumped-up hoodlum would tell her what to do in it. She pressed the silent alarm but decided there and then that the stranger would stay put until the police arrived. She took a deep breath and leaned close to the mouthpiece set into the security screen. The stranger hesitated then bent his head towards hers. Cheri fixed a cheery smile to her lips and asked, 'Do you have an account here?'

The stranger scowled and jabbed his finger at the note that was now on Cheri's side of the screen. She pretended to study the note while considering her next move. She smiled an apology and bent her head back to the mouthpiece. 'I'm sorry, this is an unusual request.' She pointed to a filing cabinet behind her. 'I'll have to get the right forms.' The stranger's brow darkened. He shook his bag at her but Cheri was on a roll. She smiled sweetly. 'Shan't be long.' She pointed to the sitting area and clicked the 'Counter Closed' sign into place. She slipped from her seat and started searching the cabinet for the non-existent forms.

The police arrived within minutes. They found a baffled bank robber and a bag containing nothing more dangerous than old telephone directories. As they applied the cuffs, the officers heard the would-be robber mutter, 'Stupid girl. She should have found the forms quicker.'

That summer, I slogged through the grind of burglary, street robbery and bounced cheques. But autumn was special; that autumn, I met a legend of the old west. At first, I wanted nothing to do with it. 'I don't have time for this,' I pleaded but the DDI was not sympathetic.

'No *time*, young man? What's *time* got to do with it?'

I slumped sulking and uninvited into a chair. 'I'm telling you, sir, it's a total waste. Philippines' cops are a bunch of headbangers.'

The DDI thumped both his fists on the desk and his voice took on a brittle edge. 'Special agents of the Philippines National Bureau of Investigation are not *headbangers*,' he said, emphasising each word with a jabbing finger. 'One: NBI agents are qualified barristers; two: they are appointed by their federal government; and three: they deal with lots of foreign law enforcement agencies.' He tried the reasoned approach. 'What's the problem? Show him some cases, buy him a beer, do anything you like.' He realised he was having no effect. 'Look,' he said, with icy finality, 'It's *your* reserve day and *you* will look after agent Vegas.' The discussion was over and I skulked back to my office.

Just what I needed, bloody babysitting a visiting bloody policeman on my bloody reserve day. He would try to look interested but all he would really want was to spend his travel allowance on booze and souvenirs. It was eight-thirty in the morning and already there was a pile of crime complaint sheets on my desk: a cheque fraud, an assault, a pickpocket.

I sensed a presence and looked up to see the DDI in the doorway. There was a pained look on his face. 'Chris. I ... *um* ... mentioned the visit from the NBI.' He gave a small cough. '*Ah*, let me introduce special agent Vegas.' Another man joined the DDI in the doorway. And he was every inch an undiluted, twenty-four carat, hoodlum. He had a square face burned to deep coffee by the Philippine sun. He styled his hair slicked back in the fashion of a Colombian cocaine lord. He wore a silver lamé suit, a black shirt and a yellow tie. Heavy gold adorned his fingers. I winced as he crushed my hand in his fist. He spoke in a throaty bass. 'Special agent Augusto Hernan Rodrigez Santiago Vegas,' he said, offering a huge grin. 'But my friends call me *Cisco*.' He pronounced it *Ceeesco*. He chuckled and held up his hands in mock surrender. 'But don't worry, I'm not Cisco, the Wild West gunslinger.'

The DDI threw me an apologetic smile and left me to it.

'Okay,' I said. 'Where to start?' I gave him a run-down of our organisation structure, manning scales and management setup. He made a good show of taking an interest. His eyes were bright and he nodded when I emphasised a point. Ten minutes later I ran out of things to say. 'So ... the ... *er* ... DDI can curtail enquiries into minor crimes if the victim is not seriously injured. Everything clear?'

'So, Chris, what kinda *gonns* do you carry?' he asked. 'Personally, I favour the automatic Colt .45 ACP.' A heavy silence hung between us. It was as if we were having two separate conversations.

I thought for a moment then told him that Hong Kong CID officers carried nothing heavier than the snub-nosed Detective Special.

Cisco blinked and shook his head like a stunned boxer. 'I understand,' he mused. But I don't think he did.

I took him into the squadroom and introduced my team. The room was full: a pickpocket had slashed a tourist's handbag with a razor, a businessman was complaining that a new client had failed to pay for a goods consignment, an assault victim nursed a bruised cheek. Cisco tried to read a statement over a detective's shoulder but gave up when he saw it was in Chinese. 'What happens if you get a lead?' he asked.

I explained that if we had a suspect, we paid him an early morning visit and searched for incriminating evidence.

'When do you do your firepower assessment?' Cisco asked.

'Firepower assessment?'

'Surely you don't use heavy weapons without doing a fire-power assessment.'

'Heavy weapons?'

Cisco looked at me as though I had just lost a loved one. 'You got no heavy weapons?'

There was a commotion and a uniformed officer bundled a young man into the squadroom. Handcuffs pinned the young man's hands behind his back and he was hurling abuse at the constable.

'What's he sayin'?'

The prisoner, I said, was telling the constable to perform an unusual act on his mother.

Cisco made a show of looking towards the door. 'Do you want I should leave while you teach him some manners?'

'No way,' I said. 'Life's hard enough without having to worry about CAPO.'

'CAPO? What is a *CAPO?*'

'Complaints Against Police Office,' I told him. 'If we even tap this guy, he'll have CAPO on us so fast our eyeballs will rattle.'

Cisco blinked. 'People *complain* about the police? Who is this CAPO? Local justices?'

'No, they're cops.'

Cisco's jaw nearly hit his shirtfront. '*Cops?* And they take complaints? From the *public?*'

For the rest of the day, Cisco stayed quiet. I talked him through our procedures for detaining suspects and I took him to the scene of a burglary. At eight that evening, Fu Jai stuck his head round my office door.

'Theft report, *Bodine's* wine bar.'

'Take a constable and try to get back within the hour,' I told him.

Fu Jai nodded and went back to the squadroom.

Bodine's was a fancy wine bar in the business district and was a favourite of the financial set. I decided to take a look. Who knows, I thought, maybe the manager would buy us a drink. It was a ten-minute walk so Cisco came too.

Bodine's was all brass, dark wood and leather. The clientele wore suits and were mostly in their late twenties. In a corner, a piano tinkled bluesy-jazz. The manager, a dapper Chinese, met us at the door. 'This is most unfortunate,' he said, shaking his head and wringing his hands. '*Most* unfortunate indeed.'

The manager ushered us to a booth where we found a fair-haired young man. His eyes were bloodshot and his head lolled. His tie was loose and the top button of his shirt was undone. He swept a lock of hair from his forehead but it refused to be controlled and instantly flopped back. 'Ah, at long last,' the young man drawled. 'It's the Royal Hong Kong bloody rozzers.' He cupped his hands to his mouth and called to a group at the bar. '*I said, it's the rozzers.*'

The manager made calming motions with both hands. '*Please,* Mister Roach. *Please* don't make a fuss.'

The three of us: Fu Jai, the detective constable and me, slid into the booth and sat facing Roach. Cisco motioned Roach to move along then eased in next to him. Roach stifled a belch and focussed glazed eyes on us.

'Well, well, what have we here?' He made a show of counting us. 'We have a white rozzer, a chinky ... no, pardon me ... *two* chinky rozzers and whatsh ...' He peered at Cisco. 'Sorry ... I mean: what's this? A sort of brownish person.' He grinned like a schoolboy. 'Oh, I get it, rozzer's brought his houseboy.' He turned to some non-existent confidante. '*Hmmm* ... I simply *must* get the name of houseboy's tailor.'

I fought the urge to march our Mister Roach to the gents and dunk his head in the urinal. Instead, I asked. 'What's the problem?'

'The problem is ...' Roach paused as if he had forgotten something then he pointed at the manager. 'The problem is that slope-eyed little bastard. He's a thief.' He called to the crowd at the bar.

'I said, he's a bloody thief.'

I thought the manager would burst into tears. 'I haven't ... I didn't. I ...'

'Why do you suspect the manager?' I asked.

Roach went through a pantomime of searching his pockets. 'Had it when I came in,' he said. 'Had it when I paid old Jackson his five hundred but when this little bastard brought the bill, my wallet had gone.' Roach made a show of looking under a drinks coaster. 'It was right here, on the table. 'Snot here now. Search the little shit. Search him right here, in front of everyone.'

Something on the floor caught Fu Jai's eye. 'What is this?' he said and ducked under the table. He came up holding a leather wallet. 'Is yours?'

Roach snatched the wallet from Fu Jai and there was a flash of a gold credit card as he flicked through the contents.

'It's all here. Bugger must have panicked and ditched it.'

'Or perhaps you drop it.' Fu Jai said, his voice flat.

'No way. I'm not pish ... I mean, I'm not pissed or anything. You should mind your chinky manners.'

Cisco put his arm across Roach's shoulder. His free hand disappeared under the table. 'My friend, you have your wallet. Please do not act like a prick.'

'A *preek*? Never had a houseboy call me a *preek*. You want to watch it ... ulp.' Roach's eyes popped, his mouth worked but he made no sound.

Cisco's voice was soft and comforting. 'It would be a shame to rip the *gonads* from one so young, is that not so?'

Roach grinned through clenched teeth.

'I think, my friend,' Cisco purred, 'you owe the manager of this excellent establishment an apology. Just nod if you agree.'

Roach nodded so hard that his hair flapped like a tarpaulin in a gale. He regained the power of speech. 'Yes. Yes, of course,' he gasped. 'I'm sorry. Really, really, really sorry.' He clambered past Cisco and hobbled to the door, one hand holding his briefcase, the other clutching his groin.

Fu Jai looked at Cisco with a mixture of awe and adoration. 'I suggest we write this off "lost and found,"' he said to me.

Cisco winked at me. 'Do you think your *CAPO* will be interested in a *Piñoy* houseboy?'

Four beers appeared on the table and the manager smiled his thanks. As we sipped our drinks, we chatted. 'Are you really a barrister?' I asked.

'Of course,' he said. 'It's a requirement of the job.'

'You don't act like a barrister.'

'You think not?' He smiled as if recalling a fond memory. 'My old professor once said: "Augusto, don't be a lawyer unless you can put someone's nuts in the vice."' He grinned at me. 'Whatsamatter? You got no lawyers in Hong Kong?'

CHAPTER 14
CHANGERS

HONG KONG'S CRIME is seasonal and Chinese New Year is the season for armed robberies. Forget flowers, the Chinese believe in saying it with gold. In the weeks leading up to the festivities, goldsmiths bring in extra stock, criminals make plans and police commanders cancel all leave. To a large part, successful policing depends on good luck but one Chinese New Year, I landed a case that proves villainy follows the same rule: without a chunk of good luck, even the smartest criminal is stuffed. Unfortunately for Jacko Chim, he was neither smart, nor was he lucky.

Jacko was an ordinary sort of villain. He was nineteen years old and like most good-looking kids, he enjoyed a bit of fun, a touch of danger and the company of pretty girls. Jacko was not a particularly violent young man but he was not squeamish about a little strong-arm extortion. Jacko worked on his petty thieving and minor scams for sixteen hours a day. It never occurred to him that life would be easier if he just got himself a proper job. Jacko was in a rut but he could not get way from his life on the street. Then one day, all that changed.

It was an accident, pure and simple. Jacko dropped into his local teahouse for a morning cup of *boh-lei*. He paid his bill but as he headed for the door, he saw a briefcase beside a vacant chair. Without breaking stride, he snapped it up, sauntered through the door and melted into the crowd. No fuss; no bother; easy. The briefcase was heavy so, bursting with curiosity, Jacko rushed back to his room in a seedy part of Causeway Bay and prised it open.

His heart sank, the case was full of papers but then, under the documents he found a stopwatch and a chunky starter's pistol. He held the pistol with a sense of reverence. It was heavy and was the nearest he had ever been to the real thing. It gleamed blue-black under a sheen of oil. He found the cylinder catch and the pistol broke open to reveal six blank cartridges. He lined the crimped little blanks along the edge of his dresser, tucked the pistol into his belt and practised his fast draw, snapping off shots at imaginary enemies.

A decent villain would have dumped the pistol into the nearest trashcan. In a city full of armed policemen, it is not a good idea to be spotted with anything that looks like a gun. But Jacko could not see that. With the weight of the starter's pistol tugging at his belt, he felt on top of the food chain. Now, Jacko could act the hard man and the idea grew that he could be a rich hard man. The future, Jacko thought, lay in the jewellery business.

At first, he only toyed with the idea. Every time he passed a goldsmith or a jeweller's shop, he found himself checking the security. In some places, the guards were alert but in others, they were not. Jacko daydreamed of charging into a plump little jewellery store, pistol in hand, and stripping the place bare. He thought about forming a gang of desperados and realised he needed only a driver and someone to bag up the loot. Jacko, of course would be the boss; after all, he was the man with the brains.

Jacko narrowed his targets down to just one shop, a jeweller in Queen's Road Central. The security was weak and there was a choice of escape routes. From Queen's Road, a car could be in Western district within minutes or it could loop around Connaught Road and head east to Causeway Bay. He spent days watching the police. There were no set patrol patterns and the policemen moved around the street with easy confidence. For the first time, Jacko saw the enormity of the risk.

He chose two friends, Chung Jai and Ah Ling. They were young and like Jacko, what they lacked in brains they made up with bravado. The plan was simple, in fact it was darn near perfect. Ah Ling would put false plates on his little Honda and on Saturday morning, all three would drive to Queen's Road. There, Jacko and Chung Jai would don carnival masks and enter the shop. While Jacko took care of the staff, Chung Jai would use a hammer to smash the nearest display case and grab what he could. They high-fived each other and spent the rest of the evening talking about fancy cars and fast women.

Saturday came and they rode Ah Ling's Honda to Central in silence. There may have been some second thoughts but no one wanted to be first to admit it. Ah Ling pulled into Queen's Road and there, right outside the target jewellers, was an empty parking space. They parked and surveyed the area. They shrank down as the manager came out of the jewellers with a policeman. The policeman gave them a passing glance, hitched his revolver holster into a more comfortable position then walked off down the street. Jacko and Chung Jai exchanged tight-lipped nods, put on their masks and opened the car doors.

When they walked into the shop, the staff fell silent, then laughed at the cartoon character masks. Jacko pulled the pistol from his waistband, pointed it at the ceiling and squeezed the trigger. The report made Jacko's ears sing but it had the right effect on the staff. The grins dropped from their faces and their hands flew up. A thrill surged through Jacko; he was in control, he could do anything he wanted. He held the pistol in both hands, his arms thrust out stiff before him. He panned the pistol from side to side and ordered the staff back against the wall. The salesmen glared at him but had to obey. Chung Jai brought his hammer crashing down onto the display cabinet. He yelped as it rebounded against toughened glass.

Outside, Ah Ling scanned the pavement for policemen. It

seemed that every passer-by turned to look at him. He eased the Honda into first gear, then back into neutral, then back into first. What was taking so long? There was a rap on his side window. His insides tightened. For a second he thought he would faint. He turned to see a woman traffic warden bending towards him. She had a face like an anvil and she jerked her thumb in a universally understood gesture: 'Move it.'

Ah Ling rolled down his window and forced a smile. 'I ... I'm waiting for someone.'

The traffic warden said nothing and again waved him on. Ah Ling looked from the traffic warden to the jewellers and then back again. If his heart beat any harder it would split. He pressed the palms of his hands together. '*Pleeease*. I won't be long, I promise.'

The traffic warden had all the pity of a Manchu tax collector. She unbuttoned her tunic pocket and pulled out a book of parking tickets. Ah Ling's eyes pleaded. He could not get a ticket; at some point, she would check his tax disc and see it did not match his number plates. Then, she would squawk like a goose with a firecracker up its arse and the police would be all over him. Ah Ling nodded. He rolled up the window and punched the Honda into gear. He eased forward a few yards then stopped and turned his head to look at the jeweller's shop. '*Comeoncomeoncomeon...*' he begged. The traffic warden set her jaw and strode after him. Ah Ling was on the verge of tears. What were they *doing*? He edged forward another few yards.

Back inside the jewellers, Chung Jai took a two-handed swing at the display case and again, the hammer bounced off. He stared at the glass as if expecting it to shatter all by itself. One of the sales assistants sidled out of Jacko's vision. Jacko swung the pistol around and the man froze. Jacko knew he could not control the situation much longer. He watched Chung Jai hammer at the display case again. Again the hammer bounced off.

Two salesmen tried to edge around Jacko's flank. Rage gleamed in their eyes and Jacko knew it was time to go. He shouted to Chung Jai and they backed into the street. Pedestrians gawked at their masks and at Jacko's pistol but no one tried to stop them. The salesmen hovered in the doorway like leashed Dobermans. Jacko kept them covered and told Chung Jai to open the car door. Chung Jai's voice was a sob. 'It's gone.'

Jacko risked a look over his shoulder and the salesmen launched themselves at him. From the corner of his eye, Jacko saw them coming. He squeezed the trigger and the shot echoed down the street. The salesman nearest Jacko felt a shock against his shirtfront. He skidded to a stop and clutched his stomach. It took a few seconds for him to realise there was no pain. He looked at his shirt; there was no blood. Seconds earlier he had been afraid but now rage welled up in him. He balled his fist and stepped forward.

The police arrived minutes later, by which time a bloodied and bruised Jacko Chim was very glad to see them.

From its granite façade to its wood panelled courtrooms, Hong Kong's high court oozed majesty. The courtrooms smelled of leather and old law books. The acoustics were church-like. Two prison wardens led Jacko in through a door at the back of the dock and unlocked his handcuffs. Jacko looked for a friendly face and finding none, he sat with his shoulders hunched and his face pinched.

There was a murmur of conversation as interpreters, court recorders, journalists, ushers, counsels and clerks filed into court. On the surface, it seemed relaxed but beneath the banter, the atmosphere was taut. A booming knock on the mahogany door of the judge's chambers ended all conversation. As his lordship entered, everyone stood and bowed to the bench. The judge returned the bow and, with a dignity unequalled on the face of this planet, everyone settled into their seats.

Our prosecutor was Stingo Webley and in wig and gown, he

cut an elegant figure. He spoke in a modulated baritone that enhanced the flat vowels of his native Australia. Stingo prided himself as a courtroom wit and had once come within a whisker of spending an afternoon in the cells. After a liquid lunch, Stingo returned to court and, somewhat unsteadily, stood to make his final address. He grasped the lapels of his robe and turned to the jury. 'Defence counsel tells you his client cannot be held responsible because he was inebriated.' Stingo had shaken his head and frowned learnédly. 'But, ladies and gentlemen, it is irrelevant whether or not the accused was as drunk as a judge.'

The court fell silent and the judge peered over the top of his *pince-nez*. 'I believe, Mister Webley,' the judge had growled, 'the correct phrase is "as drunk as a lord."'

Chastened, Stingo bowed to the bench. 'Indeed,' he said. 'I humbly defer to your greater wisdom, *my lord*.'

I always thought 'sledging' was a practice unique to cricket. It involves wicket keepers bombarding batsmen with insults, hoping to break their concentration. The Australians have raised the practice to high art but during the case of Crown vs. Jacko Chim, I found that Australian wicket keepers were amateurs compared to Australian barristers. Stingo was the model of decorum as he presented the prosecution case. He led the prosecution witnesses through their evidence and lounged in languid disdain during the defence's cross-examination. After the last prosecution witness stepped down, Stingo declared his case closed. He wrapped his gown around himself and sat down.

The judge turned to Jacko's counsel, 'Any submission, Mister Sykes?'

Counsel for the defence rose to his feet and cleared his throat. 'Indeed I have, M'lud,' he said. 'The Crown has not proved its case. My learnéd friend has shown only that the accused was present at the time of the robbery.'

Stingo leaned back in his chair, his lips barely moved. '*Frogshit.*'

The judge did not hear it, the jury did not hear it and although I heard it, I did not believe it. Stingo smiled sweetly. Sykes' cheeks reddened. He shuffled his papers, his stride rattled. '*Er ...* circumstantial evidence has no place in a case this serious.'

'*Are you farting out yer neck or talking out yer arse?*'

'I ... *um* ... just a moment, M'lud. Indeed ... there is not an ounce of corroboration ...'

'*The flaws in yer argument stick out like the bollocks on a skinny dog.*'

The judge looked up from his notes. 'Are you well, Mister Sykes?'

'Yes M'lud.' Sykes sipped water from a glass. 'Now, oh dear, where am I?'

Stingo flashed him a smile that would have warmed a Queensland beach. '*By the sound of it, mate, yer in the same deep shit as yer larrikin bloody client.*'

By the time he reached the end of his address, Sykes could hardly string a sentence together. The judge sensed something wrong but could not put his finger on it. 'Thank you, Mister Sykes,' he said. 'I find a case to answer.' He checked his watch. 'Time for lunch, I think.'

Poor Jacko did not stand a chance. The trial lasted two days and the jury retired for just half an hour. His lordship sentenced Jacko to six years and from the look on Jacko's face, that was far better than he had expected.

That spring, the Duke of Westmoreland's Light Infantry hit town. The regiment's duty was to defend the realm, but it was easy to believe they saw the real enemy as being the navy. Any navy would do, but if it was the American navy, then so much the better. As the toll of walking wounded grew, the regiment's commanding officer showed his disapproval by filling Stanley Fort's guardroom cells to overflowing. The young soldiers got the message and for a while, army and naval forces enjoyed an uneasy armistice.

The regiment discovered the 'The Duke's' bar in Wanchai and immediately proclaimed it an honorary corner of their home county. It was Saturday night when a half-dozen American sailors rolled in. Some say they were looking for trouble but it is likely they just wandered into the wrong bar. As they let their eyes adjust to the gloom, they may have wondered why the place had gone so quiet.

Mindful of the CO's warnings, the boys of the Duke's Own muttered into their beers and cleared a space at the bar. Then something wonderful happened: pockets of conversation broke the silence and the mood eased. The bar began to buzz with chatter and good spirit. Someone bought the Americans a round and to the relief of the bar staff, it seemed the evening would pass peacefully. Of course, it could not last. From somewhere a voice called, 'Ah truly do believe that you Limeys have the second best, little ole navy in the world.'

The chatter stopped. The only noise was the scrape of chairs as every soldier in the place rose to his feet. The barman began to collect empty glasses and clear bottles from the display shelves behind the bar.

The soldiers of the Duke's Own were now in a quandary. They had no love for the Royal Navy but it was their Navy; only *they* had the right to insult it. Even at that stage, a little good humour could have calmed things but in The Duke's bar, good humour was having an early night.

The man who passed the comment was a stocky seaman with a flat face dominated by a broken nose. Ignoring the well of silence deepening around him, he screwed up his eyes and spoke to nobody in particular. 'When wuz the last time the Royal, goddam Navy saw any combat?' He cast a glazed eye around the bar, pleased to find he had the undivided attention of every soldier present. 'How many Royal, goddam Navy boys got a goddam combat decoration?' He pulled a slim velvet box from his pocket. He opened the lid and the lights glinted on bright silk and burnished silver.

A soldier called Bluey Pierce squinted at the medal. He whistled in admiration. 'That's canny, that is,' he said, a note of real admiration in his voice.

Bluey's best mate, Chalky Gould stepped forward. 'Aye, that's a bonny medal all right,' he said. 'Vietnam, I suppose.' His eyes twinkled. 'Pluckiest loser, were it?'

There was the briefest of silences. Then the first table crashed over and the two groups were on each other. Glasses shattered, wood splintered, bargirls squealed and ducked behind the bar. *Mamasan* shouted for everyone to take it outside. Someone stumbled into the street and the rest of the fight followed. The Dukes outnumbered the Americans five to one but as the brawl stormed down Lockhart Road, other sailors scrambled from every bar on the strip and joined in. Rickshaw men and streetwalkers ran for cover. A rubbish bin shattered the windscreen of a parked car. A sailor smashed through the window of a tailor shop. Taxi drivers covered their 'for hire' signs, locked their doors and crouched under their steering wheels. The fight spread into the side streets and the din of battle drowned the noise of approaching sirens. The shore patrol and the military police got there first, the local police arrived a few minutes later. At first, all they could do was pluck bodies from the fight's margins and toss them into waiting paddy wagons. To those still fighting, there came a creeping realisation that the forces of law and order had arrived. The remaining fighters paused. They found themselves surrounded by a ring of white-uniformed shore patrol, red-capped MPs and khaki-clad Hong Kong policemen. Then, as if acting on an unheard starter's bell, they all burst through the cordon and sprinted off in different directions.

Chalky Gould of the Duke's Own Light Infantry found himself cut off from his mates. He ducked down an alley and emerged into a road called Fenwick Street. There he stopped for breath. He heard a shouted challenge and turned to see a solitary Hong Kong Policeman chasing him. The policeman was short and slim but brandished a three-foot riot baton as though it was a highland claymore. Chalky weighed his options then ran down Fenwick Street with the policeman close behind. Chalky's escape route was not a good one and a few seconds later, he found himself cornered on Fenwick Pier. In front of him lay Hong Kong harbour; behind him was the baton-wielding Hong Kong policeman. Chalky leaned against the harbour-front guardrail and looked into the foul-smelling waters. A mile away, across the harbour, the lights of Kowloon winked at him. The policeman shouted for Chalky to stand still. Unfortunately, the policemen spoke no English and Chalky understood no Chinese. Certain he was about to have the business end of the riot baton bounced off his skull, Chalky took a deep breath and vaulted over the guardrail. The policeman ran to the railing just in time to see Chalky swimming full speed, out to the shipping lanes.

In the Hong Kong Island command and control centre, the duty controller listened to the constable's radioed report. He telephoned his opposite number in marine police headquarters and soon, a little harbour patrol launch chugged to the waters off Fenwick Pier. The launch sergeant swept the water with his spotlight but there was no trace of Chalky.

On the off chance that Chalky might survive his dip in the harbour, the Kowloon controller sent a constable to keep watch at the Kowloon Public Pier. An hour passed and there was still no sight of Chalky so the constable slipped into the shadows for a quick smoke. Then he saw something stir on the jetty steps. The constable moved closer and there, lying sodden, bedraggled and exhausted on the bottom step was a European man. The European raised himself onto all fours and started to climb towards the landing. The constable radioed he had found the missing soldier and meaning only to help, he picked his way down the steps.

Chalky grabbed the staircase rail, pulled himself to his feet and stood swaying as he rubbed salt and oil from his eyes. The constable shone his torch at Chalky who blinked and shielded his eyes. As his vision cleared, Chalky saw the neatly creased khaki uniform, shiny leatherwork and peaked cap. '*Awww, fookin' Norah*,' he groaned. 'Not you again.' He turned, dived back into the harbour and started the long swim back to Hong Kong Island.

The harbour launch crew dragged Chalky from the water and a week later, his regimental sergeant major marched him in to face the commanding officer. Chalky pleaded guilty and the CO sighed as he read over the case facts.

'Anything to say in mitigation, private Gould?'

'Just that I was, like, defending the honour of the Royal Navy, sir.'

'The Royal *what*, private Gould?'

'Royal Navy, sir.'

The commanding officer gave a sniff and shuffled his papers. 'Seven days in the guardroom for fighting.'

Chalky grinned, it had been worth it.

'Also, private Gould,' the CO continued, 'you can have another fourteen days confined to barracks for bullshitting your commanding officer. March him out, RSM.'

It was the biggest street fight Wanchai had seen for years. Police headquarters ordered every divisional superintendent to build links with the Royal Military Police. The British land forces commander must have issued similar orders because a few weeks later, we received an invitation to visit the military police mess in Victoria Barracks. There, so the invitation read, we would partake of cold beverages and dead things on sticks.

Victoria Barracks was a green sanctuary, sandwiched between Central and Wanchai. The military police had tucked away their mess on the barracks perimeter, behind a line of trees. It was small but comfortable. The beer was cold and there was plenty of food. We made some good friends that afternoon but it was many years before I returned. When I did return, it was to enjoy the hospitality of a military unit I had long respected, but which had never before served in Hong Kong.

Summer came and I received the paperwork for my second long leave. This time the wad of forms contained a career development sheet on which I was to list my preferred posting. I ticked the box next to 'narcotics bureau' and dropped it into my out-tray. What a joke, I thought, no one ever gets the posting of their choice.

Later that year I started work with the narcotics bureau.

EPILOGUE
NEW BEGINNINGS

On June 30th 1997, sovereignty of the Crown Colony of Hong Kong passed to the People's Republic of China. From the windowless command suite of Kowloon's command and control centre, I listened to radio reports from the Tsimshatsui waterfront and wished I could be out on the streets. All day, sheets of tropical rain had disrupted celebrations and I hoped it was not an omen. Just before midnight, crowds gathered at the old clock tower next to Kowloon's Star Ferry pier. In the control room, we crowded around a TV to watch the final lowering of the British flag. An inspector popped a champagne cork. There was a catch in my throat as I took off my colonial collar tags and replaced them with new badges. Outside, police officers exchanged new cap badges for old. Mobile patrol crews had stowed spare tunics, bearing the new insignia, in their vehicles. After 156 years, the *Royal* Hong Kong Police ceased to be. I slipped the old collar tags into my pocket and gave them a rub for luck. Midnight passed. The sky did not fall and there were no riots in the streets. For years, people had asked what would happen after the handover? Now I knew the answer: nothing. In the control room the same group of quiet professionals, Westerners and Chinese, carried out the same duties they had been performing just minutes earlier.

It had been years since the bars saw such custom, but that night, there were no reports of trouble. My opposite number in the New Territories control room phoned to tell me that lorries full of Chinese troops were streaming across the border.

It was the most complex operation ever mounted by the Hong Kong police and it was nearly daylight before I ordered the control room shut down. As I drove home, a young Chinese roared up behind me on a motorcycle. A huge five-starred banner fluttered from a pole fixed to his pillion. He drew level, flashed me an eye-crinkling smile and gave the thumbs-up sign.

The next day was a public holiday and I was off duty. I drove down to Causeway Bay and strolled around the shops. It was all pretty quiet, I expect a lot of people were nursing sore heads. I stepped into a corner store and asked for a can of Coca-Cola. The store keeper was an elderly gentleman with bright eyes and a gentle smile. 'I thought all you *gwailos* had left,' he said in Chinese.

'Not quite all,' I answered. 'Some of us think this is the best place to be.'

The store keeper chuckled. 'Now we are all the same,' he said. 'Chinese and Westerners together, we are all *Heung Gong Yan* -- Hong Kongers.'

I offered him the two dollars but he waved it away. 'Special price for *ji gei yan*,' he said. He wagged his finger at me, 'Special price for one day only.'

His words stay with me today, *ji gei yan* -- one of us.

Eight months later, I was one of several officers who received an invitation from the People's Liberation Army. Our bus pulled up outside the old military police mess in Victoria barracks where a casually dressed Chinese man welcomed us. Dick Li, the assistant commissioner in charge of our group introduced him as the colonel commanding Hong Kong's PLA, military police.

We moved inside. The British army furnishings were gone and the place had the look of a five-star hospitality suite. Tientsin carpet covered the floors, concealed lighting lit the anteroom. The colonel shepherded us into an inner chamber where there were dinner tables laid out with crisp linen and fine porcelain. The colonel bustled us to our seats then went round the tables, pouring a clear liqueur into small glasses set at each place. He raised his glass and in sibilant Mandarin, proposed a toast. We downed the liqueur with a single swallow. It was fiery stuff and it hit me like a runaway truck. Throughout the evening, shaven-headed soldiers in combat fatigues served the food. Each dish was more sumptuous than the one before. The colonel proposed toasts and made speeches about friendship and mutual understanding. By the time the soldiers cleared away the remnants of our last course, we were bloated and our heads sang from the effects of the Chinese liqueur. The colonel escorted us back to our bus and shook the hand of every member of our group. Although I understood not a word of Mandarin, I found no pretence in the colonel's show of friendship; no deceit in his smile.

Nothing stays the same. Since I first stepped onto the apron of Kai Tak airport, the Hong Kong police has more than doubled in size. A five-man management team has replaced the legendary sub-divisional inspector. Now, the talk is of program management, vision statements and key performance indicators. Some officers complain the tabloid press increasingly sets the police agenda but I can assure them, there is nothing new in that.

Part of the British Empire became part of China, but on Hong Kong's streets, working police officers still risk their lives to keep the city safe. Sometimes, I check the Hong Kong Police website and allow myself a smile. The young and very able young men and women I once knew are now older and sport the rank insignia of assistant commissioner and higher.

During my service, Hong Kong's overseas officers hailed from all over the world. They came from Britain, Canada, Australia, New Zealand, South Africa and the former Rhodesia. In 1994, Hong Kong stopped recruiting its police officers from overseas.

There are some still serving but their numbers dwindle year by year. I am in touch with a few and they tell me they made the right choice to stay after the change in sovereignty. The community seems happy to see westerners in police uniform, and the bond between overseas and Chinese officers is as strong as ever.

In 2011, a Hong Kong Police delegation visited China's Public Security Ministry in Beijing. During an after dinner speech, the Public Security Minister made a special point to thank Hong Kong's overseas officers for helping to make the transition to Chinese rule so successful.

So, what legacy did colonial Britain leave behind? The rule of law, certainly. An efficient and dedicated civil service, absolutely. But what of its police force? A veteran journalist once called the Hong Kong Police 'Asia's Finest.' Had he got closer to those men and women, he would have rated them more highly. They say a community gets the police force it deserves. If so, then the hard working, open-hearted people of Hong Kong deserve a force equal to the best in the world.

Which is exactly what they have.